PASSIONATE WOMEN

FEMALE SUICIDE IN LATE IMPERIAL CHINA

# PASSIONATE WOMEN

*Female Suicide in Late Imperial China*

EDITED BY

PAUL S. ROPP, PAOLA ZAMPERINI, AND
HARRIET T. ZURNDORFER

BRILL
LEIDEN · BOSTON · KÖLN
2001

The content of this volume is a reprint of
volume 3, issue 1 of *Nan Nü*,
Men, Women and Gender
in Early and Imperial China (2001).

ISBN 90 04 12018 1

*Brill*
*Leiden · Boston · Köln*



ISSN 0022-4995

## CONTENTS

## FOREWORD

At the founding of *NAN NÜ* its Board of Editors agreed that one of the purposes of the Journal was to offer a forum for senior and junior scholars to present the first results of their research which might be developed later in other forms of publication such as monographs or collected essays. Thus, it was with great pleasure that the *NAN NÜ* Board of Editors invited participants of the panel "Passionate Women: Male Discourses on Female Suicide in Late Imperial China," organized by Paola Zamperini, at the recent Association for Asian Studies (AAS) Meeting in San Diego, March 9-12, 2000, to publish their papers. To lend perspective to the papers by the panelists Katherine Carlitz, Janet Theiss, and Paola Zamperini, which focus on male writing about female suicide, the Board also invited Grace Fong, who had given a presentation on female-authored writing on women's suicide at another AAS Meeting, to join our symposium here. Since Paul Ropp had served as both chairperson and discussant for the panel, it seemed appropriate that he and Paola Zamperini should serve as editors for this special issue of *NAN NÜ*.

The Introduction to this issue clearly indicates how the papers here build upon the important contributions of many other scholars, and how they lay new ground for others to explore. In recent publications female suicide has frequently been linked to the female chastity cult, but there is substantial literature dating from before the Qin dynasty (221-206 BC) which illustrates earlier preoccupations with the role of suicide in Chinese life. Confucius himself may have considered self-sacrifice a virtue under certain circumstances, although his later interpreters do not agreed to what extent the Master's 'saying' *shashen yi chengren* 殺身以成仁 ("to kill one self to realize humanity") recorded in the *Lunyu* (15:9) was a reflection of his particular concept of political loyalty. In any event, during China's long history both men and women have committed suicide for a variety of reasons and under varying circumstances. Nowadays, according to international newspaper reports, mainland China confronts the highest suicide rate in the world. How culturally bound to a specific Chinese ethos suicide is in China, either in the past or in the present, may be one of the many questions scholars and students need to ask, and it is hoped that in the future *NAN NÜ* readers and contributors will help address the answer.

Harriet T. Zurndorfer

# PASSIONATE WOMEN: FEMALE SUICIDE IN LATE IMPERIAL CHINA—INTRODUCTION*

BY

PAUL S. ROPP
(Clark University)

*"To starve to death is a minor thing;*
*to lose one's chastity is a great thing."*
Cheng Yi 程頤 (1033-1107)

*"She died well! She died well!"*
Licentiate Wang Yuhui 王玉輝 on his daughter's suicide in *Rulin waishi* 儒林外史 by Wu Jingzi 吳敬梓 (1701-1754)

*"If men want to make loyalty and righteousness their own responsibility, that is fine, but how does the virtue and chastity of women reflect any glory on men?"*
Yu Zhengxie 俞正燮 (1775-1840)

*"These women [chaste widows] are to be pitied. Trapped for no good reason by tradition and numbers, they are sacrificed to no purpose."*
Lu Xun 魯迅 (1881-1936)

Despite mountains of historical records, and hundreds of twentieth-century commentaries and studies, we are still in the formative stages of trying to forge a scholarly consensus about the causes, the meanings, and the significance of female suicides in Ming and Qing China. In some ways, the lack of consensus has been a constant ever since Ming-Qing times which witnessed intense scholarly and official debates on female suicide, the rights and duties of widows including "betrothed widows," and the sometimes conflicting demands of filiality, wifely duties, motherly responsibilities, family harmony, and in-

* I wish to thank Katherine Carlitz, Grace Fong, Janet Theiss, Paola Zamperini, and Harriet Zurndorfer for their insightful comments and suggestions on earlier drafts of this introduction. And I am grateful to Sara Jenkins for her expert copy-editing of this and all the other essays in this collection.

dividual integrity. Arguments over female suicide intensified in the early twentieth century, particularly in China's May Fourth Movement, and in many ways they have continued ever since. The essays in this issue of *Nan Nü* mark an effort to build on earlier scholarship, to recapture some of the voices of individual men and women from the Ming and Qing periods, and to demonstrate the wide range of sources available today for the study of this important topic.

My goal in this introduction is to place these essays in the wider context of the evolution of English-language scholarship on women and gender relations in late imperial China. I do not have the space or the expertise to cover the voluminous Chinese language scholarship on these issues. However, to enhance the value of this collection for other scholars, we include in this issue a selected bibliography of relevant and important Chinese and Western works that relate to female suicide in late imperial China.

Twentieth-century views of female suicide in the Ming and Qing have been powerfully shaped by the intellectual outlook of the May Fourth Movement and its anti-Confucian critique of Chinese culture. The leaders of the May Fourth "New Culture Movement" were all confident that the problem was the oppression of women by the patriarchal family system, particularly as inspired and reinforced by the puritanical Neo-Confucianism of the Cheng-Zhu 程朱 school. No fewer than nine of the first publications by Mao Zedong 毛澤東 were on the suicide of Miss Zhao Wuzhen 趙五貞, who killed herself in Changsha in her bridal chair on November 14, 1919, to resist marriage to a man she detested.[1] The young Mao blamed Miss Zhao's suicide on the outmoded and superstitious feudal values and customs of arranged marriages which oppressed young people, and especially women, and forced them into hopeless and self-defeating violence against their own persons.

From that time on, many intellectuals echoed Mao, and surpassed him in eloquence, in attacking the old family system and its mistreatment of women, and almost universally, these critics saw female suicide as one of the main results of the oppression of women in Cheng-Zhu Neo-Confucianism and in late imperial Chinese society. In the 1920s and 1930s, in the writings of Lu Xun and the novels of Ba Jin 巴金 (1904-), and in *Zhongguo funü shenghuo shi* 中國婦女生活史

[1] Three of Mao's essays on Miss Zhao are now available in English, in Hua R. Lan and Vanessa L. Fong, eds., *Women in Republican China: A Sourcebook* (Armonk, N.Y., and London: M. E. Sharpe, 1999), 79-83, 85-88.

(A history of the lives of Chinese women) by Chen Dongyuan 陳東原, women committed suicide because they believed in superstitious ideas about ghosts and reincarnation, they internalized the sexual puritanism (and overlooked the moral hypocrisy) of Neo-Confucian men, and as widows they succumbed to the conflicting and powerful social and economic pressures placed upon them by their in-laws. In this view, female suicide was a misguided act of self-destruction, a sign of Neo-Confucian "false consciousness," a terrible expression of individual despair and hopelessness, an unnecessary tragedy, and an embarrassing barometer measuring and revealing the depth of the sickness of Chinese society.

Chen Dongyuan's influential *Zhongguo funü shenghuo shi* can serve as a good starting point for this discussion.[2] Chen spoke of the "religionization" (*zongjiaohua* 宗教化) of the cult of chastity in Qing times and suggested that Neo-Confucian men became increasingly obsessed with female chastity, to the point that it became a kind of superstition. A widow, in the popular Qing view, was not a desirable bride because she was no longer a virgin, and her husband's death was seen as evidence that she was star-crossed or cursed by fate. In the increasingly rigid intellectual atmosphere of the Qing, widow remarriage was widely seen as disgraceful for the woman, and it was seen as a risky if not foolish proposition for any man to marry a widow. Puritanical scholars even began to apply the rules of chastity to virgins whose fiancés died before their marriages were consummated. In effect, Chen Dongyuan accused Neo-Confucian men of pressuring women to kill themselves for the sake of "family honor" and the avoidance of the disgrace of remarriage.

English-language scholarship on female suicide in late imperial China has not been quite as impassioned as the Chinese polemics of the May Fourth era, but it has still been profoundly influenced by the May Fourth critique of late imperial Chinese culture.[3] As Dor-

---

[2] Chen Dongyuan, *Zhongguo funü shenghuo shi* (1928; reprint, Taipei: Taiwan shangwu yinshuguan, 1967), esp. 241-46.

[3] I should mention here Margery Wolf's important 1975 essay, "Women and Suicide in China," in Margery Wolf and Roxane Witke, eds., *Women in Chinese Society* (Stanford: Stanford University Press, 1975), 111-41, which was refreshingly free of May-Fourth style cultural polemics. Although Wolf dealt with female suicide primarily in Taiwan during the first third of the twentieth century, she included much useful information for the student of late imperial China. She compared suicide rates in several different countries, noting the relatively higher rates of female suicide in China, and she insightfully discussed suicide in relation to Chinese women's life cycles, particularly those women of peasant class.

othy Ko has insightfully observed, "the invention of an ahistorical 'Chinese tradition' that is feudal, patriarchal, and oppressive was the result of a rare confluence of three divergent ideological and political traditions—the May Fourth-New Culture Movement, the Communist revolution, and Western feminist scholarship."[4] The May Fourth Anti-Confucians did not necessarily see Confucian patriarchy as timeless and changeless; that was largely the contribution of their Marxist successors and Western students of twentieth-century China. However, it can be said that one result of the powerful May Fourth critique was to stimulate a search for "progressive" predecessors, and to read the debates of the 1920s back into the late imperial period.

In my 1976 study of Chinese debates on the treatment of women in Ming and Qing times, I drew heavily on works by Chen Dongyuan, Lin Yutang 林語堂, Ōtsuka Hirohisa 大塚博久, Yamazaki Jun'ichi 山崎純一, and Yuasa Yukihiko 湯淺幸孫, all of whom were deeply influenced by the May Fourth critique of late imperial Chinese culture.[5] In their view, the oppression of women in the Ming-Qing period was closely tied to the strength of Cheng-Zhu Neo-Confucianism and its obsession with female chastity, an obsession symbolized for many in the Cheng Yi quotation that opens this essay. These scholars noted that some Chinese male literati (such as Gui Youguang 歸有光 [1506-71]and Lü Kun 呂坤 [1536-1618]) questioned the wisdom of suicides by "betrothed widows" whose marriages were not even consummated, some (including Mao Qiling 毛奇齡 [1623-1716] and Yu Zhengxie [1775-1840]) attacked the idea of widow suicide altogether, and some (such as the writers Li Yu 李漁 [1611-79] and Wu Jingzi and the poet Yuan Mei 袁枚 [1716-98]) mocked the puritanical obsession of male Confucians with female chastity. Yet these studies all pointed to the hegemonic power of puritanical Neo-Confucian attitudes about the seclusion and the chastity of women, and they all tended to put the onus on men for pushing, frightening, and inspiring so many women to kill themselves. As seen in the four quotations above, there is in this sense a striking intellectual continuity between the Qing dynasty authors Wu Jingzi and Yu Zhengxie on the one hand and the great May Fourth leader Lu Xun on the other.

---

[4] Dorothy Ko, *Teachers of the Inner Quarters: Women and Culture in Seventeenth-Century China* (Stanford: Stanford University Press, 1994), 3.

[5] Paul S. Ropp, "The Seeds of Change: Reflections on the Condition of Women in the Early and Mid Ch'ing," *Signs: Journal of Women in Culture and Society* 2.1 (1976): 5-23.

In *The Death of Woman Wang*, Jonathan Spence included a chapter called "The Widow" in which he drew on stories by Pu Songling 蒲松齡 (1640-1715) and the Qing legal code to illustrate the pressures on widows in early Qing society. Spence highlighted how Qing law had several unintended consequences for widows. The law provided for a widow to inherit her husband's property and specified that a widow who remarried lost control of her husband's property and her dowry. Though intended to encourage widows to remain chaste members of their in-laws' families, Qing law frequently had the effect of encouraging families to force widows to remarry against their will.[6] Ironically, some suicides were no doubt caused by unscrupulous in-laws pressuring widows to remarry. These women may have committed suicide in angry resistance to their in-laws, but the in-laws might then turn around and apply for court-sponsored honors for their chaste and heroic daughters-in-law. Since it was a prosecutable offense to cause the death of another, if families could argue that widows committed suicide strictly out of loyalty to their deceased husbands, the family could thereby remove suspicion from its still-living members. These are the kinds of messy details usually missing from virtuous widow biographies, but they often can be found in the court records of energetic and curious magistrates.

Several studies in the 1980s added more detail to our understanding of female suicide in late imperial China without necessarily challenging the May Fourth paradigm. In 1980, M. J. Meijer analyzed Ming and Qing legislation on sexual crimes including rape, fornication with consent, and indecent behavior which provoked a woman to commit suicide.[7] In the Qing period, Meijer argued, laws became increasingly harsh and puritanical so that lewd comments which provoked a woman to commit suicide became the legal equivalent of rape, and the man who made such comments could be prosecuted for "causing the death of another." As a consequence of these increasingly puritanical laws and official admonitions, women were encouraged to commit suicide by "an unhealthy craving for posthumous glory," and misery was often inflicted on "unsuspecting citizens." "The price of a *p'ai-lou*," Meijer concluded, "was excessive."[8]

---

[6] Jonathan D. Spence, *The Death of Woman Wang* (New York: Viking, 1978), 59-76.

[7] M. J. Meijer, "The Price of a P'ai-lou," *T'oung Pao* 67.3-5 (1981): 288-304.

[8] M. J. Meijer, "The Price," 304.

In 1981, Andrew Hsieh and Jonathan Spence provided a general historical overview in "Suicide and the Family in Pre-modern Chinese Society."[9] They traced the idea of female suicide as a moral imperative back to the Han dynasty *Lienü zhuan* 列女傳 (Biographies of women) by Liu Xiang 劉向 (77-6 BCE), which set the standard for female biographies in all subsequent periods. Whereas Liu Xiang featured a variety of strong women including those distinguished by their learning, wisdom, and courage in many settings, by the late imperial period, the emphasis in such compilations came to be placed almost exclusively on women's chastity and suicide in the service of chastity. While it was a crime to pressure or cause someone to commit suicide, many saw the act of suicide itself as admirable and as effective in expressing loyalty, in bringing attention to an unjust situation, and in seeking revenge against one's oppressors. Noting the abundance of sources on female suicide in legal records and in literary works, they urged scholars to utilize both in combination in order to provide a full understanding of the phenomenon.

Also in 1981, Ann Waltner noted the Neo-Confucian condemnation of widow remarriage but went on to describe the complex pressures on widows in the Ming and early Qing periods, concluding that "economic pressures to remarry were probably greater than moral pressure to remain chaste."[10] Citing a wide range of gazetteer biographies, legal records, and fictional sources, Waltner built a convincing case that widows had a variety of options, and some chose remarriage freely while others committed suicide precisely to resist pressures from their in-laws or natal families to remarry. She noted in particular that the Qing government strengthened legal protection of widows against forced remarriages. This was a net improvement rather than an erosion of the rights of widows. The result of Waltner's essay was to significantly complicate the May Fourth stereotype of the chaste widow committing suicide to fulfill the demands of Cheng-Zhu Neo-Confucianism.

In 1984, Mark Elvin chronicled the efforts of the Chinese state to promote "Confucian" virtues through its laws and administrative

---

[9] Andrew C. K. Hsieh and Jonathan D. Spence, "Suicide and the Family in Pre-modern Chinese Society," in Arthur Kleinman and Tsung-yi Lin, eds., *Normal and Abnormal Behavior in Chinese Culture* (Dordrecht and Boston: D. Reidel Publishing Company, 1981), 29-47.

[10] Ann Waltner, "Widows and Remarriage in Ming and Early Qing China," in Richard W. Guisso and Stanley Johannesen, eds., *Women in China: New Directions in Historical Scholarship* (Youngstown, N.Y.: Philo Press, 1981), 129-46, quotation from 136.

regulations.[11] Elvin noted government efforts, as early as the Han dynasty, to promote and reward virtue among its subjects, but like Meijer, he saw these efforts as gradually expanded in Song times and dramatically increased in the Ming and Qing periods. Elvin traced what he called the "democratization of virtue" in the late imperial era, as commoners were increasingly indoctrinated with, and rewarded for living up to, such elite values as widow chastity. In the Ming and Qing, for the first time, "betrothed widows" were officially honored for committing suicide or maintaining chastity after their fiancés died. Although some emperors worried about women "taking life lightly" and occasionally attempted to discourage female suicide, the reward system in the Qing period grew so much that the government finally had to curb individual arches in favor of collective arches for all the virtuous, chaste, and heroic females in each province. Elvin noted tensions and contradictions that could arise between conflicting virtues, as for example between choosing to die with one's husband or living on to serve his parents and/or raise his children, or for a "betrothed widow," between her obligations to her deceased fiancé and his parents on the one hand and her own parents on the other. The Qing state, he concluded, was unique not in what it defined as virtuous but in the extensive way it used the political system to promote and honor the private everyday behavior of its most ordinary subjects.

In her 1987 article, also drawn from Qing gazetteers,[12] Susan Mann analyzed elite male discourse on widow chastity, noting class differences in the widow chastity ideal and emphasizing the impact of mother-son ties on the commemoration of widow chastity. By the Qing period "female chastity was a metaphor for community honor," and competition for government-sponsored honors was so intense that elaborate bureaucratic procedures were established just to verify families' claims on behalf of their women. Mann was careful to note some ways in which the chastity ideal could protect widows from downwardly mobile or forced remarriage. She argued that Qing government attempts to promote female chastity were so successful in spreading the custom to commoners and lower gentry families that widow chastity began to lose some of its appeal as a status symbol among the elite.

---

[11] Mark Elvin, "Female Virtue and the State in China," *Past and Present* 104 (1984): 111-52.

[12] Susan Mann, "Widows in the Kinship, Class, and Community Structures of Qing Dynasty China, *Journal of Asian Studies* 46.1 (1987): 37-56.

The most detailed study of female suicide in late imperial China to date is *Male Anxiety and Female Chastity*, written in 1988 by T'ien Ju-k'ang [Tian Rukang].[13] Drawing on Ming and Qing local gazetteers, he analyzed the increasing number of widow suicides in the Ming and Qing dynasties, and tried to explain why this phenomenon occurred when it did. T'ien moved well beyond the May Fourth paradigm by studying regional variation in female suicide and examining a number of localities with high suicide rates in an attempt to determine plausible causes for the rising incidence of widow suicide in the late imperial period. Among the many factors involved, he cited governmental rewards for widow chastity and suicide, increasing economic pressures on widows to remarry (pressures increased by the laws concerning a widow's dowry cited above and also by the relative shortage of women caused by the rising incidence of female infanticide), a variety of superstitious and idolatrous beliefs about ghosts and spirits, and increasing literati fascination with and encouragement of widow suicide which T'ien saw as stimulated in part by the intense anxiety men faced in the increasingly competitive examination system.

Jerry Dennerline provided a very different view of widow chastity in a 1986 article on marriage, adoption, and charity in Wuxi lineages in the late imperial era.[14] He found that charitable estates for widows were important factors in the attempts of Wuxi lineages to form marriage alliances with other elite families. These estates, often established at the insistence of the women involved, assured a bride's family that she would never be cast adrift, forcibly remarried, or pressured into suicide by the untimely death of her husband. While Dennerline suggested that widow chastity was an important elite ideal in late imperial times, he went on to note that widow suicide, in his sources, was seen in a negative light. Moreover, he argued that women, even as widows, retained considerable control over family property and considerable influence over the long-term survival strategies of elite families.

These early studies were important in opening up the late imperial period to the new forms of gender analysis that became so prevalent

[13] T'ien Ju-k'ang, *Male Anxiety and Female Chastity: A Comparative Study of Chinese Ethical Values in Ming-Ch'ing Times* (Leiden: E. J. Brill, 1988).

[14] Jerry Dennerline, "Marriage, Adoption, and Charity in the Development of Lineages in Wu-hsi from Sung to Ch'ing," in Patricia Buckley Ebrey and James L. Watson, eds., *Kinship Organization in Late Imperial China, 1000-1940* (Berkeley: University of California Press, 1986), 170-209.

in the West in the 1980s. They began to move beyond the sweeping May Fourth critique of Confucian culture as the sole source of female oppression and to look at some of the economic and social pressures on women brought about by the rapid social and economic changes that swept over China from the sixteenth century onward. Dennerline, Mann, and Waltner each qualified the May Fourth anti-Confucian critique in important ways, but most of these other studies still tended to reflect May Fourth views and assumptions about the oppression of women in late imperial China and the main source of that oppression as being Cheng-Zhu Neo-Confucianism. It is highly significant that the main focus of all the above studies was on the thoughts and writings of men, as if the key to understanding female suicide lay with the attitudes of men.

In the 1990s, several major developments in the Chinese scholarly world began to change the focus of gender studies and to challenge the May Fourth paradigm that had held sway for so long. The most important was the "discovery" of writings by Chinese women, a discovery made suddenly unavoidable by the publication in 1985 of an expanded version of Hu Wenkai's 胡文楷 monumental *Lidai funü zhuzuo kao* 歷代婦女著作考 (An examination of women's writings through the dynasties),[15] which listed more than thirty-six hundred publications by women in the Qing dynasty. Hu's important work was to inspire a whole generation of scholars, beginning with a special issue of *Late Imperial China* in 1992 and continuing through the decade of the 1990s.[16] In these works, in contrast to earlier studies, the emphasis is on the voices of women themselves, as active participants in their society and shapers of their own destinies. The "female victims" of Confucian patriarchy, so prevalent in May Fourth-inspired analyses, began to give way to "female agents" who found meaningful ways to participate in late imperial Chinese society, sometimes in resistance and sometimes in accommodation, to the norms of their place and time.[17]

---

[15] Hu Wenkai, *Lidai funü zhuzuo kao* (1957; expanded and revised edition, Shanghai: Shanghai guji chubanshe, 1985).

[16] "Symposium on Poetry and Women's Culture in Late Imperial China," *Late Imperial China* 13.1 (1992). Among the many recent books and articles based largely on writings by Chinese women, perhaps the most notable ones are Dorothy Ko, *Teachers of the Inner Chambers*; Kang-i Sun Chang and Ellen Widmer, eds. *Writing Women in Late Imperial China* (Stanford: Stanford University Press, 1997); Susan Mann, *Precious Records: Women in China's Long Eighteenth Century* (Stanford: Stanford University Press, 1998); and Kang-i Sun Chang and Haun Saussy, eds., *Women Writers of Traditional China* (Stanford: Stanford University Press, 1999).

[17] Although not based on women's writings per se, and not limited to late

A second challenge to the May Fourth paradigm has come in several kinds of reassessment of Neo-Confucian philosophy and its role in Chinese history. As the field of Chinese studies has expanded in the West, scholars have increasingly come to appreciate the complexity of changes and continuities in Chinese society over several millennia, and the May-Fourth tendency to view late imperial Chinese society as a reflection of Cheng-Zhu Neo-Confucianism has lost much of its credibility. As Patricia Ebrey has observed, many more factors than Neo-Confucian philosophy have influenced the social position of Chinese women. "Should not the strength of the state, the commercialization of the economy, the character of elites, and shifts in popular piety have had effects on Chinese family life of the sort that they did in the West?"[18]

Ebrey has shown that widow remarriage was remarkably common in the Song period that witnessed the rise of the Cheng-Zhu school of Neo-Confucianism.[19] Jennifer Holmgren and Bettine Birge have demonstrated the profound influence of China's interaction with the Mongols in first inspiring state policies promoting chaste widowhood. During the Mongol conquest in the 1270s, the Mongol rulers briefly imposed on all Chinese the Mongol practice of the levirate whereby a widow stayed with her in-laws and married her husband's

---

imperial China, two other pioneering works should be mentioned as important in opening up the field of Chinese gender studies: Christina Gilmartin, et. al., eds., *Engendering China: Women, Culture, and the State* (Cambridge: Harvard University Press, 1994), ; and Harriet T. Zurndorfer, ed., *Chinese Women in the Imperial Past: New Perspectives* (Leiden: E. J. Brill, 1999). A useful overview of the development of gender studies in the China field is Jinhua Emma Teng, "The Construction of the 'Traditional Chinese Woman' in the Western Academy: A Critical Review," *Signs: Journal of Women in Culture and Society* 22.1 (1996): 115-51. Three articles that survey much new work of the early 1990s are: Susan Mann, "What Can Feminist Theory Do for the Study of Chinese History? A Brief Review of Scholarship in the U. S.," *Research on Women in Modern Chinese History* 1 (1993): 241-60; Paul S. Ropp, "Women in Late Imperial China: A Review of Recent English-Language Scholarship," *Women's History Review* 3.3 (1994): 347-83; and Ann Waltner, "Recent Scholarship on Chinese Women," *Signs: Journal of Women in Culture and Society* 21.2 (1996): 410-28.

[18] Patricia Ebrey, "Women, Marriage, and the Family in Chinese History," in Paul S. Ropp, ed., *Heritage of China: Contemporary Perspectives on Chinese Civilization* (Berkeley: University of California Press, 1990), 200.

[19] Patricia Ebrey, "Women, Marriage, and the Family," 220; Patricia Ebrey, "Women in the Kinship System of the Southern Song Upper Class," in Richard Guisso and Stanley Johannesen, eds., *Women in China* (Youngstown, N.Y.: Philo Press, 1981), 113-28; and Patricia Buckley Ebrey, *The Inner Quarters: Marriage and the Lives of Women in the Sung Period* (Berkeley: University of California Press, 1993), esp. 204-16.

younger brother. Remaining chaste was, at that point, the only way a widow could escape a levirate remarriage. This policy, which seemed to many Chinese like forced incest, was quickly relaxed, but a far-reaching consequence was to import into Chinese law the steppe-inspired notion that a wife was, in a sense, purchased property. From the 1260s to the 1320s, Chinese inheritance laws were changed to grant to a widow's in-laws both the control of her dowry and the power to arrange for her remarriage.[20] These were profound changes that seriously constricted the available options for widows in Chinese society. As Bettine Birge concluded, "What later Confucians took to be classically inspired laws promoting timeless standards were in fact the result of changes made possible by a confusing encounter between Chinese and Mongolian culture."[21]

In her 1997 study of shrine-building in the Ming period, Katherine Carlitz demonstrated how the ideals of widow chastity came to serve a variety of interests in the Ming period.[22] The Ming founder had emphasized the importance of the Three Bonds (daughter to parents, wife to husband, mother to sons) and Five Relationships (ruler-subject, husband-wife, parent-child, older-younger sibling, older-younger friend) in defining "proper Chinese" virtues. In these relationships, women's fidelity was recognized as the analogue of male loyalty, and as the Ming proceeded to build and expand its bureaucratic rule, local officials in the fifteenth century began to build shrines to "local worthies," including women, who exemplified extraordinary loyalty. Some of these shrines were intended to replace "efficacious" shrines to deities or spirits and to inspire and encourage virtue in the populace in "non-superstitious" ways. Carlitz shows how the cult of widow suicide served the dynasty in promoting a "recognizably Chinese web of loyalties," while it provided local officials a way to promote the interests of their regions and local elites with an appealing "aura of pathos" in praising and building their own lineages.[23]

---

[20] Jennifer Holmgren, "The Economic Foundations of Virtue: Widow Remarriage in Early and Modern China," *The Australian Journal of Chinese Affairs* 13 (1985): 1-27; and "Observations on Marriage and Inheritance Practices in Early Mongol and Yuan Society, with Particular Reference to the Levirate," *Journal of Asian History* 20 (1986): 127-92; Bettine Birge, "Levirate Marriage and the Revival of Widow Chastity in Yuan China," *Asia Major* 8.2 (1995): 107-46.

[21] Birge, "Levirate Marriage," 146.

[22] Katherine Carlitz, "Shrines, Governing-Class Identity, and the Cult of Widow-Fidelity in Mid-Ming Jiangnan," *Journal of Asian Studies* 56.3 (1997): 612-40.

[23] Carlitz, "Shrines," 636.

All of these recent studies show how complex was the rise of the cult of widow chastity in the late imperial period. Neo-Confucian scholars promoted the cult, to be sure, but many legal, economic, and institutional factors were at least as important as Neo-Confucian ideals in the development of the cult. There are still, to be sure, feminist critics of Neo-Confucian philosophy, but no scholar today would make the sweeping charges against the Cheng-Zhu tradition that were made in the May Fourth period. And some scholars have made a spirited defense of Confucianism with regard to its treatment of women. In *The Sage and the Second Sex: Confucianism, Ethics, and Gender*, edited by Chenyang Li, Patricia Ebrey summarizes the book's argument in her introduction.

> The authors whose work is presented here challenge the New Culture reading of the links between Chinese women and Confucianism in three principal ways: they suggest that women's situations were not as bad as supposed; that core Confucian teachings had little to do with anything bad about their situations; and that Confucianism offers an ethical vision compatible with feminism.[24]

Not all scholars will accept these conclusions, but in the scholarship of the 1990s, late imperial Chinese culture is seen to reflect not simply Neo-Confucian values but also social, intellectual, legal, and economic forces of a society in great ferment.

A third form of challenge to the May Fourth paradigm has taken place in literary studies, as the Maoist paradigm declined in China, and literary specialists both there and in the West began to move beyond the May Fourth tendency to categorize literary works as "progressive" or "regressive" vis-a-vis a society perceived as in need of transformation. Instead, literary scholars have attempted to reconstruct the meanings of literary works in their own time, quite apart from the question as to whether they were socially or politically "progressive." Andrew Plaks, David Rolston, Stephen Roddy, and Martin Huang have made important contributions in this regard.[25] Some authors working in this vein have also addressed gen-

---

[24] Patricia Ebrey, "Foreword," in Chenyang Li, ed., *The Sage and the Second Sex: Confucianism, Ethics, and Gender* (Chicago and La Salle, Illinois: Open Court, 2000), x.

[25] Andrew Plaks, *The Four Masterworks of the Ming Novel* (Princeton: Princeton University Press, 1987); David Rolston, "Theory and Practice: Fiction, Fiction Criticism, and the Writing of the *Ju-lin wai-shih*" (Ph.D. diss., University of Chicago, 1988); David Rolston, ed., *How to Read the Chinese Novel* (Princeton: Princeton University Press, 1990); Martin W. Huang, *Literati and Self-Re/Presentation: Autobiographical Sensibility in the Eighteenth-Century Chinese Novel* (Stanford: Stanford Univer-

der questions directly, including Li Wai-yee, Louise Edwards, Keith McMahon, and Maram Epstein.[26] In each case, these authors have challenged, or ignored, the May Fourth (and the Chinese Marxist) assessment of the novels under study and instead applied other criteria (sometimes structuralist, sometimes feminist, sometimes traditional literati readings) to evaluate and make sense of the works.

Finally, in recent years, increasingly detailed studies of social and political institutions have shed much new light on the position of women in late imperial Chinese society. In her 1993 article, Angela Leung demonstrated that widow homes became increasingly commonplace from 1873 until the Qing collapse, as a way of providing widows from poor families some of the guarantees of safety and support that the charitable estates studied by Jerry Dennerline had provided widows of elite families. Leung argued that widow homes reflected a determined effort to maintain the cult of widow chastity in an increasingly hostile environment in which gangs of young ruffians regularly kidnapped widows for sale and remarriage. These violent attacks on poor widows escalated with the weakening of the Qing social order, especially after the Taiping uprising of the mid-nineteenth century. In the nineteenth century in particular, women themselves became active in promoting and managing such homes.[27]

Thanks to the opening of new archives in China in the 1990s, there have been several important studies of late imperial Chinese legal institutions which bear on our theme of the cult of chastity as it influenced official interpretation of the rights and duties of widows. Kathryn Bernhardt, in *Women and Property in China, 960-1949*, argued that the growing cult of chastity in the Qing period had some favorable consequences for widows, as magistrates gave them increasing power to name an heir of their own choice, precisely out of respect for the widows' desire to remain chaste. Whereas Ming law had stipulated that widows must adopt a specified heir in strict order

sity Press, 1995); Stephen J. Roddy, *Literati Identity and Its Fictional Representations in Late Imperial China* (Stanford: Stanford University Press, 1998).

[26] Wai-yee Li, *Enchantment and Disenchantment: Love and Illusion in Chinese Literature* (Princeton: Princeton University Press, 1993); Louise P. Edwards, *Men & Women in Qing China: Gender in "The Red Chamber Dream"* (Leiden: E. J. Brill, 1994); Keith McMahon, *Misers, Shrews, and Polygamists: Sexuality and Male-Female Relations in Eighteenth-Century Chinese Fiction* (Durham: Duke University Press, 1995); Maram Epstein, *Competing Discourses: Orthodoxy, Authenticity, and Engendered Meanings in Late Imperial Chinese Fiction* (Cambridge: Harvard University Press, 2001).

[27] Angela Ki Che Leung, "To Chasten Society: The Development of Widow Homes in the Qing, 1773-1911," *Late Imperial China* 14.2 (1993): 1-32.

of seniority and closeness of relationship, magistrates in the Qing regularly disregarded this statute, and by 1775 a widow's right was formally recognized to choose her own heir from among her nephews, as long as generations were not mixed.[28]

In his studies of sexual offenses in Qing law, Matthew Sommer illustrated how women, often of modest means, could be active agents in appealing to the cult of chastity explicitly in order to defend their own interests, to insure their inheritance rights, and to protect themselves against unscrupulous in-laws and other family members. The chaste widow ideal could empower a widow and reward her with a high degree of independence and even freedom under the law, as long as she could make a convincing case that she used her freedom in the service of chastity and dedication to her deceased husband and his heirs.[29]

In her recent doctoral dissertation, Janet Theiss examined "how norms of female virtue worked in social practice for ordinary people by studying criminal cases that involve infringement of those norms or conflicts over them."[30] Among the many revelations in her study, Theiss demonstrated that some magistrates condoned the power of lineages to punish non-criminal wrongdoing in their own families, that many women had natal families who were active in defending their daughters' rights long after their marriages, and that there existed a wide gulf between moral handbooks and non-elite practices and expectations concerning male-female contact outside the family. The intensity of concern for female chastity, coupled with the commonplace contact between men and women outside the elite, meant that women were easily provoked to suicide by casual actions or remarks that might in any way call into question their chaste reputations. Suicide was particularly appealing to a wronged woman whose family failed to come to her defense or to confront the offending male. In such a case, a woman's suicide was seen as proof of her

---

28 Kathryn Bernhardt, *Women and Property in China, 960-1949* (Stanford: Stanford University Press, 1999), Ch. 2, "The Inheritance Rights of Widows from the Song Through the Qing," 47-72.

29 Matthew H. Sommer, *Sex, Law, and Society in Late Imperial China* (Stanford: Stanford University Press, 2000), especially Ch. 5, "Widows in the Qing Chastity Cult: The Nexus of Sex and Property in Law and in Women's Lives," 166-209; and "The Uses of Chastity: Sex, Law, and the Property of Widows in Qing China," *Late Imperial China* 17.2 (1996): 77-130.

30 Janet M. Theiss, "Dealing with Disgrace: The Negotiation of Female Virtue in Late Imperial China" (Ph.D. diss., University of California at Berkeley, 1998), 34.

chastity, and it assured that her harasser would be charged with a serious crime.

As Theiss revealed, it was precisely in the eighteenth century that the cult of chastity was most important, not because it was a particularly virtuous age, but on the contrary, because "social and economic status were volatile and tenuous and the boundaries between inner and outer, between the acceptable and the unacceptable and between assumed norms and contested preferences were more blurred than they had ever been."[31] In such an atmosphere, chastity was an important status marker for a woman and her entire family. Yet women were also taught that assertiveness was not a desirable female trait; the line dividing the chastity heroine from the shrew was a fine one. The rich archival evidence of Theiss's study suggested that women, with the largest stake in the chastity cult, and easily caught between the demands of chastity, the pressures of age and status hierarchies, and family concerns for saving face and avoiding scandal, had even more reasons than men to suffer from anxiety.

Bernhardt, Sommer, and Theiss all effectively used legal records to illuminate the ways that ordinary people, including ordinary women, internalized, adapted, and manipulated the cult of chastity in their daily lives. Among many other things, these scholars have revealed that many pressures on women, and widows in particular, had little to do with Cheng-Zhu Neo-Confucian orthodoxy per se and much more to do with inherited community standards and practices, property and inheritance laws and customs, family wealth, status and concerns about face, and the peculiarities of the individual personalities of emperors and officials and the informal relationships between them.

As a consequence of all the above developments—new attention to the voices of women themselves, a reassessment of Neo-Confucian philosophy and its role in shaping late imperial society, new paradigms of literary analysis, and new studies of Qing social institutions, especially using newly available sources in Chinese archives—the old May Fourth paradigm is rapidly being transcended in contemporary scholarship on late imperial China.[32] Equally im-

---

[31] Theiss, "Dealing with Disgrace," 310.

[32] Two essays that deal in part with widows and widow suicide, and that explicitly address the ways a more nuanced understanding of late imperial China calls into question the May Fourth paradigm, are my own "A Confucian View of Chinese Women in the Ch'ing Period," *Chinese Studies* (Taipei) 10.2 (1992): 399-

portant, as a result of the ongoing revision of the May Fourth legacy and the rapid development of gender analyses in the past two decades, the study of late imperial China today has become an intensely interdisciplinary enterprise. The boundary lines between history, literature, law, philosophy, anthropology, and sociology are happily and beneficially blurred as never before. The four essays in this collection all make important contributions to these trends.

We begin with Katherine Carlitz's essay which explores the writings of two prominent Ming literati, Kang Hai 康海 (1475-1541) and Wang Jiusi 王九思 (1468-1551). This essay continues Carlitz's work in tracing the various meanings of female suicide for male literati in the Ming period. (She also notes the paucity of female-authored writings on suicide in the Ming.) Whereas the May Fourth critique focused on blaming male attitudes for encouraging female suicide, Carlitz is more concerned with discovering why Ming literati were so fascinated with female suicide and so quick to admire its practitioners. She makes very substantial revisions in the picture presented by T'ien Ju-k'ang and by the scholars quoted at the beginning of this introduction. She demonstrated in her earlier articles how male literati praised female chastity and suicide for a variety of reasons: to write movingly of female suicide in order to promote their own literary fame and/or the moral reputation of their friends, family, and local region.[33] Here, she emphasizes how such writings were used to encourage, solidify, and publicize deepening ties of literati friendship and the building of social networks. Even more impor-

---

435; and Paola Paderni, "Between Constraints and Opportunities: Widows, Witches, and Shrews in Eighteenth-Century China," in Zurndorfer, ed. *Chinese Women in the Imperial Past*, 258-85. I argue that the Qing male literati who wrote poems in praise of chaste women who committed suicide did so out of admiration for the women's courage and strength of will, and also sadness and pity over their loss of life. These men did not urge suicide as a proper course of action, but felt obliged to honor such acts of self-sacrifice. Paderni demonstrates how women could and often did manipulate the Qing value system, including the cult of chastity, in pursuit of their own self- interest. She casts her essay in response to Dorothy Ko's critique of any simple dichotomy between women as victims or agents, and argues that women in the eighteenth-century had considerable room to maneuver between constraints and opportunities.

[33] In addition to her essay on shrines cited above in note 22, see Katherine Carlitz, "The Social Uses of Female Virtue in Late Ming Editions of the *Lienü Zhuan*," *Late Imperial China* 12.2 (1991): 117-48; and "Desire, Danger, and the Body: Stories of Women's Virtue in Late Ming China," in Gilmartin, et. al., *Engendering China*, pp. 101-24. Another article that nicely complements Carlitz's work is Paola Paderni, "Le rachat de l'honneur perdu. Le suicide des femmes dans la Chine du XVIIIe siècle," *Études chinoises* 10.1-2 (1991): 135-60.

tant, she relates the male fascination with female suicide to the Ming cult of *qing* 情, passion. This effectively scrambles and modifies one of the articles of faith of the May Fourth paradigm in which the cult of *qing* represented "progressive" forces that stood in opposition to the puritanism of Cheng-Zhu Neo-Confucianism. Carlitz demonstrates that the rise of pro-suicide writings in the fifteenth century was *not* orchestrated by the state on behalf of a conservative and puritanical orthodoxy. Rather it was a spontaneous development among Ming literati of a variety of intellectual persuasions and included such an unorthodox aesthete and connoisseur of courtesans as Wang Jiusi. At least by the sixteenth century, passionate love—whether between husbands and wives, husbands and concubines, or literati and courtesans—had become a key ingredient in the male literati understanding and representation of female suicides. This is a far cry from the earlier view that female suicides were chiefly inspired by Cheng Yi's harsh admonition on the importance of preserving chastity over life itself. Carlitz's analysis shows how many different agendas could be met by the male praise of female suicide.

If Carlitz modifies our understanding of literati encouragement of female suicide, Janet Theiss complicates the May Fourth view of the role of the state in the growing cult of female chastity and suicide. In passing, Carlitz notes that young women who committed suicide usually did so in violation of some of their duties under the five Confucian relationships. In examining Qing state policies toward female suicide, Janet Theiss gives us our most detailed look to date at court debates over what might be called an official "containment" policy, as a succession of emperors worried about women "taking life lightly" and committing suicide in irrational acts of passion. Theiss notes that by the end of the Shunzhi 順治 reign, the court made a clear distinction between "good" or "proper" and "bad" or "improper" suicides. Emperor Yongzheng 雍正 attempted to bureaucratize the cult of chastity, to bring it under state control, and to use it to bolster the prestige and power of the state. But he was not simply an opportunist trying to harness a social phenomenon for state purposes. In his view, widow suicide was far less admirable than living out a long chaste life and continuing to raise one's children and serve one's in-laws. Like other Qing emperors, he was fundamentally ambivalent toward the phenomenon of female suicide. Such ambivalence resulted in periodic edicts outlawing suicide and/or curtailing state honors for most suicides, only to be followed by an avalanche of requests from local officials for exemptions in "special cases" which, in the officials' views, deserved state recognition and honors.

Theiss highlights the evolution of official Qing policy toward female suicide and shows how Emperor Yongzheng's state-building efforts collapsed in the nineteenth century amidst the chaos of civil war and the breakdown of the imperial order. In such an atmosphere, the number of requests for honors skyrocketed, and the Qing government lowered the requirements for official honors, giving rise to unprecedented numbers of awards for "chaste and heroic" women. As Carlitz reveals the complex mix of literati motives in praising female suicide, Theiss demonstrates the complex ways that Chinese scholar-officials' motives interacted, sometimes in convergence and sometimes in tension, with Qing imperial goals and policies. In Theiss's view, Qing policies toward female chastity and suicide had less to do with orthodox definitions of morality and more to do with issues of ethnic identity, the personal proclivities and sometimes-conflicting political agendas of emperors and their officials, and the ever-changing vagaries of social life and political circumstances.

In surveying female suicides in a wide range of Ming-Qing fiction, Paola Zamperini adds several more dimensions in complicating the May Fourth paradigm. She notes that fiction writers mirror the ambivalence of official discourse on female suicide, but she also highlights important contrasts as fiction writers tend to see in the women who commit suicide many motives quite at variance with the orthodox chastity concerns featured in so much nonfiction writing on the topic. Here is perhaps the strongest contrast with the kind of female suicides envisioned by Lu Xun and Mao Zedong. The suicidal women portrayed by Zamperini are anything but passive, defeated, and despairing. Rather, they commit suicide in their quest "for justice, freedom, and independence." They seek to avenge wrongs and "to convey to eternity the strength of their passions, from love to hatred, from jealousy to thirst for revenge." Echoing one of the themes of Carlitz, Zamperini also notes the importance of love in prompting many women in fiction to commit suicide. While she recognizes the varied concerns of fiction writers—from satire and social criticism to titillation and voyeurism to the workings of karma through multiple reincarnations—she also shows how fiction reveals a more complex set of motives for female suicide than suggested in most conventional epitaphs and chaste widow biographies.

Grace Fong's essay on women's suicide writings in the Ming-Qing period opens perhaps the newest and least explored territory on female suicides. Here are voices that were not recognized in the May Fourth critique of late imperial Chinese culture. Although these writings were mostly by anonymous women, and some of them may have been "ghost-authored" by men (though Fong believes they were not), they suggest a powerful sense of female agency in the autobiographical rationale for the suicidal act itself. Two of the women Fong discusses killed themselves to preserve their chastity and prevent their defilement by the Manchu troops who captured them (one in 1654 during the later stages of the Qing conquest and one in 1864 during the demise of the Taiping rebellion). These women had a strong sense of loyalty to history and to the core Chinese values of the subject's loyalty to the sovereign. In effect, they surpassed most men who, lacking their courage and determination, more often submitted to their captors. The third case examined by Fong is a young widow accused of sexual misconduct by her mother-in-law. Just before starving herself to death, she wrote an autobiographical postscript to three hundred of her own poems, written in secret and detailing the hardships of her three years of widowhood and her steadfast loyalty to her deceased husband. In all three cases, Fong notes, these women accomplished their objective, as their writings were preserved and published, providing posthumous vindication. Through the moral praise of subsequent generations, they attained a kind of cultural immortality.

Each of the essays in this issue marks a significant revision of the May Fourth view of women and their role in late imperial Chinese culture. Together they reveal a complex world of tensions, conflicting demands and expectations, and a variety of means by which women and men made moral sense of their lives. Neither all men nor all women necessarily agreed on the proper way to view female suicide. But it is abundantly clear from these studies that female suicide was not necessarily a sign of weakness, despair, "false consciousness," or "enslavement" to Neo-Confucianism.

# THE DAUGHTER, THE SINGING-GIRL, AND THE SEDUCTION OF SUICIDE

BY

KATHERINE CARLITZ
(University of Pittsburgh)

*Abstract*

This paper examines how the suicides of singing-girls and young gentry women were commemorated by the poets Kang Hai (1475-1541) and Wang Jiusi (1468-1551) whose devotion to wine, women, and song were, and still are, legendary. Witnessing the suicides of mutually-related female family members as well as a concubine of a mutual friend, these two poets valorized these deaths in terms of *qing* (passion). The girls of good family defy their elders in order to consummate their suicides, and Wang's songs for the concubine singing-girl are filled with evocations of sensual satisfaction. Thus, in the writings of Kang and Wang we see how the norms of the chastity cult were made not restrictive but alluring; the author suggests that this helped the poets to conquer the imagination of the governing class, with the ultimate results that they were able to diffuse these images throughout the whole of society.

The poets Kang Hai 康海 (1475-1541) and Wang Jiusi 王九思 (1468-1551) are legendary for their celebrated friendship and for their devotion to wine, women, and song. The chroniclers of Ming literati life have kept the memory of that friendship alive, but less well-known are the ties of fidelity and family tragedy that bound the two men. They betrothed their children (Kang's son and Wang's daughter) in 1508, at the high tide of their brief careers at court,[1] but two decades later, Kang and Wang were both exiled from government, Wang's daughter had died, and the death of Kang's son was followed not only by the virtuous suicide of his second wife, but by the death of the second wife's brother, and the suicide of *his* wife. At Kang Hai's request, Wang Jiusi wrote funerary essays for all of these young people.

At the very beginning of this cascade of misfortune, the two men

[1] Strictly speaking, the children were promised in 1508 when they were born, but betrothed formally only in 1516, when both men were back home. See Wang's epitaph for his daughter, cited below.

had been using the rhetoric of fidelity to praise a very different sort of heroine. In 1526, the year that Wang lost his daughter, their friend Zhang Yupeng 張予鵬 died at the secluded retreat he had chosen after leaving government. Zhang was married, but had taken a singing-girl, Wang Lanqing 王蘭卿, as a concubine. Some months after Zhang's death, Wang Lanqing committed suicide. Wang Jiusi, deeply moved, wrote a suite of songs in the Southern style that he and Kang were helping to bring into fashion. Kang Hai then wrote a *zaju* 雜劇 play about Wang Lanqing, showcasing Wang Jiusi's suite of songs as the dominant arias of the fourth act.

What links can we see between the songs, drama, and essays that Kang and Wang wrote for all these young women? Why do the links matter for the study of suicide? The answer is that the cult of fidelity, of which suicide was a canonical expression, soon became less a matter of rules than of emotions. The court's criteria for awards were based on age and length of widowhood, but a note of pathos dominated the standard petitions by the earliest years of the Ming.[2] This emphasis on the feelings blurred the difference between a singing-girl and a girl of good family and, in a sort of feedback loop, made the fidelity cult ever more attractive to literati men as the value of *qing* 情 or affection took root in literati culture.[3]

We must recognize the importance of women's chastity to elite men's culture if we are to understand why the reporting (and doubtless the actual cases) of women's virtuous suicide surged during the Ming dynasty. Fidelity-suicides (to avoid remarriage, to avoid rape, or—in a motif newly honored in the Ming—to follow a husband in death) account for roughly a third of the women recorded in Ming local histories, virtually all of which devote a chapter to *lienü* 列女 (notable women).[4] By contrast, most extant Song and Yuan dynasty gazetteers record no women's names at all, and accounts of fidelity ordeals are found in only a small fraction of those that do.[5] What

[2] See the early Ming essays from Kunshan 崑山 cited in Katherine Carlitz, "Shrines, Governing-Class Identity, and the Cult of Widow Fidelity in Mid-Ming Jiangnan," *Journal of Asian Studies* 56 (1997), 616.

[3] Enthusiasm for *qing* is conventionally considered a late-Ming phenomenon, but Kang and Wang are already, in 1519, using the language that would be standard in late Ming discourse on *qing*. They justify *qu* poetry, understood as poetry about the passions, in terms of *qing*, considered as fundamental to human nature and all nature. See Han Jiegen 韓結根, *Kang Hai nianpu* 康海年譜 (Shanghai: Fudan University Press, 1993), 155.

[4] For the one-third figure, see Carlitz, "Shrines," pp. 613, 636.

[5] Based on gazetteers collected in the set *Song Yuan difangzhi congkan* 宋元坊志叢刊

changed? Any answer must be complex, involving a fusion of new philosophical trends and bureaucratic structures in the late Yuan and early Ming, the spread of examination orthodoxy that equated women's chastity with men's loyalty, and social changes that put this examination culture in reach of more and more families.[6] But what we must remember is that the chastity cult originated in male culture. Neo-Confucian thinkers of the Song dynasty took China's profoundly gendered philosophical heritage and made women's chastity and fidelity the feminine expression of the *dao wu gou* 道無垢 (the "Dao without flaw,"), and the value of chastity, as Patricia Ebrey shows, was already gaining ground among the elite of the late Song.[7] Beverly Bossler demonstrates that Yuan literati, in new genres of "exemplar texts" that celebrated both virtuous men and women, accorded unprecedented prominence to wifely fidelity.[8] By Ming times, when the cult of fidelity took root in society at large, it was male writing in the public sphere—memorials, biography, epitaphs—that crystallized the conventions later used by both sexes to describe suicide for fidelity.

Why did literati men commit themselves to the ideal of women's chastity? I will be looking here at the early sixteenth century, when it cannot be argued that men were simply responding to the dictates of state policy vigorously pursued. The Ming founder had established procedures for awards to chaste widows and their families, but

---

(Beijing: Zhonghua shuju, 1990). In this set, one quarter of the gazetteers include a section devoted to *lienü* 列女 and *zhenfu* 貞婦, but most of the exemplars are companions to famous mythological males and have nothing to do with *ru* 儒 norms of fidelity. Ten percent of the gazetteers contain a significant number of cases with a recognizably *ru* tone. They are the 1192 *Wujun zhi* 吳郡志 (thirteen cases), the 1201 *Huiji zhi* 會稽志 (seven cases), the 1268 *Lin'an zhi* 臨安志 (eleven cases), and the 1344 *Jinling xin zhi* 金陵新志 (sixteen cases). This does not reflect the full extent of literate society's commitment to fidelity ideals; gazetteers, which typically compressed essays by notable literati, inevitably lag a bit behind. See citation to Beverly Bossler below.

[6] This was not solely a matter of Chinese ideological purity. As Bettine Birge shows, the spread of the fidelity cult during the Yuan was due in part to a fortuitous convergence of Mongol and Neo-Confucian ideals. See "Levirate Marriage and the Rise of Widow Chastity in Yuan China," *Asia Major,* 3rd Series, 8.2 (1995): 107-46.

[7] See Patricia Buckley Ebrey, *The Inner Quarters: Marriage and the Lives of Chinese Women in the Sung Period* (Berkeley: University of California Press, 1993). Family prestige was a factor, since the new attitudes toward chastity were associated with the examination culture that gained social power over the course of the Song.

[8] Beverly Bossler, "Faithful Wives and Heroic Martyrs: State, Society, and Discourses of Loyalty from Song to Yuan." (forthcoming).

after the Hongwu 洪武 and Yongle 永樂 eras, the court itself made very little coherent effort to regulate morals. No Ming emperor took women's chastity as seriously as did the Qing dynasty Yongzheng 雍正 emperor, whose measures are described by Janet Theiss in this volume. Local officials and gentry in the late fifteenth century were very active in establishing *ru* 儒 or "Confucian" shrines to men *and* women, but they did not do so in response to directives from the court. Rather, the localities took the initiative and used state-sanctioned rhetoric to aggrandize themselves.[9]

Similarly, individual men who wrote about chastity did so because such writing satisfied their own needs and desires. In another paper I discussed evidence showing that literary fame, career advancement, and community self-advertisement could serve as reasons men wrote about women's ordeals of chastity, once the state had established a channel whereby they could achieve recognition for doing so.[10] It was men who produced the enormous preponderance of the literature of fidelity, and they did so because such writing could fit perfectly into the ideal life pattern of elite men, namely the continuum from the personal to the public. Men could vie for *public* recognition by adopting state-sanctioned rhetoric and establishing shrines to faithful women, and at the same time, they could and did forge personal ties to other men, by writing epitaphs or poems for their friends' mothers, wives, daughters, and concubines. The evocation of passion, including the passion-driven gesture of suicide, was a signal to other men of one's capacity for friendship. (Men might, upon request from friends, write eloquent poetry about women they had never seen and barely heard of.)[11]

Sensuality of various kinds was part of the appeal of these stories of purity. Tales of singing-girls, whose fidelity to elite norms triumphed over their supposedly depraved milieu, can be found in Song dynasty sources dating from the earliest stirrings of the chastity cult.[12] Ming law attempted to keep these *jian* 賤 (debased) women in

---

[9] See Carlitz, "Shrines," and Wing-kai To, "Local Shrines, Family Rituals, and the Cult of Loyalty in Mid-Ming Guangdong." (paper presented at the Annual Meeting of the Association for Asian Studies, San Diego, March 2000.)

[10] Carlitz, "Shrines." In "Faithful Wives," Beverly Bossler demonstrates that Yuan literati who celebrated virtuous women had similarly complex motives.

[11] An outstanding case is the long poem that Secretary Lu Shidao 陸師道 (1511-74) of the Ministry of Rites wrote to defend the reputation of a young woman suicide Zhang 張 who was being championed by the essayist Gui Youguang 歸有光 (1507-71). See "Dao Zhang zhenfu 悼張貞婦," in the1605 *Jiading xianzhi* 嘉定縣志, 21.48a-52a.

[12] See for example two tales in the Song dynasty compendium *Yijian zhi* 夷堅志

a separate sphere from those of respectable commoner (*liang*) 良 status, but the fact that Kang Hai and Wang Jiusi could move so fluently between their *liang* and *jian* heroines suggests that the singing-girl, with her explicit appeal to the passions, has a great deal to tell us about the actual content of the *liang* ideal.

By mid-Qing times, as Janet Theiss has demonstrated from extant court records, the chastity cult was woven into the texture of social life at every level. Women had assimilated the ideal of chastity and fidelity to the point of using suicide aggressively, to embarrass men who tainted them.[13] We have no such trove of Ming dynasty court materials, which would give us women's voices at many social levels.[14] Poems, letters, and diaries of elite women afford our best opportunity to hear Ming women's voices, but references to suicide—whether approving *or* disapproving—are rare in these sources. Women wrote exemplary texts given to girls, but these texts emphasized fidelity and propriety far more than they talked about suicide.[15] Women did *not* write the biographies, the petitions for state awards, the epitaphs that established the conventions for writing about suicide in the public record, namely the local histories in which pathetic accounts of ordeals of fidelity were a standard feature from early Ming times on. Unlike footbinding, conventionally thought to have been imposed on women by men but now shown to have originated and continued as one of the mysteries of the women's quarters,[16] the spread of the chastity ideal apparently got its start in the way literati men talked to *each other*, holding their heroines up as models or as objects of passionate concern.

---

(Beijing: Yanshan chubanshe, 1997), "Chang'an Li Mei 長安李妹," 2521, and "Yi chang zhuan 義倡傳," 3041.

[13] Janet Theiss, "Dealing with Disgrace: The Negotiation of Female Virtue in Eighteenth-Century China" (Ph.D. diss., University of California, Berkeley, 1998).

[14] Sparse legal materials from the very *late* Ming suggest the same aggressive use of suicide by women. See the cases of Xu Dui 徐對, 190, and Liu Shijun 劉士俊, 671, in the 1634 casebook *Xunci* 譖辭 by Zhang Kentang 張肯堂 (Taibei: Taiwan xuesheng shuju, 1969 [facsimile reprint]).

[15] See the texts introduced by Theresa Kelleher in "Women's Education," Wm. Theodore DeBary and Irene Bloom, eds., *Sources of Chinese Tradition*, vol.1, 2nd ed. (New York: Columbia University Press, 1999), 819-40.

[16] See Ebrey, *Inner Quarters*, and Dorothy Ko, *Teachers of the Inner Chambers: Women and Culture in Seventeenth-Century China* (Stanford: Stanford University Press, 1994), 147-51.

*Kang Hai and Wang Jiusi*

Kang Hai and Wang Jiusi were born into high-gentry, office-holding families in Shaanxi 陝西 province, Kang Hai in Wugong 武功 county and Wang in nearby Hu 鄠 county. Both passed the *jinshi* 進士 examination in their twenties, Wang in 1496 and Kang Hai as the top graduate of 1502. Both were assigned to the Hanlin 翰林 Academy, and their participation in the group of essayists who would come to be known as the Seven Early Masters of classical style assured them fame that far outlasted their time at court. Their good fortune must have seemed complete when both their wives became pregnant: if one child was a boy and one a girl, they agreed, the babies would be betrothed.[17] But the fall of their notorious fellow-provincial, the eunuch Liu Jin 劉瑾, meant the end of their careers at the heavily factionalized court. Neither was willing to entertain later requests to serve, and they lived out their lives as private gentlemen, though their repeated poems and letters about the dangers of holding office suggest underlying disappointment at the demise of the brilliant careers they must have expected.[18]

The "Seven Early Masters" was actually a fairly fleeting association, and it was during the long years after the fall that Kang and Wang deepened their personal ties. Like most elite men of their era, they traveled continually to visit friends, and, with those friends, went on pilgrimages to famous sites. (We know of these travels from the endless literary exchanges they produced, since no visit could be considered complete without a poem or essay to commemorate it.) Kang and Wang were already united by their shared history at court and the planned marriage of their children; they deepened their friendship with poems on rhymes they borrowed from each other and with prefaces to each other's work.

And just as they had been masters of the essay at court, in retirement they became literary pioneers of song-poetry or *qu* 曲, helping to create the national fashion for Southern melodies, and writing *zaju* plays in the new style that mixed Northern and Southern tunes.[19] This put them at the center of another modus of Ming

[17] Wang already had an eight-year-old son by his deceased first wife. Wang and his first wife had been betrothed because of the friendship of their fathers, and Wang would choose his second wife because of his friendship with her father's younger brother. See the epitaph for his wives, cited below.

[18] L. Carrington Goodrich and Chaoying Fang, *Dictionary of Ming Biography* (New York: Columbia University Press, 1976), 692-94 and 1366-67.

[19] Tilemann Grimm makes this point in his biographical sketch of Wang Jiusi. See *Dictionary of Ming Biography*, 1367.

friendship, the realm of banquets and singing-girls, since the performance of drama and song was central to the culture of literati visiting. *Qu* were performed at banquets or at the temples or lakes where romantic gatherings were convened, and these banquets and gatherings were then further commemorated in *qu*.

Two very different personalities emerge from Kang's and Wang's writing, even their writing for each other. Kang's literary persona is reserved and scholarly. A *zhuangyuan* 狀元 or top graduate, he had been much in demand as writer of prefaces for Shaanxi county gazetteers, and he produced a celebrated gazetteer of his own Wugong county.[20] Wang always refers to him as "The Historian." Kang's essay on the nature of friendship has no hint of the lively banquets he and his friends organized; rather, it presents the orthodox view of friendship as a means of moral development.[21] Wang Jiusi is the expressive member of the pair, writing numerous playful poems to singing-girls of his acquaintance (he uses Kang's rhymes for some of these), and in his suites of songs for the birthdays of everyone from respectable dowagers to himself, he paints every feast as the equal of those in the Daoist paradise.[22] The difference in their temperaments is clear in the epitaphs they wrote for their wives: Kang Hai, while apparently deeply moved, is nevertheless laconic, emphasizing his wife's sternness, competence, and rectitude ("The household women all feared and respected her.")[23] Wang's epitaph, by contrast, overflows with details of his own career, his children's careers, and the affecting details of his two wives' deaths. Like Kang Hai, Wang makes sure we know how competent his wives were (both "personally prepared all the food for my parents"), but his emphasis is on the losses suffered not only by himself and his sons but by the wives themselves, who lost children while alive and did not live to see the achievements of their surviving children.[24]

Kang Hai's preface to Wang's collected essays praises Wang in the highest terms of Kang's repertoire (he compares Wang to Sima

---

20 *Wugong xianzhi* 武功縣志 (preface dated 1519).

21 "You lun 友論," *Duishan ji* 對山集. Siku quanshu ed., 1.13a-15a.

22 These *qu* are collected in Wang Jiusi, *Bishan yuefu* 碧山樂府, reprinted in the 1640 edition of Wang's collected works *Meipo ji* 美陂集. See the *Mingdai lunzhu congkan* 明代論著叢刊 facsimile edition (Taibei: Weiwen tushu chubanshe, 1976), vol. 3.

23 "Wang qi an ren Shangshi muzhiming 亡妻安人尚氏墓誌銘," *Duishan ji*, 7.20b-23a.

24 "Qi zeng ruren Zhaoshi jishi feng ruren Zhangshi he zang muzhiming 妻贈孺人趙氏繼室封孺人張氏合葬墓誌銘," *Meipo ji*, *Mingdai lunzhu congkan* ed., 604-10.

Qian 司馬遷),[25] but this sober praise pales in comparison to Wang's outpouring of poems for Kang Hai, who seems to have been the brightest star in Wang's emotional firmament. There are poems to Kang Hai from every decade of their friendship: poems about scenery and singing-girls, composed while they were drinking together;[26] a poem for Kang's sixty-first birthday; in which he laments that their early glory vanished "like a dream;"[27] a poem teasing Kang Hai for his shyness:

> In your youth, no thoughts of love
> But once the silk cords bound you fast,
> You'd fall into gloom when you couldn't see her,
> And lose your voice whenever you did![28]

Wang wrote poems for numerous other friends as well ("Teasing Zhang Haozhou" suggests that Zhang had none of Kang Hai's inhibitions),[29] but no one else was singled out for the repeated effusions he bestowed on Kang Hai. When Wang matches a "ladies' lament" (*gui yuan* 閨怨) of Kang Hai's, writing, as was the fashion, in the voice of a woman longing for her lover, it is tempting to read the note of longing as having at least something to do with the depth of his feeling for Kang Hai.[30]

The most searing evocation of that friendship is Wang's epitaph for his own daughter, who had been married to Kang Hai's son in 1523, when both were seventeen *sui*. Wang was clearly very proud of his daughter: he writes that she was a favorite of Kang's wife, and as Kang's wife died before the wedding took place, Wang's daughter "dreamed of restoring the household to what it had been under her mother-in-law," discussing with her new husband "all the details of food offerings and sacrifices, of spinning and weaving, of what to feed the pigs and chickens. Vegetables, fruits, pickles and sauces—with none of these was she unconcerned." Wang and his wife were in anguish over her death in childbirth, and apparently the heavens concurred; Wang writes that "a strange fragrance pervaded the room and lasted for more than ten days." And in Wang's view, his

---

25 "Meipo xiansheng ji xu 美陂先生集序," *Duishan ji*, 3.3a-4b.
26 "Ci Duishan yin zhong zhi zuo 次對山飲中之作," *Bishan yuefu*, 1178-79.
27 "He Duishan xiansheng liushi yi shou 賀對山先生六十一壽," *Bishan yuefu*, 1228-33.
28 "Xi Duishan zi 戲對山子," *Bishan yuefu*, 1325-26.
29 "Xi Zhang Haozhou 戲張毫州," *Bishan yuefu*, 1325.
30 "Ci Duishan sishi gui yuan 次對山四時閨怨," *Bishan yuefu*, 1328-30.

daughter had died because she felt as strongly about Kang Hai as he did:

> In the summer of the third year of [my daughter's] marriage, namely the fourth month of the *bing xu* 丙戌 year [1526], my mother died. My daughter came home to Hu county to mourn with us. Since she was pregnant, she remained in Hu county. On the eighth day of the ninth month, she gave birth to a boy.[31] But the infant uttered not a sound, and we were unable to revive him. At this time, the Historian was fifty-two years old, and had only one son.[32] Day and night he longed for a grandson—and now this. My daughter wept in angry despair, and after three days the pains of regret and remorse attacked her stomach. She took medicine but her condition only worsened. On the seventeenth day of the month she died; we were unable to save her. She was just nineteen *sui*. Oh, how painful![33]

Wang had written a congratulatory poem when Kang Hai's son was born;[34] the poem promised Kang a long line of illustrious descendants, and now, Wang seems to have felt, his daughter had blighted Kang's hopes, and died of the resultant despair.

### *Wang Lanqing*

After passing the *juren* 舉人 examination, Kang's and Wang's friend Zhang Yupeng was appointed *tuiguan* 推官 in the Shandong prefecture of Qingzhou 青州, a position he left to mourn his father's death in 1519. Kang Hai's play suggests that Zhang retired permanently, to escape a vendetta being prepared against him by opportunistic colleagues. Whatever the reason, he does seem to have retired to the Zhouzhi 盩厔 county village of Nuan quan 煖泉 (Warm Springs) in 1519. Kang Hai and his friend Lü Nan 吕柟 visited him there that year.[35] Poems show us that Kang Hai and Wang Jiusi had a circle of friends in Zhouzhi county, and it was doubtless those friends who sent word of Zhang Yupeng's death and Wang Lanqing's suicide.[36] She is listed in the *Lienü* (virtuous women) chapter of the Qing dynasty Qianlong 乾隆-era Zhouzhi county gazetteer as follows:

---

31 The baby was premature; by Chinese reckoning pregnancy lasted ten months.

32 Wang, by this time, had two sons, and at least one of his two grandsons may already have been born. See the epitaph for his wives, cited above.

33 "Kangshi nü muzhiming 康氏女墓誌銘," *Meipo ji*, 521-24.

34 "He Duishan de zi 賀對山得子," *Bishan yuefu*, 1245-47.

35 Han Jiegen, *Kang Hai nianpu*, 153. *Tuiguan* was a judicial position at the prefectural level.

36 See for example Wang's poems in *Bishan yuefu*, 1333, 1351, and 1356.

> Wang, named Lanqing, was originally a singing-girl. She was taken as a concubine by the *tuiguan* of Qingzhou prefecture, Zhang Fu'ao 附翱 [Yupeng].[37] Fu'ao died of an illness, and Wang sacrificed herself by taking poison.[38]

This grand gesture on the part of a singing-girl clearly impressed the Zhouzhi county historians more than did the suicides of ordinary women. (Zhang Yupeng's brother's concubine, for example, also followed her husband in death, but the gazetteer gives her only a laconic entry stating her name and his). Wang Jiusi was similarly impressed. He had a fixed idea of what drew a man to a singing-girl:

> *A poem for my friend to give to the singing-girl Meilian*
> Lively as can be, with her sweet tongue and her clever ideas—
> Ready for love in a thousand coquettish ways.
> Dreams of her, warm and yielding, will land you in the abyss of affection—
> With everything she's ready to give you, it's hard to stay upright!
> The red lotus is the best flower of them all,
> And she's even better than that.[39]

And he had a fixed idea of how singing-girls suffered when their men were absent:

> My soul is sick with missing him—
> Before he dies in that distant land, my own grief will carry me off.
> It's the fragrant springtime, but my slippers are covered with dust,
> and my silk kerchief's stiff with sweat.
> As long as I wait for him, my eyes will swim with tears.[40]

In many another Yuan and Ming author's hands, these poems of longing (which were set-pieces that both men and women wrote) shaded over into resentment, but Wang Jiusi was sure that Wang Lanqing had willingly given her all, and his response was to imagine the lively singing-girl of his typical poems reserving all of her passion for his friend. He responded to the news with a set of songs striking in their open talk of love and their sensuous presentation of death, as we can see from the second and fourth songs in the suite:

> (*No. 2, to the tune "Liangzhou xu* 梁州序")
> She's studied Meng Guangnü 孟光女, who held the tray at eyebrow-height,[41]
> She's *better* than Liu Panchun 劉盼春, whose perfume bag withstood the fire.

---

[37] Fu'ao is his *ming* 名, Yupeng his *zi* 字. In Kang Hai's play he is referred to as Zhang Yupeng.

[38] 1749 *Zhouzhi xianzhi* 盩厔縣志, 8. The existence of Kang's play may have caused Lanqing's prominence in the gazetteer.

[39] "Dai you ren zeng ji Meilian 代友人贈妓美蓮," *Bishan yuefu,* 1100.

[40] "Diao Xianyang ji 吊咸陽妓," *Bishan yuefu,* 1185.

[41] Meng Guangnü was a Han dynasty paragon of wifely obedience, famous for holding dishes before her eyes so as not to gaze too familiarly upon her husband.

Who says it's all just lies with ladies of the night?
And you don't need to swear those vows on the mountains or the seas
You don't need to cut your hair off, or set incense-sticks alight—
Just a pinch of poison fills your mouth like sugar, sweetening your throat
Swallow it down, and you'll soon drift off to dreamland,
Where you'll be spirits, hand in hand in the moon's light,
Or tall trees in the mist at evening, with your roots and branches intertwined,
Or a pair of butterflies in springtime, touching wings as you take flight.
Think of it
Consider it
Isn't indiscriminate love a moral blight?
I'm not descending to empty praise here,
But isn't she just like the loyal men of war and state
Her virtue pure as snow and ice?

(*No. 4, to the tune "Gan huang en* 感皇恩")
Alas—
I want to maintain my single state
But they'll buzz around me just like bees and butterflies.
Better to leave springtime behind,
Return to the green wilds, be buried in a yellow mound
And keep company with the clean breeze and the moon's light.
That's the way to fulfill our eternal ties.
Because, because I met my gentleman
I think, I think he loved me
I long, I long to follow him and die.[42]

The effect is to infuse the ideal of fidelity with the aura of longing, presenting death in a way that has nothing to do with the Five Relationships of official orthodoxy.

The evocation of sensuality is central to Kang Hai's play also, but here it carries a very different charge. Wang Jiusi's is a sentimental heroine, but Kang Hai's is a sentimental heroine with a backbone of steel. Wang Jiusi writes about love; Kang Hai makes Wang Lanqing a sharer of her husband's literati ideals. Kang Hai does not, however, alter Wang Jiusi's lyrics.

The opening scene of *Wang Lanqing* introduces the singing-girl Lanqing, who has just pledged herself to Zhang Yupeng, and her mother, who respects her decision and is not forcing her to take customers. In the first act of the play, Zhang Yupeng's mother sends gifts and a matchmaker to welcome Lanqing as a secondary wife for her son. Lanqing's maid is incredulous that her mistress would give

---

[42] "Ge'er Wang Lanqing shi Nuanquan Zhang zi Zhang zi si nai yi yin yao si yu wen er yi zhi wei ci ci chuan yan 歌儿王蘭卿侍煖泉張子張子死乃亦飲藥死予聞而異之為此祠傳焉," *Bishan yuefu*, 1242-44.

up a life of luxury to marry into an "empty chamber." (Yupeng has gone off to his post in Qingzhou). Lanqing replies that becoming a Three Bonds wife is infinitely superior to the moral "stink" of the brothel. She waves the matchmaker away ("Yupeng and I are beyond all that"), since she and he are destined spouses, intimates, and old friends. "Never cease," she calls out to him in song, "your efforts to solve the emperor's problems!"

In the second act, Zhang Yupeng's father dies, and Yupeng returns to arrange his funeral. He tells Lanqing that opportunistic colleagues are frustrating his initiatives and working to have him fired. The two plan an idyllic life in the country (he farming, she weaving).[43] But by the third act, when they have lived in Warm Springs for several years, Yupeng has become ill. Lanqing sings that he is wasting away ("Where are the laughter and sweet pleasures we shared? Where is my handsome husband?"). When Zhang Yupeng injures her feelings by suggesting she remarry, she asks, in canonical fashion, how he could think that she would take a "second Heaven?" And when he does die, she takes complete charge of the family. There will be no "superstitious" funeral (no Buddhists, no Daoists, no "sevens"); rather, the wife (whom we meet for the first time) must bring the boys up to be a credit to their father. When a rich neighbor conceives designs on Lanqing and plies both her own mother and Yupeng's mother with gifts, she realizes that only suicide will enable her to remain faithful. Calmly, she arranges a feast for Yupeng's wife and mother, talks again about how important it is that the children be brought up properly, and retires to the next room to take poison. When she is discovered she asks that no one try to save her. Again, she admonishes the women to bring the children up properly and tells her mother-in-law to take care of her health. She is going to a place where she and Yupeng will be happy.

The final act of the play is built around Wang Jiusi's songs. The spirit of Mt. Tai (Tai bai shan ren 太白山人) vows to learn what the people of Warm Springs are saying about Lanqing, and when he finds that local officials are neglecting her because her family is poor, he lectures the local students in song about her nobility in leaving behind the "clouds and rain" to live in a scholar's hut. (Here

---

[43] In *Technology and Gender: Fabrics of Power in Late Imperial China* (University of California Press, 1997), Francesca Bray points out that in Ming and Qing China, "farming and weaving" functioned as an orthodox formula for gender distinction. Thus Yupeng and Lanqing are characterizing themselves as exemplars of Confucian virtue.

Kang Hai is inserting himself into the play, as "Tai bai shan ren" was one of his courtesy-names.) He says he has heard that a Scholar Wang has written a suite of commemorative songs, and he has Wang Jiusi's songs performed by singing-girls and musicians. He then causes the transfigured Yupeng and Lanqing to appear to the students, which awes and enlightens them.

Kang Hai's aims will be even clearer to us if we catch an allusion that he surely intended. The second of Wang Jiusi's songs compares Lanqing to Liu Panchun, whom lovers of *zaju* would have recognized as the heroine of Zhu Youdun's 朱有燉 early fifteenth-century play *Xiang nang yuan* 香囊怨 (The perfumed sachet). The plot of *Sachet* has the same overall structure as *Wang Lanqing*. In *Sachet*, the singing-girl Liu Panchun, hounded by her mother to take customers, instead vows fidelity to a young man of good family. When the boy's father keeps them apart, she supports her family by singing at banquets but takes no other lovers. When the pressure to take a wealthy lover becomes unbearable, she hangs herself. When she is cremated, onlookers are astounded to see that a small sachet containing her lover's poem remains unburnt. Her young man appears and takes her bones away to await joint burial with his own. (He vows lifelong fidelity.)[44]

*The Perfumed Sachet* is in fact a far better play than *Wang Lanqing*, with just enough comedy to make Panchun's tragedy truly moving. But Kang Hai wanted to take this standard reformed-courtesan plot in a slightly different direction. *Sachet's* young man is a bit of a cipher, whereas Zhang Yupeng is clearly a frustrated official, through sharing whose aims Lanqing can ennoble herself. *Sachet* is a play about theater itself (Panchun rattles off a list of *zaju* titles when she is asked to perform), whereas the whole idea of skill in drama performance would valorize Lanqing's original milieu and is thus alien to the way Lanqing talks about herself. And while Panchun's gift of her virginity to her lover is the supreme sign of their union (a feast celebrates this *shu long* 梳攏, a standard ritual in the courtesans' quarters), Wang Lanqing is more than willing to forego or postpone sex in the service of higher aims. (She marries into an "empty chamber"; she urges her husband on at his distant post.)

Nevertheless she brings her own sensuality with her. The conventional justification of a virtuous singing-girl simply emphasized her

44 This play is summarized and analyzed in W. L. Idema, *The Dramatic Oeuvre of Chu Yu-tun (1379-1439)* (Leiden: E.J.Brill, 1985), 164-71.

repudiation of her world, but a valid reading of such a plot, I think, is that the singing-girl fascinated the literatus precisely because of the sensuous aura of her origins. In *Wang Lanqing* we are never allowed to *forget* the delicate food, the fine clothing, the music, ornaments, and wealth Lanqing has left behind. (People keep asking her about them.) But these hints of her sensual experience are not the whole of Lanqing's attraction for Kang Hai. There is another kind of sensuality involved, namely freedom from convention. In Kang Hai's play as in many a poem or suite of songs, the courtesan is the woman who can truly comprehend a man's aspirations and offer companionship free of constraint. The note of cool competence in Kang's depiction of Wang Lanqing may recall the way he wrote about his wife, but a wife, for men like Kang Hai and Wang Jiusi, was someone who freed her husband by taking care of household matters: clothing, pickles, pigs. Their famed associate Li Mengyang 李夢陽 (1473-1529) lamented that he never really knew his wife until she died, and the animals were going unfed and his clothing unmended.[45] (A few decades later, the essayist Gui Youguang 歸有光 was so governed by these conventions that he wrote contradictory epitaphs for the father and mother of his friend Pan Shiying 潘士英 (fl. 1530-60). Gui's epitaph for the father states that he was an outstanding household manager, maximizing the family's wealth and expanding their dwelling. But in his epitaph for Pan's wife, Gui claimed that it was *she* who used her dowry to build them a fine house and free her son for study, while Pan "enjoyed wine and paid no attention to the family finances.")[46]

This is the rhetoric of separate spheres for the two sexes, central to Ming ideas of ritual propriety. But however much Lanqing may have wanted to be a Three Bonds wife, her attraction was that she was *not* locked away in a separate sphere but was free to share Yupeng's life in a way that a wife, precisely in order to be esteemed, was not.[47] Lanqing—the competent administrator of funerals and

[45] "Feng yiren wang qi Zuoshi muzhiming 封宜人亡妻左氏墓誌銘," in Li Mengyang, *Kongtong ji* 空同集. Siku quanshu ed., 45.7b-10a.

[46] "Pan Yongzhong muzhiming 潘用中墓誌銘," in Gui Youguang, *Zhenchuan xiansheng ji* 震川先生集 (Shanghai: Shanghai Guji chubanshe, 1981), 495-96, and "Pan fujun shi Shen ruren muzhiming 潘府郡室沈孺人墓誌銘," 501-3.

[47] Over the last decade work by Ellen Widmer, Dorothy Ko, Susan Mann, and others makes it clear that gentry women could have an extremely lively and expressive lives within their walls. But this does not alter the fact that gentry norms made it unconventional at best for a wife to be idealized in the same free-and-easy terms as the courtesan.

education, denied recognition by corrupt officials—mirrors Zhang Yupeng to such an extent that the two almost fuse, and she thus frees him from constraint by embodying freedom herself. By inserting both himself and Wang Jiusi into the finale of *Wang Lanqing*, Kang Hai made a gift of her freedom and sensuous appeal not only to the departed Zhang Yupeng but to Wang as well. By presiding over Lanqing's death and transfiguration, he evoked a realm where the desire for a truly sensuous self-realization (poison "filling your mouth like sugar") could be satisfied. And the structure of this final scene reminds us that heroines of fidelity were not simply exemplars held up by men to *women*. *Wang Lanqing* ends with a male spirit edifying the next generation of male literati.

### *Daughters and Daughters-in-law*

After the death of Wang Jiusi's daughter, Kang Hai betrothed his son in 1527 to the daughter of Yang Shu'an 楊叔安, a high-ranking official from Lingbao 靈寶 county.[48] The marriage was celebrated in 1528. (This was also the year that Kang published *Wang Lanqing*.)[49] In 1529, Kang's son contracted a respiratory illness and died. The young widow struggled against his family and her own and finally managed to follow him in death. But before we look at the epitaph that Wang Jiusi wrote for her, we need to examine the way experience was packaged in the standard Ming genres for writing about women.

Neither Kang Hai nor Wang Jiusi was a prolific writer on women's virtue, but like many literati for whom this was one of many conventional topics, each of them has a piece about a chaste widow who lived on instead of committing suicide. Wang Jiusi wrote an epitaph for an aged lineage aunt who had been widowed when young and had resisted her father-in-law's concubine's pressure to remarry and leave.[50] The widow's husband's brothers took her side against the concubine and settled her on enough land that she could support herself. Wang's father urged the young Wang Jiusi to take the steps to have the aunt's fidelity officially recognized, but only when Wang entered the Hanlin academy (by this time his aunt had

---

[48] Epitaphs suggest that the Kang and Yang lineages had a pattern of intermarriage. Thus Kang Hai's betrothal of his daughter to Wang Jiusi's son must be seen as a sign of a particularly strong friendship, since it broke the pattern.

[49] Han Jiegen, *Kang Hai nianpu*, 204.

[50] "Zu gu Zhu jiefu muzhiming 祖姑朱節婦墓誌銘," *Meipo ji*, 793-96.

been widowed for forty years) did he have enough influence to make the magistrate notify the court. The Wugong county widow Li, whom Kang Hai eulogized in a ballad and accompanying essay, was forced out of her home by her husband's parents and brothers when her father-in-law was posted elsewhere and decided to sell the family's holdings. Ever conscious of his vocation as a historian, Kang was exercised at the way another Wugong county chronicler had described her as the modern equivalent of the Warring States exemplar Shuji of Jin 晉叔姬. Kang pointed out that Shuji, the wife of a ruler, had been able to live out her days under the protection of her dead husband's family, while the Wugong county widow, a commoner whose family had scattered after the famine of 1484, had no place to go except for the space grudgingly rented to her by an uncle.[51]

The outlines of the cases suggest that both of these widows were faced primarily with subsistence problems, surely brought on at least in part by the diminution of widows' property rights under Ming law. The two accounts are essentially stories about women and land, not chastity—but both are packaged as stories about chastity. Wang's essay reflects his efforts to have his aunt's virtue recognized, which meant following a standard template showing her length of widowhood and her refusal to remarry. (The Wang family must have wanted the local prestige and the tax advantages that went with having an officially designated chaste widow, and Wang needed to fulfill his father's request.) Kang's essay moralizes explicitly about chastity: after complaining at length about the inappropriate historical parallel, he goes on to praise widow Li for being "one in spirit" with Shuji of Jin, and he finishes by stating that thus do *women* fulfill the Sages' caveat that "the Dao is without flaw." (Only in his song does he say that widow Li refused remarriage, but this seems implied in the essay as well, with its repeated references to her body's being "without stain.")

Neither man, however, is an uncompromising moralist in the Song dynasty mold. Far from *exhorting* their widows to suffer rather

---

[51] "Li jiefu ge 李節婦歌," *Duishan ji*, 10.91-11b. Shuji of Jin, who appears earliest in the *Zuozhuan* 左傳, is one of the "humane and wise" exemplars included in Liu Xiang's 劉向 (c.79-78 BCE) classic *Lienü zhuan*. She is discussed by Lisa Raphals in *Sharing the Light: Representations of Women and Virtue in Early China* (Albany: SUNY Press, 1998), 43-44. The local gazetteer, cited in Han Jiegen, *Kang Hai nianpu*, 150-51, says that she raised and found a husband for her daughter, and then mother and daughter lived out their virtuous widowhood together.

than submit, they are in deep sympathy with the sufferings that their widows have already undergone. Wang Jiusi is aghast at the behavior of the evil concubine, and Kang Hai is indignant that the historical comparison diminishes what his own heroine has endured. The same sympathy is evident in the other two set-pieces that Kang and Wang wrote about virtuous women, Kang's "Song for the Filial Daughter-in-law Nie" and Wang's "Biography of a Filial Daughter." The widowed daughter-in-law Nie shoulders the entire burden of her mother-in-law's care and ignores her own exhaustion, and her dying mother-in-law weeps and praises her.[52] Wang Jiusi's paragon is the youngest and best-beloved daughter of Old Wu 吳, whom Wang had met while serving in Shouzhou 壽州 after his demotion. As Old Wu lay on his deathbed, his daughter revived him with soup made from the flesh of her arm. When Old Wu realized what she had done he wept, but she assured him that she had spilled no blood and felt no pain. Thereupon he burst into lamentation, crying out, "My child! How could I bear to consume your flesh?"[53] Young and old in both these accounts experience transports of self-sacrifice and gratitude.

Kang and Wang were following the Ming conventions for writing about virtuous women, emphasizing the heroic endurance of ordeals and narrating these ordeals in tones of deep emotion. This bias in favor of the ordeal is evident in Ming local histories, whose chapters on women were almost exclusively devoted to widow-chastity and the filial piety of daughters-in-law. Typically, about two thirds of the women live on, but it was the suicides and those who disfigured themselves who were given shrines.[54] Kang Hai was far from alone, in fact, in feeling that he had to describe ordeals and responsibilities so as to justify Widow Li's decision *not* to commit suicide. (He points out in his essay and again in his song that while she may have *wanted* to commit suicide, her daughter was still a babe in arms.)

This glorification of suicide had multiple roots: the totalizing trend evident in the teaching that "the Dao is without flaw," the Neo-Confucian emphasis on embodying the Dao in one's own conduct, and the way the dynastic histories, starting in the late Yuan, exalted women who resisted rape by foreign invaders. Ming law, which took rape very seriously, was crafted to keep patrilineal descent lines clear

---

52 "Nie xiaofu ge 聶孝婦歌," *Duishan ji,* 10.11b.
53 "Xiao nü zhuan 孝女傳," *Meipo ji,* 634-37.
54 See Carlitz, "Shrines."

and class hierarchies distinct, and Ming beliefs about death must have considered suicides dangerous to families and whole communities. But *stories* about rape, chastity, or the forced transfer of one's body to a second husband kept those issues concealed behind a swirl of appeals to Dao, empire, and Chineseness itself. By the early fifteenth century, these resonances made suicide attractive enough that court and localities were willing to honor suicide in the absence of any ordeals at all. Ordeal stories were still ubiquitous, but now spontaneous suicide could also be thought of as an uncompromising commitment to fidelity, or as a sort of pre-emptive strike against the unchaste alternatives a widow might face if she lived on.

And suicide could also be represented as an attempt to rejoin one's departed husband. Since Ming *ru* ideology discouraged romantic feelings between husbands and wives, this motivation never appears in official commendations. But a widow was a woman alone, and it was a quick step to fuse the icon of the widow with language of the "ladies' laments" that were already an established genre in Tang and Song. This fusion was well underway by the time of the Yuan-Ming transition, as we can see in these lines from Wang Feng's 王逢 poem *The Faithful Wife Xu of Jiading County*:

> A single goose is left without a mate
> And pecks her lonely meals out in the wild.
> Xu Miaozheng 徐妙正, that beauty, never leaves
> Her solitude inside the ladies' chambers.
> Frosty moonlight passes through the curtains,
> Her solitary cup holds chilly wine.
> In sleep and dreams she finds her only pleasures,
> But when she wakes, she cannot stop her tears.[55]

The poem goes on to describe Xu Miaozheng teaching her children, feeding her mother-in-law, and generally putting duplicitous men to shame. Archetypally good women were still able, in this language, to long for their mates.

We will see below that Ming dynasty men were perfectly able to imagine, in fiction and drama, amorous girls of good family—coquettish girls with the same range of responses as Wang Jiusi's courtesans. But in epitaphs, gazetteer entries, and petitions for official commendation, the essay forms in which suicide was most often described, women's experience was packaged primarily as fidelity, filial piety, and wifely probity. With the rise of spontaneous suicide

[55] 1673 *Jiading xianzhi*, 18.22a-b.

stories, however, fidelity trumps filial piety. Wang Jiusi's young *liang* women, determined to follow their husbands, do everything in their power to evade the elders they are supposed to obey.

Wang Jiusi's epitaph for Yang Shengrong 楊升容, the young woman who was married to Kang Hai's son after Wang's daughter died, is if anything *more* dramatic than Kang Hai's play.[56] On his deathbed, Kang Li 康栗 tells his wife to prepare three coffins: one for himself, one for his first wife, and one for herself. Weeping, she says that this is just what she intended to do. Kang Hai and his wife realize that she is planning her own suicide, and they try to prevent it. Nevertheless she manages to take some rat poison. The Kang parents revive her and send her home to her own family, in hopes that her mother and father can change her mind. Nothing works. Her parents send her back to the Kangs. As soon as she arrives, she embraces her husband's coffin in her joy that he has not been buried without her. And this time she is cleverer, pretending to agree with whatever the Kang family wants:

> The next day, Yang got along very well with everyone who was watching her. Whenever one of them left, she would say, "Please don't go—I'll be frightened!" This led the servants to think she needed less attention, but Madame Zhang [Kang Hai's wife] knew otherwise, and she saw to it that Yang was watched even more strictly than before.
>
> And indeed, a few days later, at the *ji hai* 己亥 hour of dawn on the seventh day of the eleventh month, Yang arose, bathed, and deceived her guards by adding soup of pickled vegetables to the dinner order. She lay down in the inner chambers and drank the soup, but took two or three doses of arsenic with it. She went to the toilet, and when she got back she knew the poison was working and that no antidote would be effective. Again she deceived her guards, saying, "Just now when I went to the toilet, I was very slow to void." Again she asked for soup of pickled vegetables, and drank three bowls in a row, saying that it made her feel a bit better.
>
> Madame Zhang entered and was alarmed by Yang's appearance. Her suspicions were aroused, and she felt Yang's sleeve, where some arsenic remained. Madame Zhang cried out, and the rest of the household ran in to help with the rescue. But Yang said to them, "My reason for returning was to die and follow my husband beneath the ground. What I said was jewelry in my bag was actually arsenic. I worried that Mother-in-law would suspect me, so I spoke falsely, but now I have taken it all. People say that there is no antidote to arsenic taken with pickled vegetables, and I felt that any antidote would deter me from my purpose. That is why I did what I did. Do not try to save me—it will put you to a lot of trouble, and you won't succeed. Just call my sister-in-law to make the final arrangements."

[56] "Kang liefu Yangshi muzhiming 康烈婦楊氏墓誌銘," *Meipo ji*, 589-96.

The family does of course try mightily to save her:

> Her brother and sister-in-law were called in, and they tried to give her an antidote. She refused it, and when they attempted to force her, she bit the cup and broke it. Again they tried to give her medicine, but she clenched her teeth and refused it all. They tried to open her teeth with an iron chopstick, but she bent the chopstick. They could not force her teeth apart.

These scenes of violence contrast with the sense of peace and fulfillment that attend her when she is allowed to die:

> Her sister-in-law opened Yang's clothing-chest and took out her garments, all of which she had just recently sewn. Every one of her burial garments had been exquisitely prepared. The family had no choice: they dressed her in the grave clothes, and as soon as they finished, she died. Her appearance was peaceful, with no sign of turmoil. Spirits apparently were with her and kept the poison from disturbing her countenance.

But this peaceful and principled death is motivated by her *own* sense of loss:

> Alas! No sooner did Kang Li die than her heart was riven with grief, such that no one could prevent her death.

And the epitaph ends with an image of reunion:

> Before his death, Kang Li requested that he and his wives be buried together, and his request has not been ignored. Those in the realm of darkness have no cause for regret.

Yang Shengrong's death carried in its wake two others. Her brother contracted a respiratory illness from running back and forth between his home and Kang Hai's, and when he died, his own wife (a girl from Kang Hai's lineage) followed him in death, dismissing her parents-in-laws' arguments out of hand:

> Her parents-in-law were aware of her plans. Her father-in-law was the Provincial Administration Commissioner Yang Shu'an, and her mother-in-law was Lady Xu, daughter of the Minister of Ritual Xu Xiangyi 徐襄毅. Again and again they implored her not to die, but to remain with them and make a name for herself as a filial and faithful widow. "Wouldn't that be admirable?" they said. "Why do you stubbornly insist on dying now, so as to become famous later? And aren't you even thinking about your daughter?"
>
> But Martyr Kang replied: "I know nothing of fame—I know only that I have a husband. When I die, do not grieve for me. And if not even I am to be pitied, how much less should you pity my daughter?"[57] Back and forth the words flew, but in the end Kang would not consent to live.

---

[57] Despite the cultural preference for sons, the conventions of essays like these made it perfectly possible to valorize a daughter. The faithful widow Li for whom

The heroine's mind is made up, and the rest of the story is much like Yang Shengrong's. Once again we have the arsenic, the servants who let down their guard, the mother-in-law who tries but fails to protect the heroine from herself, the advance preparation of the grave clothes. Like Yang Shengrong, she dies at peace:

> Ah, how heroically virtuous! She had prepared in advance her burial clothing and everything needed for her funeral, and she gave up parental love for the sake of righteousness. Her countenance was not at all perturbed or disorderly, but dignified and calm, as though the spirits attended her in death. She resembled Kang Li's wife exactly.[58]

In a variation on the usual story, Kang Li had demanded the suicide of his second wife. More typically, the dying husband offers his wife the freedom to remarry, which she emphatically refuses. Often the refusal invokes the Five Relationships ("Can a minister serve two rulers?"). But Yang Shengrong's passion is quite typical of this genre—young women faint, or throw themselves onto coffins or into the ashes where money or incense are being burned. The way Kang and Wang write about all of these young women is genre-appropriate: songs and a play for the *jian* heroine who could have performed them and standard epitaph-essays for the girls from *liang* families. Nevertheless, the seduction of suicide spans these genres. In all of them, the heroines do remarkably similar things. All of them make big gestures of renunciation, and for all of them, death is sensuous fulfillment and *union* with the departed. For Wang Lanqing, arsenic is as sweet as sugar, and as for Yang Shengrong, her husband summons her from his coffin; her grave-clothes—like bridal clothes—are exquisitely prepared, and he waits to be buried with her. For Yang Shengrong as much as for Wang Lanqing, death is a passionate gesture.

### *Conclusion: The Problem of Passion*

Wang Jiusi may have been grateful for the conventions of the fidelity cult when he wrote these epitaphs for Yang Shengrong and her sister-in-law. He had watched his daughter die in his own house, and he could imagine what the Kang and Yang households had suffered. The first lines of his epitaph for Yang Shengrong show us that his own feelings were still raw:

---

Kang Hai wrote the poem discussed above chose to live on rather than commit suicide, precisely because she had a daughter.

58 "Yang liefu zhuan 楊烈婦傳," *Meipo ji,* 647-49.

> My son-in-law was the student Kang Li (courtesy-name Zikuan 子寬) of Wugong county. When he was buried, I composed his epitaph. Now his second wife Yang has taken poison to sacrifice herself for him. Kang Li's father, the historian Kang Hai, sent a messenger rushing to tell me, saying, "The pain of her death penetrates my very heart and bones; how can I bear to speak of it? But she cannot go without an epitaph, so I dare to trouble you once again." When I heard this I could not restrain my tears. Can it really be that another young woman has died, just like my own daughter?

By writing the epitaphs he did, he could valorize his friend's relatives and ritualize their grief and his own. Here the ritualization is extreme: Wang presents the two deaths as nearly identical and creates preternaturally peaceful deathbed scenes to resolve the turmoil into which both girls threw their households.[59]

But of course it is the turmoil that is actually validated. Literati culture had eulogized political martyrs for centuries, and these young women were, after all, standing up for a canonical value, just like male martyrs to principle. Nevertheless, ambiguity hovers. These young women stand up to their families in the name of something that is *perhaps* principle and *perhaps* desire. And it is just this ambiguity that blurs the boundaries between *liang* and *jian*, licit and illicit. Wang's young women follow their own feelings. His resolute heroines are typical of chastity-martyrs eulogized throughout the empire, but these chastity-martyrs, who use stealth and guile to find opportunities for suicide, are actually, in their turn, congruent with the heroines of love stories who arrange clandestine meetings. To a degree rarely discussed, Ming literati seem to have seen young women—including young women from *liang* families—as vessels of *qing* or passion (and thus in danger of overflowing!).[60] We can see this

---

[59] Popular funeral ritual in modern times assumes that the spirits of suicides are dangerous, and even though Wang Jiusi and Kang Hai were part of a ritually correct ideological wave that repudiated popular funeral customs (recall Lanqing's strictures), and even though the girls died for a canonical value, it seems plausible that people in the household would have been more likely to fear these suicides than to admire them. Emily Martin makes this point in "Gender and Ideological Differences in Representations of Life and Death," in James L. Watson and Evelyn S. Rawski, eds., *Death Ritual in Late Imperial and Modern China* (Berkeley: University of California Press, 1988), 177; and a similar point about Japanese war memorials is made by Klaus Antoni in "Yasukuni Jinja and Folk Religion," in Mark R. Mullins, Shimazono Susumu, and Paul L. Swanson, eds., *Religion and Society in Modern Japan* (Berkeley: Asian Humanities Press, 1993), 121-34. The potential for pollution in these "virtuous" suicides is a topic that needs further exploration.

[60] Women as well as men idealized the sensuality of young *liang* women. Dorothy Ko, in *Teachers,* 160-69, and Ellen Widmer, in "Xiaoqing's Literary Legacy and the Place of the Woman Writer in Late Imperial China," *Late Imperial China*

in the moralizing of a Lü Kun 呂坤 (1536-1618), ever-vigilant about keeping the sexes adequately separated from each other,[61] and we can see it in the kinds of fiction and drama that were popular from the earliest years of the dynasty. *Xixiang ji* 西廂記 (The romance of the Western Chamber) stayed in the performing repertoire longer than any other Yuan *zaju* and was rewritten as drama fashions changed.[62] Jia Zhongming 賈仲明 (b.1343) wrote *zaju* about singing-girls, but he also composed romantic dramas with *liang* heroines.[63] Erotic novellas featured amorous young women: the Cantonese gentry heroine of the fifteenth-century *Zhongqing liji* 鍾情麗集 (An elegant compendium of sentiments conjoined) is as sexually forward as any young man. She and her lover read and discuss *Xixiang ji* and *Jiao Hong ji* 嬌紅記 (The tale of Jiao and Hong)—whose own heroines are *liang* girls.[64] And by the late Ming, the reading public swooned over the gentry heroine of Tang Xianzu's 湯顯祖 *Mudan ting* 牡丹亭, who died of longing and was resurrected by love.[65]

The heroines of these love stories evade their elders in order to have secret meetings; just so do Yang Shengrong and her sister-in-law evade their elders to seek death. Whether such death was "righteous" adherence to principle or motivated by attraction between the young couple was a point the tradition never resolved, and the ambiguity even hovers over the stories of bereaved fiancées, who might never have seen their intended husbands. A case in point is Miss Xu 徐 of Jiading county, who in 1527 hung herself in her bedroom because she was not allowed to remain faithful after the

13 (1992):111-55, have written at length about the general cultural enthusiasm for tragic, beautiful young women poets, and Ko (*Teachers*, 168) quotes a remarkable poem in which a seventeenth-century gentry mother recognizes the budding womanhood of her daughter.

61 See Katherine Carlitz, "The Social Uses of Women's Virtue in Late Ming Editions of *Lienü zhuan*," *Late Imperial China* 12 (1991):117, 122, 132-33.

62 The original Song dynasty tale of a young gentry woman who visits her lover at night was rewritten (with a happy ending) in the Jin dynasty as a *zhugongdiao* 諸宮調 or prose-verse medley; in the Yuan as a *zaju* cycle, in the Ming as a *chuanqi* 傳奇, and in the Qing as a staple of Peking and numerous other local opera styles.

63 See Idema, *Dramatic Oeuvre of Chu Yu-tun*, 220-33.

64 For a discussion of the amorous gentry heroine in texts as different as *Xixiang ji* and *Zhongqing liji*, see Katherine Carlitz, "On *Yingying zhuan*, by Yuan Zhen," in Pauline Yu, Peter Bol, Stephen Owen, and Willard Peterson, eds., *Ways with Words: Writing about Reading Texts from Early China* (Berkeley: University of California Press, 2000), 192-97.

65 Ko, *Teachers*, 68-114, and Judith Zeitlin, "Shared Dreams: The Story of the Three Wives' Commentary on *The Peony Pavilion*." *Harvard Journal of Asiatic Studies* 54.1 (1994): 127-80.

death of her betrothed. Her father's friend wrote an epitaph praising her action as dedication to the principles of the patriline ("I was betrothed to the Gan 甘 family, so now I am a Gan family wife"),[66] but thirty years later, the compiler of the 1557 county gazetteer redirected Xu's passion toward her husband, using some of the same imagery that Wang Jiusi had used for Wang Lanqing:

Certain am I that these heroic souls
Have since become a pair of noble trees
Their branches twined in mutual support
Leaves interwoven one upon the other.
And there, devoted pairs of nesting birds
Fly off each day, and every night return
To this their ever-verdant resting-place
As long as heaven lasts and earth endures.[67]

Faithful courtesans stories, with their automatic associations of sensual attraction, may in fact have entered the stream of chastity-writing because they realized the latent sensual potential of the *liang* archetypes. And since *liang* men were married to *liang* wives, it was perhaps comforting to accord wives—otherwise idealized for probity and competence—this reserve of emotion.

But whether she acts from principle or desire, the young widow's heroic fidelity automatically pits her against the older generation, who at worst are trying to remarry her and at the very least are trying to thwart her suicide. How did this formula for rebellion sweep the empire, whose explicit moral grammar was the Five Relationships? Part of the answer must lie in the story's rich potential for vicarious experience. The male narrator can experience *himself* as the object of desire and simultaneously share the heroism of the heroine standing up to authority. For the narrator this was a perfectly safe sort of mental rebellion, since it was acted out by Others, and in fact the suicide story was boxed in by an equally powerful set of conventions extolling filial daughters-in-law, who sacrificed themselves for the very parents or parents-in-law whom they defied in the suicide stories. For literati men the standard suicide story doubtless functioned as a sort of repressive sublimation, to resurrect the Marcusian notion: a way to express dissatisfaction with the power structure, or with the confines of traditional social roles,

---

[66] Guo Shan 郭山, "Xu lienü zhuan 徐烈女傳," 1605 *Jiading xianzhi,* 19.37a-38a.

[67] "Dao Xu lienü 悼徐烈," 1605 *Jiading xianzhi* 21.46b-48a. The author of the poem, Pu Nanjin 浦南金, compiled the 1557 Jiading gazetteer, now only extant in a long fragment in the Nanjing Library.

permissible because it did not in fact pose any danger to the power structure. And the ideal of the courtesan, as men constructed her, offered a chance to step outside those roles altogether. Wang Jiusi and Kang Hai availed themselves of both ideals, the heroic widow and the devoted courtesan, though the satisfactions of the widow-suicide story must have been barely adequate to their sorrow.

# MANAGING MARTYRDOM: FEMALE SUICIDE AND STATECRAFT IN MID-QING CHINA*

BY

JANET THEISS
(University of Utah)

*Abstract*

During the first 150 years of Qing rule, the suicides of women were the subject of unprecedented quantities of legal and ritual legislation and a frequent topic of debate in imperial, official, and literati discourses on law, ethics, and social order. This legislation often appeared contradictory, banning honors for suicide in principle, yet granting frequent exceptions. This article examines the complex array of political, cultural, and social factors that produced this intensification of state and elite interest in female suicide and created the apparent inconsistency of state policies. It argues that evolving Qing policies toward female suicide reflected a surprising convergence of statecraft goals, Qing imperial agendas, Han literati interest in promoting orthodox social norms, Manchu ethnic concerns, and the enduring fascination that the pathos of the female martyr held for male rulers and officials in general.

## *Introduction*

In late seventeenth-century China, female suicide was a thorny issue, politically complicated, culturally sensitive, socially disruptive, and impossible for early Qing rulers to ignore. The Qing inherited two problematic traditions of valorized female suicide, Han and Manchu, each with its own set of dangers and attractions for rulers engaged in consolidating the legitimacy of their new, non-Han dynasty. The mature edifice of the Qing state chastity cult was pieced together as Qing rulers and their officials grappled with the political legacies and social consequences of these traditions during the first

---

* This article grew out of my paper presented at the Association for Asian Studies meeting in March 2000 and, in somewhat different form, at a symposium at the Center for Chinese Studies at the University of California at Berkeley in April 2000. In its several incarnations, the paper has benefitted enormously from the comments and criticisms of many people, including Katherine Carlitz, Tobie Meyer-Fong, Susan Mann, Susie Porter, Paul Ropp, Paola Zamperini, and Harriet Zurndorfer. Remaining errors and weaknesses are my own.

century of the dynasty. State policies toward female suicide and chastity in general reflected both the principles of universal rulership that guided Qing governance of the expanding empire and the personal proclivities of individual emperors and their policy-making officials. As they evolved, these policies were ideologically and institutionally intertwined with the political agendas of imperial expansion and state-building. What emerged by the mid-eighteenth century was a complex bureaucratic system for the regulation of expressions of chastity which defused the transgressive implications of chastity martyrdom by banning unacceptable forms of suicide and taming others with state approval. Enacting an activist, paternalist vision of the state's normative role, the new imperial chastity cult was embedded in a complex of social reform policies which reconfigured state-society relations to intervene more comprehensively and systematically in social life than ever before.

As the chastity cult developed over the eighteenth century, the passionate, eroticized figure of the Ming female suicide who was the dominant symbol of heroic chastity was subjected to intense bureaucratic scrutiny and statecraft intervention. Designed to control the practice of female suicide and harness the interpretation of martyrdom to suit broader political goals, the new cult channeled the seductive passion of the chastity martyr into either irrational female fury or sober, self-sacrificing duty. The forceful and sometimes flamboyant martyr gave way in state discourse to either a pathetic victim, requiring the help and education of a paternalistic, civilizing state, or a model of obedient loyalty to family and political order.

By categorizing, regulating, and manipulating women's moral fervor, the state chastity cult sought, in effect, to manage martyrdom by bureaucratizing pathos. Such oxymorons hint at the many contradictions inherent in Qing chastity policies, which banned widow suicide yet extolled martyrdom and systematized award processes while reinforcing imperial prerogative to grant exceptions. Yet they also encapsulate the radical institutional effects of state policies that intervened in local cultural life to an unprecedented extent. This article will trace evolving imperial and official constructions of female suicide and the political context that shaped them during the critical period of the Qing chastity cult's development over the Kangxi 康熙, Yongzheng 雍正 and Qianlong 乾隆 reigns.[1]

[1] The latest contribution to the substantial literature on the late imperial chastity cult is Mark Elliot, "Manchu Widows and Ethnicity in Qing China," *Comparative Studies in Society and History* 41.1 (1999): 33-71.

*Interpreting Martyrdom in the Multi-ethnic Empire*

Early Qing rulers inherited a troublesome Ming cult of female chastity which was inextricably enmeshed in literati culture and reached the peak of its popularity and political resonance during the conquest. At its center was the dramatic figure of the chastity martyr committing suicide to follow her husband or lover in death. Celebrated by late Ming literati as the embodiment of *qing* 情 (passion), indeed, often quintessentially imagined as a courtesan, the chastity martyr became one of the most compelling symbols of Ming loyalism and endured long after the conquest as a potent emblem of Han cultural identity under the Manchu regime.[2] This linkage between loyalism and female chastity complicated what was usually a fairly perfunctory gesture for founders of new dynasties: the establishment of state awards for the chaste and filial.

Confusing the issue further was the fact that the Manchus had their own distinct tradition of following-in-death, with roots in Inner Asian funerary practices in which men were often accompanied in death by wives, servants, and personal possessions. The Manchu form of widow suicide was embedded in notions of women's incorporation into their marital families and the dependence and subservience owed by subordinates to their lords and masters.[3] Rather than facilitating affirmation of chastity martyrdom, however, the existence of this Manchu custom apparently heightened the opposition of Qing rulers to suicides of any kind. For although following-in-death had many parallels in ancient Chinese culture and throughout much of the Ming period when imperial and princely consorts occasionally accompanied their royal husbands in death, it lacked the overtones of principled martyrdom which fueled the respectability and popularity of widow suicide in the late Ming. In association with other non-Han customs like the levirate, it was thus tainted for Han and Manchu observers as a remnant of uncivilized ways long abandoned by the Han themselves.[4] In the memorial which prompt-

---

[2] There is a rich body of literature on the nexus of gender, martyrdom, and *qing* in Ming culture. See, for example, Katherine Carlitz, "Shrines, Governing Class Identity, and the Cult of Widow Fidelity in Mid-Ming Jiangnan," *Journal of Asian Studies* 56.3 (1997): 612-40; Dorothy Ko, *Teachers of the Inner Chambers: Women and Culture in Seventeenth-Century China* (Stanford: Stanford University Press, 1994), 68-112; Kang-i Sun Chang, *The Late Ming Poet Ch'en Tzu-lung: Crises of Love and Loyalism* (New Haven: Yale University Press, 1991).

[3] My discussion of Manchu approaches to widow suicide relies heavily on the findings and insights of Elliott, "Manchu Widows."

[4] On the Manchu custom of following-in-death and its association with "bar-

ed the Shunzhi 順治 Emperor to ban the imperial practice of accompanying in death (*xunzang* 殉葬), Censor Zhu Pei 朱裴 read the custom precisely this way, invoking the civilizing mission of a prosperous and powerful dynasty to justify his critique: "There is nothing more deeply rooted than superstitious beliefs about life and death," he wrote. "Love life and hate death: this accords with human reason. Taking life lightly by giving it up is not fitting for a glorious age (*shengshi* 盛世)."[5] Such moral and political principles aside, the custom took on intimate significance for the two emperors who articulated most forcefully the dynasty's opposition to widow suicide, Kangxi and Yongzheng, as their widowed mothers wrestled with clan pressures or their own inclinations to follow their husbands in death.[6]

The civilizing role of the ruler, his duty to reform barbaric and inhumane customs, was integral to the idea of universal emperorship that guided Manchu rulers as they consolidated control over their multi-ethnic, multi-religious empire and it informed the political discourse that set the terms for early Qing policies on awarding chastity. Breaking with Ming and Manchu female suicide traditions, the dynasty forged new regulations which manipulated aspects of both into a new paradigm of chastity and its political significance. Placing equal stress on the universality of the emperor's benevolence and the particularity of his patronage of distinct ethnic groups with varying political status, the regulations stipulated that Han subjects, Manchu, Mongol, and Han-martial bannermen and members of the imperial clan would all be equally eligible for awards as "filial sons,

---

barian" Altaic culture, see Elliot, "Manchu Widows," 42-47. Hongtaiji banned the practice of the levirate in 1631 and 1636. See Evelyn S. Rawski, *The Last Emperors: A Social History of Qing Imperial Institutions* (Berkeley: University of California Press, 1999), 130.

[5] *Qingshigao* 清史稿, 529 *juan* (reprint; Beijing: Zhonghua shuju, 1997), *juan* 264.9926. The concept of the glorious or prosperous age (*shengshi*) pervades High Qing discourse on many subjects. For a discussion of the mid-Qing as *shengshi*, see, for example, Philip Kuhn, *Soulstealers: The Chinese Sorcery Scare of 1768* (Cambridge: Harvard University Press, 1990), 30-48.

[6] Facing conflicting pressures from Manchu traditionalists advocating the custom of following-in-death and others arguing against it, Kangxi's mother died, suspiciously, according to Silas Wu, within the two-year mourning period for the Shunzhi Emperor. Yongzheng's mother reputedly wished to follow Kangxi in death, was dissuaded by her son, but then died soon after, having refused medication for an illness. See Silas Wu, *Passage to Power: K'ang-hsi and His Heir Apparent, 1661-1722* (Cambridge: Council on East Asian Studies, Harvard University, 1979), 14-15, 195-96, n. 5.

obedient grandsons, righteous husbands, and faithful widows," but each group was subject to different, parallel procedures and the forms of award varied.[7] The parallel structure of the chastity award system was maintained throughout the dynasty as regulations changed and the system was extended to accommodate new ethnic groups incorporated into the expanding empire, those under the jurisdiction of *tusi* 土司 or frontier garrisons.[8] As precedents were set in response to individual cases involving commoner or bannerwomen the two sets of regulations diverged, only to be realigned soon after by imperial edicts whose explicit intent was to make "all regulations on testimonials of merit for Manchus and Han uniform again."[9] Consistent with the mid-Qing trend toward extending commoner status and normative expectations to formerly debased social groups, the chastity system also gradually expanded to encompass new social categories previously considered unworthy of canonization, like Daoist nuns, wives of yamen runners and criminals, freed bondservants, and women from prostitute families.[10]

Although the structure of the Qing chastity cult played up difference, it promoted a unified standard of virtue which reflected more the political concerns of Qing rulers than the practices and values of

[7] Petitions for Han commoner awardees passed through review at each level of the bureaucracy, while those for bannerwomen were reviewed by the various levels of the banner command structure. For both, awards consisted of a testimonial of merit (*jingbiao* 旌表), thirty *liang* of silver for the family to construct a memorial arch (*paifang* 牌坊) and, after 1661, rice for chaste widows. Awards for members of the imperial clan were reviewed by the Imperial Clan Court (*zongrenfu* 宗人府) and consisted of sacrificial wine, mutton, paper, and differential quantities of silver and satin depending on rank. *Da Qing huidian shili* 大清會典事例 (1899; hereafter, DQHDSL), 1220 *juan, juan* 403, SZ 9, 10, 11.

[8] Such parallelism was not maintained for filiality awards: the Qianlong Emperor curtailed filiality awards for bannermen in 1767. See Elliott, "Manchu Widows," 64, and DQHDSL, *juan* 403, QL 32. Regulations on chastity awards dominate the sections of the *Da Qing huidian shili* that outline honors for the chaste and filial, implying that chastity was far more complicated and politically important than filiality in the Qing.

[9] The wording here is from an edict of the Qianlong Emperor in 1762, bringing awards for betrothed chaste banner maidens into line with those for commoners. See also the edict in 1771 working in reverse to bring awards for commoners into line with banner policies (DQHDSL, *juan* 403, QL 27, 36).

[10] For a description of Yongzheng era policies eliminating certain hereditary debased classes and their social effects, see Susan Naquin and Evelyn S. Rawski, *Chinese Society in the Eighteenth Century* (New Haven: Yale University Press, 1987), 117-23. For an in-depth discussion of the intentions of this so-called emancipation and its judicial implications, see Matthew H. Sommer, *Sex, Law and Society in Late Imperial China* (Stanford: Stanford University Press, 2000), 260-304.

any of their constituents. Consonant with its cultivation of the notion of the ruler as civilizer of his subjects, the dynasty from early on criticized suicide in the name of any sort of virtue as uncivilized and ignorant. With an edict of 1652 it forbade state honors for those who killed themselves in acts of extreme filial piety, like *gegu* 割股, thus establishing a clear opposition to unnecessary expressions of virtue that resulted in death.[11] By the end of the Shunzhi reign, honors for imperial women who accompanied their husbands in death were curtailed, and in 1688, the Kangxi Emperor categorically banned widow suicide and forbade awards for it.

Suicides of women who died defending their chastity in the midst of rebellion presented the first challenge to this principle of absolute intolerance for female suicide, but were readily categorized as a completely different phenomenon from widow suicide or *gegu*. In 1660, the dynasty established a crucial precedent by canonizing and bestowing money for commemorative arches and steles on women from Guangxi Province who killed themselves to preserve their chastity in the midst of the ongoing conquest of the region. Ming loyalist discourse on female martyrdom had conflated chastity suicides associated with loyalty to the dynasty and those expressing loyalty to a husband. By sanctioning the former and banning the latter, the Qing coopted the politically charged symbolism of loyalist martyrdom. More important, from the perspective of later developments in the chastity cult, by establishing the principle of distinguishing between acceptable and unacceptable suicides, the dynasty asserted the prerogative of the state to set the conceptual boundaries for the interpretion of female martyrdom. The state was intervening for the first time in the negotiation over the cultural and political meanings of chastity suicide that had until then been structured by the physical gestures of individual women and the empathetic encomia of the male literati who revealed their deaths to history.

In the new state hermeneutics of female suicide, various forms of suicide were categorically differentiated by the use of distinct terms implying approval or disapproval. The phrase used to describe the

[11] This was despite lingering, limited acceptance of following-in-death until late in the Shunzhi reign. In 1656, sacrifices were instituted within the palace to honor women of the imperial clan who "martyred themselves for chastity"(*xunjie* 殉節). DQHDSL, *juan* 403, SZ 13. Not incidentally, early Qing rulers were at the same time voicing opposition to excessive and wasteful expressions of filiality in funerary and mourning rituals. See Norman Kutcher, *Mourning in Late Imperial China: Filial Piety and the State* (Cambridge: Cambridge University Press, 1999), 90-91.

chastity suicides of the Guangxi martyrs, *xunnan* 殉難, refers to heroic sacrifice of one's life out of loyalty to the country. This term was also commonly used to describe the sacrifice of male martyrs who were canonized during the conquest. When the Kangxi Emperor banned widow suicide in an edict of 1688, the object of his opposition was not, strictly speaking, martyrdom (*xun* 殉), but "following-in-death" (*congsi* 從死), the term used to translate the Manchu phrase for accompanying in death.[12] Alluding to the ongoing popularity of widow suicide, in this edict he elaborated for the first time on the nature of dynastic opposition to suicide as an expression of virtue:

> Recently we have noticed that there are still many women in the capital region and in the provinces who are following in death (*congsi*). The consequences for human life are tremendous. Death is really a pitiable thing. Nature takes its course in determining the length of a lifetime. How can one recklessly sacrifice one's life? Taking life lightly by following in death (*qingsheng congsi* 輕生從死) is uncanonical. If we continue to commend [such behavior] then I fear that many more lives will be destroyed. If from now on there are no longer any honors for following in death, then [the practice] should cease. Following in death is forever forbidden for everyone from princesses of the imperial clan down to commoner women. If there is a woman who feels she must sacrifice her life out of principle (*shenxun* 身殉), then she should plead her case to appropriate officials of the Board [of Rites] and seek their permission.[13]

According to the Emperor, there is nothing admirable or canonical about widows unnecessarily sacrificing their lives to follow their husbands to the grave. The ban on such suicides and their canonization, he suggests, will prevent such needless deaths. His final caveat to the ban appears to contradict this goal; however, he carefully uses another term to distinguish this acceptable suicide from the unacceptable *congsi*, which is characterized as "reckless" (*wang* 妄) and "taking life lightly" (*qingsheng* 輕生). This term, *shenxun*, refers to the sacrifice of one's life for one's beliefs or principles. Principled suicide undertaken after careful deliberation is thus understood to be categorically different from taking life lightly and, the Emperor asserts, only the state can judge whether a suicide is principled or not. He perhaps also assumes that the introduction of a cumbersome procedure for advanced approval of suicide would give would-be chastity martyrs time to come to their senses and refrain from killing themselves.

---

[12] Here I am following the interpretation of Elliott, "Manchu Widows," 47-49, as I do not read Manchu myself.

[13] DQHDSL, *juan* 403, KX 27.

The choice of the Manchu-associated term *congsi* for unacceptable widow suicides and the use of *xun* with its links to Han ideas of martyrdom for acceptable ones seems to suggest validation of Han customs and rejection of the Manchu. Yet, if we look at how the dynasty interpreted these categories as it dealt with requests for exceptions to the ban on widow suicide honors, it becomes clear that what was being valorized was a new notion of chastity which compromised both traditions while reflecting the personal proclivities of Qing rulers. In the past scholars have made much of the Qing Dynasty's promotion of lifelong widowhood over widow suicide, and personal abhorrence of women's suicide was surely a factor in the minds of emperors devoted to a mother, grandmother or consort who had to face customary pressures to commit suicide as widows.[14] However, imperial rhetoric on the chastity cult suggests that the critical concern was not merely the inhumanity of suicide, but the relative importance of familial duty and the role of the state as the arbiter of female moral integrity. In 1728, the Yongzheng Emperor made this clear in an edict that provided perhaps the most thorough articulation of the dynasty's definition of female virtue and the relationship of suicide to it. He was responding to a memorial from the Manchu Governor of Fujian, Changlai 常賚, requesting honors for a filial son who died after cutting out a piece of his liver to feed his dying mother. The Board of Rites, conforming with the longstanding position of the dynasty on this practice, denied honors, calling this behavior "the ignorant filiality of common people who take life lightly," a phrase that the Yongzheng Emperor himself used on more than one occasion.[15] Intriguingly, though, the Emperor himself had very mixed feelings in this case and mused at great length on the moral conundrum posed by such virtuous suicides. "We think that although the practice of cutting the liver to cure [a parent] is uncanonical, yet it was done out of the urgent desire to save his mother.

---

[14] On Kangxi's devotion to his grandmother, see Wu, *Passage to Power*, 13-20, and Kutcher, *Mourning*, 92-97. On Yongzheng's attachment to his mother, see Wu, *Passage to Power*, 195-96, n. 5. On Qianlong's devotion to his empress, Xiaoxian, see Kutcher, *Mourning*, 153-89 and Norman Kutcher, "The Death of the Xiaoxian Empress: Bureaucratic Betrayals and the Crises of Eighteenth-Century Chinese Rule," *Journal of Asian Studies* 56.3 (1997): 708-25.

[15] Yongzheng uses the same phrase, for instance, in his rescript rejecting another memorialist's request for canonization of a woman who committed *gegu*. Memorial by Ochang 鄂昌 (d. 1755, nephew of Oertai), YZ7.8.23. *Yongzheng zhupi zouzhe, neizheng lei* 雍正硃批奏摺內政類, *juan* 94.

Truly this is rare behavior and deeply deserving of sympathy."[16] He grants honors in this one case as an exception demonstrating his great benevolence.

Having granted this exception, however, Yongzheng then agonizes over its justification. He launches into a long, rather tedious review of the uncanonical status of *gegu*, quoting Han Yu 韓愈 (768-824), Zhu Xi 朱熹 (1130-1200), and Qing rulers' criticisms of the practice. Equating widow suicide with *gegu*, he notes the still significant numbers of "foolish men and women" who "sacrifice their lives to save their parents or martyr themselves for their husbands" because they do not have a proper understanding of virtue and the dynasty's laws. He worries that "if we do not bestow honors on them, I fear there is nothing with which to make known their bitter determination and console their lonely spirits. So for several decades now, despite the statute forbidding such honors, we have shown extreme benevolence in allowing exceptions in response to memorialized requests."[17] Although he criticizes the ignorance of such suicides and the failure of local officials to educate people in these matters, Yongzheng is clearly moved by the pathos and sincerity of such acts. Despite his sympathy, however, Yongzheng decides finally that *gegu* amounts to an unnecessary sacrifice of life. Quoting Confucius and Mencius on the body as a gift from parents and the proper expressions of filiality as service to parents in life, mourning and regular sacrifice after death, he concludes that such suicides are committed "in the heat of the moment disregarding the importance of ancestral sacrifices and family continuity."[18]

With this emphatic advocacy of fulfillment of familial duty over impassioned suicidal expressions of family feeling, the Emperor moves on to an equally exhaustive critique of widow suicide:

> As for the duty of women to follow one [husband] and never marry again (*congyi zhi yi, jiao er bu gai* 從一之義，醮而不改), this is indeed the orthodox way of all under Heaven. However, there is a difference between chaste widows (*jiefu* 節婦) and widow martyrs (*liefu* 烈婦) .... Widow martyrs die to martyr themselves for their husbands (*yi si xunfu* 以死殉夫), nobly following them down under the earth. This is certainly difficult for people to do. Yet if widow martyrdom is difficult, then chaste widowhood is even more difficult. For those who follow in death (*congsizhe* 從死者) show resolve only for a moment, while those who maintain chastity [for a lifetime] must have perpetual regard

[16] DQHDSL, *juan* 403, YZ 6.
[17] DQHDSL, *juan* 403, YZ 6.
[18] DQHDSL, *juan* 403, YZ 6.

> for their husbands. Those who follow in death sacrifice their lives and that is the end of it. Those who maintain chastity must be prepared to undergo hardships. Moreover, the circumstances under which widow martyrs martyr themselves for chastity and sacrifice their lives (*xunjie juanqu* 殉節捐軀) vary. Some suicides are pressured by poverty and lack of means of support. Some occur out of indignation and failure to think about the future. [These women] do not realize that after the husband has died, the duties that a wife must fulfill are even greater [than before]. Above her are her parents-in-law whom she must serve and nurture as a substitute in the way of the son. Below her are her descendants, whom she must educate as a substitute in the way of the father. If she prepares the sacrifices and manages household affairs, her duties are countless. How can it be that her responsibilities cease as soon as she dies? This is why the honoring of chaste widows is stipulated in the laws and regulations [of the dynasty]. But widow martyrs are not mentioned in the statutes because [they] give up their lives just like those who cut their livers and thighs out of ignorant filiality. If many people imitated them, then there would be great loss of life, a prospect that we cannot tolerate.[19]

Perhaps because of the persistent admiration for widow suicide among Han elites and even some Manchus, Yongzheng couches his opposition to the practice within a fairly even-handed discussion of the relative merits of widow chastity and suicide, initially admitting the virtuous intent of widow suicide by describing it as martyrdom: *xunfu* and *xunjie*. He suggests that the critical issue in assessing the legitimacy of a suicide is not the particular form of womens' expressions of virtue, suicide or lifelong widowhood, but the implications of their behavior for social order. Properly carried out, he argues, both suicide and lifelong widowhood could serve as fulfillments of wifely duty. That being said, however, the Emperor evinces great skepticism toward the integrity of women's intent when they follow their husbands in death, ultimately associating their suicides with banned practice by referring to them as *congsizhe*. As he sees it, following-in-death is essentially an expression of individual emotional fervor or personal distress. Given the magnitude of the widow's ritual and familial duties after her husband's death, suicide is, like *gegu*, not merely irrational and unnecessary, but fundamentally selfish and irresponsible. On this basis he reiterates his father's ban on honors for "foolish people who take life lightly" through *gegu* or widow suicide.

For Yongzheng wifely duty was not narrowly conceived as personal devotion and loyalty to one's husband, a sentiment that was

---

19 DQHDSL, *juan* 403, YZ 6. My translation of this passage varies somewhat from that of Mark Elvin in "Female Virtue and the State in China," *Past and Present* 104 (1984): 111-52.

usually imbued in the late Ming and early Qing with passionate moral and emotional fervor and understood to justify chastity martyrdom. Rather, he understood it to have much broader social and, indeed, political implications as obedient lifelong service of the living to the family interest as a whole and thus, implicitly, to the social order. He hints at the political resonances that chastity and martyrdom hold for him when he elaborates on the state's responsibility to cultivate proper understanding of wifely and filial duty. He attributes the perpetuation of suicidal expressions of "ignorant virtue" to the failure of local officials to "enlighten and guide the common people by educating them on the ethical way of the sages and worthies, and the state's loving support." This last term for loving support (*aiyang* 愛養) derives, according to Pamela Crossley, from Manchu terms for fatherly support which invoked notions of paternalism and loyalty based on a master-slave model of ruler-subject relations, emphasizing an exchange of total service for protection and affection.[20] This kind of paternalism and absolute loyalty contrast subtley but significantly with the ethically inspired understanding of hierarchy in Confucian tradition, in which loyalty is the response to a ruler's virtue, and authority is wielded through moral emulation.[21] Likewise, the dutiful wife as chaste widow is, in some sense, the model of the proper subject: civilized by a benevolent ruler and expressing absolute loyalty to the new imperial social and political order through obedience and dutiful service to family and state. Consistent with the dynasty's eclectic approach to culture and ritual in other policy realms, the Qing model of female virtue, in a sense, grafted Manchu notions of loyalty and duty onto the Ming model of chastity and martyrdom.

The simple dichotomy of acceptable and unacceptable suicides was meant to fix the meaning of chastity martyrdom, suppress politically disruptive interpretations of it, and harness it as a tool of universal rulership. But although the bans appear to have gradually reduced the numbers of widow suicides, the practice did not disap-

---

[20] The term was also used prominently in the Yongzheng Emperor's "Great Righteousness Resolving Confusion" (*Dayi juemi lu* 大義覺迷錄), a collection of documents compiled to respond to the anti-Manchu writings of Zeng Jing 曾靜 (1679-1736) in 1730. Pamela Kyle Crossley, *A Translucent Mirror: History and Identity in Qing Imperial Ideology* (Berkeley: University of California Press, 1999), 140-41, n. 15.

[21] On the differences between Manchu and Confucian concepts of loyalty and hierarchy, see Kutcher, *Mourning*, 153-94 and Crossley, *Translucent Mirror*, 125-127, 138-141.

pear completely.[22] And the widow martyr was far too compelling and malleable as a symbol of feminine virtue, loyalty, Han culture, eros, and passion to be readily abandoned. Veneration of widow martyrs persisted in Chinese society and even spread among Manchus and bannermen.[23] Ongoing debate among officials and literati about the practice revealed the fundamental instability of the concept of chastity martyrdom, and exceptions to the ban on widow suicide honors spurred continual reinterpretations and clarifications of the categories of proper and improper suicide.[24]

As they responded to these requests, mid-Qing rulers, beginning with Kangxi, betrayed their own continuing fascination with the improper chastity martyr, expanding the types of acceptable female martyrdom, albeit with reference to the established paradigm. Kangxi granted state honors to women who died or killed themselves resisting rape, if they were not actually raped (1672). Beyond this revival of Ming practice, he also established new precedents for canonization of betrothed girls who mourned the death of a fiancé for the full three years by the side of the grave and then killed themselves (1712); betrothed girls who, upon hearing of the death of their fiancé, were so resolved to maintain chastity that they starved themselves to death (1713); and widows committed to raising their

---

[22] The effectiveness of the imperial bans on widow suicide is debatable and probably varied greatly across different regions. Using gazeteer listings of chastity martyrs and chaste widows, Susan Mann argues that the ban succeeded in reducing numbers of suicides in the Lower Yangzi region in "Suicide and Survival: Exemplary Widows in the Late Empire," in *Chūgoku no dentō shakai to kazoku: Yanagida Setsuko Sensei koki kinen ronshū* (Family and society in traditional China: Essays in honor of Professor Yanagida Setsuko), (Tōkyō: Kyūko shoin, 1993), 23-39. However, in a forthcoming paper entitled "Bound Feet, Splendid Slippers, and the Women of Huizhou (Anhui) Who Killed Themselves: Gender and Changing Regional Identity in Late Imperial China," Harriet Zurndorfer argues that the ban was completely ineffective in Huizhou where the chastity cult became ever more popular over the course of the nineteenth century (personal communication).

[23] On the incidence of chaste widows and chastity martyrs among Manchus, see Elliot, "Manchu Widows."

[24] Documented requests for exceptions in the *Da Qing huidian shili* and occasional comments on numbers of such requests in edicts and memorials suggest that they were small during the Kangxi and Yongzheng reigns but increased dramatically over the Qianlong reign and into the nineteenth century. Standards of chastity and gender norms more generally were similarly contentious in local communities. Many widows remarried by choice or under family pressure. And families often opposed the suicides of betrothed daughters. See Sommer, *Sex, Law and Society*, 166-209, and Janet M. Theiss, "Dealing with Disgrace: The Negotiation of Female Virtue in Eighteenth-Century China" (Ph. D. diss., University of California, Berkeley, 1998).

sons and maintaining their chastity who killed themselves after being pressured by relatives to remarry (1715).[25] Yongzheng began canonization of women who committed suicide in response to a proposition (1733).[26] Qianlong approved honors for *tongyangxi* 童養媳 (girls raised by their fiancés' families prior to consummation of the marriage) who died resisting illicit sex with their fiancés (1742).[27]

These exceptions to the ban on suicide honors were framed by the distinction between reckless and principled suicide. All were justified on the basis that these women were fundamentally "unlike those who ordinarily take life lightly" (*yu xunchang qingshengzhi bu tong* 與尋常輕生者不同) or that their suicides "were not committed out of an extremist desire to take life lightly" (*yuan fei jilie qingsheng* 原非激烈輕生). After all, the objectionable part of suicide, according to the imperial paradigm, was not the loss of life per se, but rather the glorification of women's romantic and, from the standpoint of family duty, impractical impulses. So the suicides of betrothed maidens who starved themselves, completed mourning rituals for their husbands, or died to defend their chastity were acceptable and proper because they were carefully and long-considered acts committed some time after the death of the husband or fiancé.[28] They were not inspired in the heat of the moment by irrational, let alone erotic, passion, a sudden, romantic desire to die with one's husband, but by an immediate and severe threat or a well-thought out sense of familial duty, manifested in observance of the full mourning period or the raising of sons.

If defense of chastity under threat, even a verbal one, presented a compelling example of principled heroism, the logic of duty seems rather stretched as a justification for canonizing betrothed girls. Solid ritual and humanistic arguments were available to Qing rulers had they chosen to extend the ban on widow suicide to include such

---

[25] DQHDSL, *juan* 403, KX 11, 51, 52, 54.

[26] DQHDSL, *juan* 403, YZ 11. See also the Yongzheng edict in the same year initiating criminal penalties for men whose propositions led to such suicides. DQHDSL, *juan* 806.

[27] DQHDSL, *juan* 403, QL 7.

[28] Another inspiration for the singling out of starvation deaths as particularly worthy of canonization may have been the common view that suicide by starvation was more painful, for the victim herself and her family, than faster forms of death like hanging. From this perspective, too, it required higher levels of resolve than other forms of suicide. See T'ien Ru-k'ang, *Male Anxiety and Female Chastity: A Comparative Study of Chinese Ethical Values in Ming-Ch'ing Times* (Leiden: E.J. Brill, 1988), 56-60.

girls. The ritual propriety and moral integrity of fiancée suicide was hotly debated among the most prominent literati moralists in the mid-Qing. Some argued that the practice was uncanonical, inhumane, and contrary to a proper understanding of female duty because girls who were merely betrothed and had not even laid eyes on their prospective husbands had neither ritual nor emotional bonds with them. Others argued that despite its questionable ritual justification, it represented an admirable expression of the highest level of female loyalty.[29] Qing rulers evaded this controversy. Despite their fulminations against following-in-death and their concerted efforts to rationalize a fundamental distinction between martyrdom and widow suicide, they refrained from making any categorical statements of principle about fiancée suicides, while consistently canonizing such girl martyrs whose cases numbered between about ten and forty a year through the end of the eighteenth century.[30]

These exceptions to the general logic of Qing canonization policies may have served as a politically benign and pragmatic gesture of support for the values of Han conservatives whose movement for revival of ritual and moral orthodoxy was gaining momentum at the time.[31] Yet the undeniable inconsistency of this policy, whatever justification was used to rationalize it, also suggests that the pathos, particularly of the young female suicide, still had a powerful allure for the Kangxi, Yongzheng, and Qianlong Emperors. Hidden in a rhetoric focused on the technicalities of assessing female suicide was an abiding sympathy with these perenially romantic figures. James Cahill and Wu Hong's recent uncovering of the deeply hypocritical yet irrepressible fascination of these three emperors with erotic images of forbidden Jiangnan-style Han beauties offers a framework for understanding this contradictory recognition of the improper,

---

29 On this debate, see Harriet T. Zurndorfer, "Han-hsüeh, 'Evidential Research,' and Female Chastity: A Re-Examination of Intellectual Attitudes and Social Ideals in 18th Century China," in W.L. Idema and E. Zürcher eds., *Thought and Law in Qin and Han China: Studies dedicated to Anthony Hulsewé on the occasion of his eightieth birthday* (Leiden: E.J. Brill, 1990), 208-24 and Chow Kai-wing, *The Rise of Confucian Ritualism in Late Imperial China: Ethics, Classics, and Lineage Discourse* (Stanford: Stanford University Press, 1994), 204-14.

30 Year end totals for canonizations in various categories, including chaste maidens (betrothed marytrs) (*zhennü* 貞女), were listed with demographic statistics at the end of each year in the Veritable Records.

31 On this orthodox revival and the role of gender norms within it, see Chow, *Rise of Confucian Ritualism.*

young, and almost always Han chastity martyr.[32] Wu suggests that when the Yongzheng Emperor sat in a palace chamber surrounded by life-sized paintings of the Twelve Beauties dressed in forbidden Han attire, he partook of the classic scholar-beauty romance featuring himself as lover/conquerer of an exotic Chinese beauty. "All her passivity, subordination, and suffering thus gained overt political significance: the possession of her and her space fulfilled not only a private fantasy but also a desire to exercise power over a defeated culture and nation."[33] The proper and the improper female suicide were two inseparable aspects of the same politicized figure of the chaste woman. The disapproved-of chastity martyr resided along with the Han beauty in the *nei* 內 of imperial politics, forbidden yet still the object of undiscussable fascination, while the chaste widow and the martyr for the country occupied the *wai* 外—publically sanctioned, politically central, and endlessly discoursed.

### *Managing Martyrdom through Bureaucracy*

For the Yongzheng Emperor, the state's "loving support" for his subjects who were feminized as objects of fascination and conquest was not merely a gesture of moralizing rhetoric but was to be enacted through bureaucratic institutions designed, in the case of the chastity cult, to promote state-defined models of female virtue and social order in every corner of the expanding empire. If the first two reigns of the dynasty saw the creation of a new state discourse on chastity suicide, it was the Yongzheng Emperor who constructed the institutional edifice that promoted the cult to the peaks of its popularity in the mid-eighteenth century. While chastity suicide in the early Qing was caught up in the political dynamics and priorities of dynastic consolidation, for the Yongzheng Emperor, it was inseparable from his state-building agenda. His reign saw a dramatic process of bureaucratization in many areas, including normative policies regarding filiality and the chastity cult.[34] In the pursuit of en-

---

[32] James Cahill, "The Three Zhangs, Yangzhou Beauties, and the Manchu Court," *Orientations* 27.9 (1996): 59-68, and "The Emperor's Erotica," *Kaikodo Journal* 111 (1999): 24-43. Wu Hung, "Beyond Stereotypes: The Twelve Beauties in Qing Court Art and the 'Dream of the Red Chamber,'" in Ellen Widmer and Kang-i Sun Chang, eds., *Writing Women in Late Imperial China* (Stanford: Stanford University Press, 1997), 306-65.

[33] Wu, "Beyond Stereotypes," 358.

[34] On Yongzheng's administrative reforms see Pei Huang, *Autocracy at Work: A Study of the Yung-cheng Period, 1723-1735* (Bloomington: Indiana University Press,

hanced efficiency and centralized control in administration, fiscal management, bureaucratic communications, and policy-making procedures, Yongzheng and his most trusted top officials shared the view that imperial expansion and state-building involved a civilizing process intended to promote social order and loyalty to the state.[35] Both newly incorporated peoples in frontier regions and the Han people in the heartland were to be morally and culturally transformed in conformity with state-defined norms.

Within the short span of his reign, the Yongzheng Emperor issued numerous regulations, unprecedented in quantity and detail, and designed to enhance the reach, prominence, efficiency, and integrity of the state's system for awarding chastity. The goal was a thoroughly bureaucratized chastity cult, linked unmistakably to the prestige of the imperial state and completely under centralized state control. The political prominence of the cult was to be manifested physically in the form of a shrine to chaste and filial women in every provincial, prefectural, and county seat in the empire where officials would preside over sacrifices twice a year. Yongzheng ordered these shrines to be constructed in accordance with strict guidelines, designated local tax monies to fund construction and maintenance, and called for regular oversight by the Board of Works. Local officials were to ferret out models of virtue in the poorest, most remote regions of the empire and submit rosters of those eligible for honors in these shrines on a fixed yearly schedule. Finally, the emperor laid out detailed procedures for families wishing to apply for canonization of their women, requiring affadavits from relatives and neighbors and review at various levels of the bureaucracy.[36]

---

1974); on his reform of fiscal administration see Madeleine Zelin, *The Magistrate's Tael: Rationalizing Fiscal Reform in Eighteenth-Century China* (Berkeley: University of California Press, 1984). On the increasing bureaucratization of the dynasty's approach to managing official mourning leaves, see Kutcher, *Mourning.*

[35] The mandate of rulers to "civilize" their own people and non-Han "barbarians" has a long history in Chinese political discourse reaching back to the Classics. The term used for such moral and cultural transformation is usually *jiaohua* 教化. For an overview of the history of this concept, see Wang Gungwu, "The Chinese Urge to Civilize: Reflections on Change," *Journal of Asian History* 18.1 (1984): 1-34. Wang suggests that this "urge to civilize" was relatively weak, largely noninterventionist, and lacking in "missionary zeal." However, I am suggesting here that the nature of this civilizing mission changed fundamentally in the Qing as political strategies for reforming people's behavior evolved beyond education and model emulation to more direct and sometimes coercive forms of intervention in social life.

[36] DQHDSL, *juan* 403, YZ 1.

Thoroughly bureaucratized and thrust into unprecedented political prominence, this micro-managed state chastity cult was put to work promoting the chaste woman as a model of imperial subjecthood in the Han heartland and in non-Han frontier regions. The pacification of rebellious non-Han peoples in the southwest was accompanied by civilizing policies which included the establishment of local chastity shrines and official promotion of state orthodoxy with regard to marriage practices and kinship systems.[37] Some canonizations of Inner Asian women followed in the wake of the conquest of Xinjiang, although the feasibility of extending the chastity award system into non-Han frontier regions appears to have been in question in the late eighteenth century.[38]

Over the course of the Yongzheng, Qianlong, and Jiaqing 嘉慶 (1796-1820) reigns, there would be many instances of strategically timed recognition of chastity martyrs at critical junctures in the process of imperial expansion and in the suppression of rebellions. In 1726, Ortai 鄂爾泰 (1680-1745), then leading campaigns against the Tai in southern Yunnan as Governor-general, requested special honors for the wife and concubine of a *jiansheng* 監生, normally ineligible because of their husband's degree status, who killed themselves to preserve their chastity in the face of a bandit attack, and for commoner women in Yunnan who martyred themselves (*xunnan*), leaving sons behind. He cited as a precedent the Shunzhi emperor's edict of 1660 granting honors to Guangxi women martyrs during the conquest. Committed as he was to the civilizing mission of the Qing, Ortai seemingly saw chastity martyrs as useful symbols of loyalty in the context of imperial conquest. The Yongzheng Empe-

---

[37] See William T. Rowe, "Education and Empire in Southwest China: Ch'en Hungmou in Yunnan, 1733-38," in Benjamin A. Elman and Alexander Woodside, eds., *Education and Society in Late Imperial China, 1600-1900* (Berkeley: University of California Press, 1994), 417-57, and "Women and The Family in Mid-Qing Social Thought: The Case of Chen Hongmou," *Late Imperial China* 13. 2 (1992): 1-41.

[38] Investigations for chastity canonization among nomadic peoples moved from Heilongjiang 黑龍江 to garrisons in Yili 伊犁 were forbidden in 1767 (DQHDSL, *juan* 403, QL 32). However, an edict of 1799, though noting the difficulties of investigating chaste widow claims among nomads, suggests that canonizations be granted to certain tribal (*buluo* 部落) women of the Soluns, Chahars, Oirats, and (Turkic) Muslims in the Yili garrisons "in order to demonstrate Our intention to show benevolence uniformly among subjects of all tribes" (DQHDSL, *juan* 403, JQ 4). The specific criteria for making chastity awards among such women is not clear in the *Daqing huidian shili*, but this aspect of Qing chastity policies deserves further research. I am indebted to James Millward for sorting out the status of the peoples referred to in these edicts.

ror apparently agreed with him, granting the honors.[39] In 1738, the Qianlong Emperor granted the request of Zhang Guangsi 張廣泗 (d. 1749), Governor-general of Guizhou, who had just successfully led the campaign to suppress the Miao Rebellion, for honors for a woman and her two daughters who killed themselves to defend their chastity in the midst of a Miao bandit attack.[40] The Qianlong Emperor made similar awards in the context of suppression of the Wang Lun Uprising in Shandong in 1774.[41] After the conquest of new territories or pacification of tribal groups within the borders of China proper, chastity honors were often inaugurated for newly incorporated non-Han peoples, providing local models of the dutiful loyalty expected of Qing subjects. In 1782 and 1783, for example, shortly after the suppression of the aboriginal Jinchuan rebels in Sichuan, Qianlong set precedents for granting chaste widow honors to "barbarian women (*fanfu* 番婦)" in *tusi* families "in order to demonstrate the intention to pacify barbarians with impartial kindness."[42]

The state's new normative agenda was not limited to providing exemplars for the populace to emulate. The Yongzheng Emperor frequently emphasized that local officials were to monitor social customs and work actively to reform them through education and enforcement of the dynasty's laws and regulations. He thus blamed the survival of the uncivilized practices of *gegu* and widow suicide on local officials and concluded his critique of female suicide by ordering that

> all local officials should broadly proclaim, striving to instruct every family and household in the most isolated and backward areas, so that ignorant people all realize that one can only be a filial son or a chaste widow by taking the long road and that preserving one's life is in accordance with orthodox principles.... If, after the issuing of this edict, there are still those who do not love life...we will generally no longer honor them, thus allowing this to become a fanatic craze in the countryside or prolonging the custom among ignorant people of taking life lightly.[43]

Officials were to function as agents of a paternalistic imperial state seeking to raise its subjects out of ignorance and save them from the

---

[39] DQHDSL, *juan* 403, YZ 4.

[40] DQHDSL, *juan* 403, QL 3.

[41] DQHDSL, *juan* 403, QL 39. On the Wang Lun uprising, see Susan Naquin, *Shantung Rebellion: The Wang Lun Uprising of 1774* (New Haven: Yale University Press, 1981).

[42] DQHDSL, *juan* 403, QL 47, 48.

[43] DQHDSL, *juan* 403, YZ 6.

tragic consequences of their fanatic beliefs. In his expansion of the chastity cult, as with his other administrative reforms, Yongzheng sought to fine-tune bureaucratic institutions to intervene in and regulate society ever more efficiently and thoroughly.

His high expectations for the effectiveness of the state in reforming social customs are evident in an edict of 1734, in which he chastised the Governors of Zhili 直隸 and Jiangsu 江蘇, Li Wei 李衛 (1687?-1738) and Gao Qizhuo 高其倬 (1676-1738), for submitting some ten requests for widow suicide honors within the space of a few days.[44] He notes that the state's ban on suicide honors had been so effective that "for many years... the number of requests for honors for chastity martyrs has been very small so I have shown benevolence and granted honors as exceptions." Yet, he concludes, such a spate of widow suicides indicates that

> obviously, local officials have not spread knowledge of my edicts broadly enough and ignorant villagers still do not know how...we cherish their lives. Thus the number of commoner women who sacrifice their lives in extremist fashion is even greater than before. If I continue to generously grant honors, I fear that people will revert [to this bad custom] in imitation, readily causing deaths.[45]

Yongzheng sees the state, through the agency of its officials, as directly responsible for the persistence of widow suicide, yet readily capable of stopping the practice. He thus orders more thorough propaganda efforts among the populace and announces he will no longer grant any such exceptions, to avoid "the development of a zealous craze in the countryside." He suggests here that the imperial state should be the central arbiter of the normative order, not merely by setting an example and punishing egregious transgressions, but by regulating social interaction with ever more precision. Of course Legalists had long advocated using rewards and punishments to encourage upright behavior. What was new in this articu-

---

[44] DQHDSL, *juan* 403, YZ13. Li Wei was one of Yongzheng's closest advisors and a point man in his fiscal reform policies and anticorruption campaigns. See Zelin, *Magistrate's Tael*, 160-1, and Arthur W. Hummel, ed., *Eminent Chinese of the Ch'ing Period* (United States Government Printing Office, 1944), 720-21. Gao Qizhuo was twice Governor-general of Yunnan-Guizhou under Yongzheng and a critical player in conquest of the southwest. His wife, Cai Wan 蔡琬, was a well-known poetess and daughter of a Han bannerman who played a major role in Manchu conquest in the Shunzhi-Kangxi periods. It is said that she wrote many of his memorials. Her mother may have been a former concubine of Wu Sangui, captured by her father. See Hummel, *Eminent Chinese*, 721, 735, 920, and Charles Patterson Giersch, "Qing China's Reluctant Subjects: Indigenous Communities and Empire Along the Yunnan Frontier" (Ph. D. Diss., Yale University, 1998).

[45] DQHDSL, *juan* 403, YZ 13.

lation of the state's normative role, particularly when we place this memorial in the larger context of mid-Qing legislation, was the level of precision and effectiveness expected of state intervention to shape individual behavior. The state was meant to be not merely an exemplar or even a source of punishment, but a social engineer.

This vision of an activist, paternalistic state was widely shared by officials during the Yongzheng and Qianlong periods who shaped its enactment through voluminous memorials suggesting new legislation to promote chastity-centered moral and social order by intervening in diverse realms of social life. Prominent among their agendas were increasing punishments for adultery, incest, and prostitution; making the reward system for chastity more strict; controlling heterodox sects whose illicit activities often included improper relations between the sexes; restriction of women going to temples; maintenance of sex segregation and propriety in prisons and among those exiled as punishment for crimes; enforcement of "proper" marriage rituals and control of unscrupulous matchmakers; and promotion of women's weaving and proper gender distribution of labor.[46] These memorials resulted, among other things, in a dramatic expansion of the Qing Code, honing it to function as another bureaucratic tool for moral transformation. Between the beginning of the Yongzheng reign and the early years of the Jiaqing reign (1730-1810), huge numbers of new substatutes were created in the sections of the Code dealing with illicit sex, illegalities in the contracting of marriages (some twenty-five new substatutes), homicides arising out of sexual assaults, adultery and prostitution (altogether over forty new substatutes), and causing a woman to commit suicide through improper behavior.[47] They defined with ever greater precision, indeed, with hair-splitting detail, the parameters of proper family behavior and gender relations.

The new laws on female suicide created new categories of chastity martyrdom. Yongzheng opened up an entirely new category of state-recognized female martyrdom in 1733 by inititating canonization for women who killed themselves in response to a sexual propo-

[46] On state promotion of "proper" women's handicrafts, see Susan Mann, "Household Handicrafts and State Policy in Qing Times," in Jane Kate Leonard and John R. Watt, eds., *To Achieve Security and Wealth: The Qing Imperial State and the Economy 1644-1911* (Ithaca, New York: Cornell University East Asia Program, 1992), 75-95.

[47] For an overview of substatutes dealing with adultery, see M. J. Meijer, *Murder and Adultery in Late Imperial China* (Leiden: E.J. Brill, 1991).

sition. In the same year a new substatute was added to the Qing Code spelling out for the first time distinct penalties for men who forced women to commit suicide by propositioning them, as distinct from attempting to rape them. Between 1733 and the end of the Qianlong reign, some fifteen new substatutes were appended to the statute on "causing a person to commit suicide" in the Qing Code. Among these a dozen or so dealt with women committing suicide under various circumstances in the wake of rape, attempted rape, or unwanted propositions; unintended sexual insult or "improper familarity;" "indecent remarks," "dirty jokes," or "obscene gestures" made in her presence, in the context of an argument with her, or about her; adultery; or gossip arising out of any of these incidents.[48] Chaste women who killed themselves under such circumstances were all deemed eligible for canonization.

Collectively, these myriad new substatutes reflected widespread anxiety among mid-Qing elites about increasing challenges to fidelity and a heightened distrust of women's moral fortitude. The meaning of chastity in this diverse legislation expands to include not just sexual loyalty to one husband but proper female behavior in social interactions with men in general. But although in some sense a logical extension of honors for resisting rape, this new legislation on suicide also came with a new attitude toward women and their capacity for virtue. Contrary to the oft-stated imperial goal of reducing the numbers of female suicides, they sanctioned a form of suicide that appears to have become increasingly widespread over the mid-Qing and could well be considered more reckless and irrational than following in death. The criminal case record suggests that the circumstances leading to such suicides were often controversial and difficult to decipher. Touched off by a woman's interpretation of a man's wording or tone of voice, such suicides represented, on one level, a powerful form of female agency.[49] It would appear that for all the attempts of the Qing state to control the practice and interpretation of women's suicide, the behavior of women themselves played a vital, if not easily traceable role in the development of Qing policies. The moral zeal and ethical anxiety of civilizing officials was

[48] For an overview of the substatutes dealing with female suicide, see M. J. Meijer, "The Price of a P'ai-lou," *T'oung Pao* 67 (1981): 288-304.

[49] For more on the social meanings and motives for such suicides, see Theiss, "Dealing with Disgrace," 188-208. See also Paola Paderni, "Le rachat de l'honneur perdu. Le suicide des femmes dans la Chine du XVIIIe siécle," *Études chinoises* 10.1/2 (1991): 135-60.

matched in this period by the equally fervent sensitivity of women themselves, whose struggles to negotiate ever more stringent norms of virtue and preserve their honor in a context of increasing social mobility and unsettling economic development are amply documented in the records of the cases produced by these new statutes.[50] At a time of increasing disjuncture between prescriptive gender norms and the realities of women's everyday lives, such sensitivity was eminently practical, and suicide, which usually vindicated the victim's reputation in cases of sexual assault or insult, could make sense.

To fit such suicides into the state's paradigm, however, they had to be interpreted as acts of pathetic desperation, not assertive, transgressive revenge. If the chaste widow represented the ideal loyal subject of a paternalistic state, the chastity martyr became either a victim or an ignorant woman in need of reform. The memorials and edicts developing such legislation during the Qianlong reign were marked by a reformist ardor that was notably lacking the fascinated empathy of earlier chastity discourse. The female suicide caught in the zealous gaze of reform-minded officials in the late eighteenth century was more than ever the object of bureaucratic intervention seeking to deconstruct her motives, alter her behavior, and control the public interpretation of her death. The bureaucratization of pathos required not just the regulation of suicide through categories of proper and improper, but the transformation of the heroic martyr into an object of state charity.

### *Pathos Become Pathetic: The Martyr Demystified*

While Kangxi and Yongzheng era discourse often portrayed the female suicide as ignorant of proper virtue, it rarely questioned the sincerity of her motives. But during the Qianlong reign, the paradigm of proper and improper suicides was applied increasingly to dissect the motives of potential awardees and eliminate categories of women deemed inherently ineligible because of their social status. In

---

[50] For analysis of the nature of women's agency and their interests as revealed in criminal cases see Paola Paderni, "Between Constraints and Opportunities: Widows, Witches, and Shrews in Eighteenth-Century China," in Harriet T. Zurndorfer, ed., *Chinese Women in the Imperial Past: New Perspectives* (Leiden: E.J. Brill, 1999), 258-85, and "I Thought I Would Have Some Happy Days: Women Eloping in Eighteenth-Century China," *Late Imperial China* 16.1 (1995): 1-32. See also Matthew Sommer, "The Uses of Chastity: Sex, Law and Property in Late Imperial China," *Late Imperial China* 17.2 (1996): 77-130.

1749 the dynasty made its first effort to limit awards by introducing a distinction between ordinary chastity and extraordinary chastity, with only the latter deserving of silver for a private arch. This was in part a reflection of the effectiveness and efficiency of Yongzheng's bureaucratized chastity cult. By the latter half of the eighteenth century it was making between five hundred and fifteen hundred awards per year, prompting attempts to deal with overextension in the granting of awards and with the excessively perfunctory attitudes of local officials who quickly collected names of prospective awardees at the end of the year without making great efforts to seek out the specially worthy. Such efforts occurred, moreover, as increasing numbers of officials and the Qianlong Emperor himself began to question the purity of chastity martyrdom.[51] Some critiques were inspired by compassion, some by a zealous desire to promote orthodoxy. Yet memorialists and the emperor shared a fundamental distrust of the virtuous intent of female martyrs, assuming them to be either conniving and self-serving or weak and irrational.[52]

In 1758, the Judicial Commissioner of Jiangsu, Cui Yingjie 催應階, memorialized to call for more exhaustive investigation into the marital status of putative martyrs who died resisting rape, suggesting that honors be denied if they happened to be remarried widows.

> The substatute on awarding chastity martyrs is intended to promote the transformation of customs....[It] originally referred to those women who maintained chastity by following one [husband] , but this is not stated clearly....[Therefore] no one questions whether the woman is an unmarried virgin, a properly married woman, or a married woman who remarried after her husband died. So among [those awarded] there are inevitably women who have already lost their chastity, but then suddenly sacrifice their lives defending [themselves] against violence and fortuitously acquire public praise and citation.[53]

This, he insists, is inconsistent with the agenda of "energetically encouraging the maintainence of a reputation for chastity." Although he believes "leniency for violent attacks certainly should not

---

[51] Matthew Sommer has noted a similar trend in judicial discoure, arguing that over the mid-Qing there is a shift in definitions of chastity from a notion of chastity as objective status to chastity as purity of intent. He sees the 1803 change in canonization rules to allow honors for rape victims who were penetrated as a key indicator of this shift. Sommer, *Sex, Law and Society*, 312-16.

[52] Such sentiments are commonly expressed also by magistrates in judicial proceedings for the criminal cases that often arose from female suicides. See Theiss, "Dealing With Disgrace," 126-168.

[53] Memorial of Cui Yingjie, QL 23.4.24.*Zhupi zouzhe* 硃批奏摺 (hereafter ZPZZ), *neizheng lei* 內政類, *bao* 22, *juan* 45.

be tolerated" nor should "imperial benevolence be requested recklessly." Cui's suggestion was initally rejected with the rescript "this is not reflective of a spirit of benevolence and generosity," but by the end of the reign it was incorporated into the rules for canonization.[54]

In an edict of 1775, refusing canonization for a concubine who followed her husband in death, the Qianlong Emperor applies similar logic. He cites the ban on widow suicide and notes that he has usually granted exceptions in the few cases submitted for special consideration. But in this case he feels an exception would not be proper because of the woman's status as a concubine which he judges in the context of Manchu custom, indicating its ongoing salience in imperial thinking about chastity.

> According to our old Manchu system, all concubines, even if they have produced sons and daughters, still are not buried with the husband because social position cannot be transgressed. Moreover, with this sort of martyrdom for chastity (*xunjie*), how can we know that [the concubine] did not have conflicts with the first wife and killed herself on principle (*shenxun*) because she feared future insult and abuse from her? This [suicide] did not necessarily arise out of righteous fervor (*yilie* 義烈). How can we distinguish precisely [in matters of intent]? And how does giving honors to many such people help to improve customs?
>
> Furthermore, this memorial states that "in fulfilling her role as concubine, she was always cherished in the quilts and sheets (*chang bao qinchou* 常抱衾裯)." This wording is particularly improper! The existence of concubines in the inner quarters is a matter for the feudal princes (*zhuhou* 諸侯). How can it be that [this custom] is wantonly being adopted among commoners? Zhong Yin 鐘音 (the memorialist) is an examination graduate and formerly very accomplished in literary pursuits. Yet he ignorantly makes use of such indiscriminate wording. This is perverse enough to warrant investigation.[55]

The Emperor here dismisses *shenxun* as personal pique, no longer qualifying as principled martyrdom. With its categorical rejection of concubines as widow martyrs and its testy criticism of the Manchu memorialist Zhong Yin's inappropriate language, this edict reflects a moral fundamentalism diversely inspired by concerns about Manchu identity and by orthodox Han literati standards of etiquette.

Such rigorous attention to literal and orthodox interpretation of the standards for martyrdom led Qianlong in 1776 to refuse the request of the Manchu Governor of Zhejiang, San Bao 三寶, for filial martyrdom honors for the young unmarried daughter of the magis-

---

[54] Memorial of Cui Yingjie, QL 23.4.24. (ZPZZ), *neizheng lei, bao* 22, *juan* 45.

[55] DQHDSL, *juan* 403, QL 43.

trate of Shouchang County, Shandong 山東, who hung herself after hearing the news that her father had been killed defending his *yamen* from the Wang Lun rebels.[56] He argues,

> Although ... the sentiment here is pitiable, nevertheless, carrying out sacrifices at the grave is the ritually correct path of filial piety. If everyone were to follow their fathers in death (*xunfu* 殉父), then who would be responsible for affairs after their deaths? This is why the ritual classics admonish against allowing oneself to waste away to the point of death in mourning. Sons are successors, but daughters are headed outside [the family] from birth. So how can their taking life lightly be considered filial? If this [woman's] death is judged under the statute on members of one family dying to defend the country (*xunnan*), then honors for righteousness are possible. But honors for filiality are not possible. Loyalty, filiality, these two characters concern the teaching of the sages on the Three Bonds. They cannot be falsely claimed in bits and pieces. Words must be followed by deeds. It is improper to frivolously bestow [honors].[57]

The logic here is reminiscent of Yongzheng's seminal edict, emphasizing the duty of the living over the moral ardor of the dead. The edict also emphasizes that to deserve canonization, one had to follow the state's rules. State honors were not a blanket recognition of vaguely understood but well-intended virtue. This young woman did not understand proper filiality and, since the dynasty does not recognize filial martyrdom as a virtuous act, following one's father in death can only amount to a "false claim" of filiality.

Even women recognized as proper chastity martyrs were increasingly portrayed as pathetic objects of bureaucratic intervention. In a memorial of 1745, from the head of the capital Office of Transmission, Zhang Ruoai 張若靄 (d. 1746, son of Zhang Tingyu 張廷玉, 1672-1755), treats women's suicides in response to propositions or verbal insults as a social problem arising out of women's propensity to overreact to slights on their chastity. Based on his experience processing incoming documents from the provinces, he notes the large number of women who commit suicide in response to a verbal insult and then reviews the creation of new substatutes in the Yongzheng and Qianlong periods to punish men who cause a woman's suicide with verbal harassment. But after praising the benevolence and wisdom of these laws, which criminalized sexual harassment and gave state recognition to such suicides for the first time, he launches into a litany of cases in which women killed themselves

---

[56] Memorial of San Bao, QL 41.2.20. *Lufu zouzhe* 錄副奏摺 (hereafter LFZZ), document #0301-008, reel 20, p. 1096.

[57] DQHDSL, *juan* 403, QL 41.

only after a prolonged delay of some days or even weeks after an insult. He observes that in these cases delay or failure of the family, neighbors, or village leaders to report the verbal harassment to the local magistrate for punishment, or the magistrate's own delay or failure to punish the offender, caused the women to feel that "their grievance went unredressed and because of this to take life lightly." Zhang suggests that officials inform people that they should report such cases to the magistrate and that he be required to arrest the offender within three days and punish him with the cangue. "In this way, the woman's humiliation and anger can be assuaged and the offender can avoid having to atone with his life....The laws of the dynasty have reached into popular sentiment. [When the people] know fear and feel ashamed of their customs, then perhaps such customs can gradually be eradicated and one aspect of the Emperor's benevolence can be extended."[58] His memorial resulted in the creation of a new substatute in the same year, which for the first time mandated specific punishment for sexual harassment itself and criminalized the failure to report any incident of sexual assault or harassment to state authorities. Such concerns led further to an edict in 1759 calling for local officials to inform people that families should immediately report sexual harrassments to the magistrate so that the offenders could be publicly punished with the cangue to assuage the humiliation and fury of the insulted woman. Officials who failed to deal with such cases and caused a suicide were to be punished themselves.[59]

Zhang adopts the tone of a paternalistic official calling for the state to protect women from the worst effects of their frail, irrational, and hypersensitive natures. He implies that such suicides are neither moral nor heroic but merely the helpless gestures of women too readily prone to outrage. With his comment about avoiding death sentences for male offenders in these cases he even seems to suggest that the law places too much blame for these suicides on the male offenders, punishing them too severely. Positing an intimate state intervention in local society through the mechanism of the law, he implies that through laws which embody certain normative values and create incentives and punishments to uphold them, the state directly influences the choices individual women make about how to deal with an insult. Assuming the potency of the state's influence, he

---

[58] Memorial of Zhang Ruoai, QL 10.11.2. ZPZZ, *neizheng lei*, *bao* 33, *juan* 46.
[59] DQHDSL, *juan* 403, QL 24 and *juan* 825.

suggests honing the law to be a more effective instrument for preventing women's suicides.[60]

Numerous memorials like this one indicate that by the middle of the Qianlong reign, female martyrdom was a statecraft problem that had more to do with handling the vagaries of women's behavior and motivations than with honoring the heroic expression of virtue. Increasingly, too, such a matter-of-fact approach to female suicide transcended differences of opinion about the nature of virtue and appropriate policy directions. This demystification of the chastity martyr is strikingly evident in an exchange between He Wei 何煟 and Qianlong in 1765. He suggested that honors for women who killed themselves in response to a proposition or harassment be limited to those who acted purely out of humiliation or desire to prove their chastity. In his edict responding to this suggestion, the emperor calls for greater attention to the details of individual cases but refuses to make a hard and fast rule, arguing that

> Women who take life lightly may perhaps do so because they wish to assuage their fury and use this as a pretext to obtain hidden merit. But they are not so different from those who become vegetarians and recite Buddhist scriptures. Within the women's quarters sincerity and insincerity are obscured. There is no consistent pattern. Sometimes wives and daughters originally do not want to die, but are pressured by husbands or parents to do so. And we cannot protect them from doing so. How is it benevolent to promulgate a statute to distinguish [these motivations] clearly?[61]

Memorialist and emperor share a dim view of women's moral integrity, though they disagree about the best way to deal with feminine foibles. The edict argues that one should not question the sincerity of women's suicides because their motives are always mixed. In effect, then, women are ultimately incapable of principled martyrdom. This basic assumption of the fickleness and irrationality of women's motivations appears frequently during the Qianlong reign in routine memorials reporting such suicide cases in which magistrates often comment on women's vulnerability to insult and tendency to overreact furiously when they think their chastity has been

[60] The criminal case record confirms to some degree Zhang Ruoai's hunch about the state's power, demonstrating that many women did indeed see the magistrate's *yamen* as the only acceptable source of public redress for humiliation. Yet criminal cases also suggest the limits of the state's role at the local level, indicating that from the local standpoint, it was only one among several sources of normative authority that worked to define parameters of behavior and arbitrate transgressions. See Theiss, "Dealing With Disgrace."

[61] DQHDSL, *juan* 403, QL 30.

impugned.[62] They also appear commonly in the writings of mid-Qing moralists like Chen Hongmou 陳宏謀 (1696-1771), himself the quintessential activist official, who, though he promotes stringent standards of separation between the sexes to avoid the suspicion of impropriety also criticizes women for being overly sensitive and prone to suicide at the slightest provocation. Chen comments in a handbook on women's education, "Residing deep within the inner apartments, women know nothing of the affairs of the world or its hardships. They develop haughty and truculent dispositions...and unavoidably become humiliated at the slightest suspicion."[63] With such disdainful dissection of the motives–indeed, the moral fiber–of the female suicide, the demystification of the chastity martyr was complete.

*Epilogue*

The transformation of the romantic chastity martyr into a statecraft project did not bring about the end of the imperial state's interest or stake in female chastity. In the last years of the Qianlong reign and on into the nineteenth century, the numbers of "benevolent" exceptions granting honors to widow martyrs and technically ineligible chaste widows grew enormously. However, after one modification to the statutes on chaste martyrdom in 1803, extending honors to rape victims who were violated before they died, there were no new legislative initiatives in the state chastity cult until the Tongzhi 同治 Emperor restored honors for widow suicides in 1851, as the Taipings mounted the greatest challenge since the conquest to the legitimacy of the empire. The state almost dispassionately canonized an increasing flood of chastity martyrs, many of them victims of the numerous rebellions and bandit attacks that were symptomatic of social breakdown in the last decades of the dynasty. In 1871, the dynasty finally lowered the requirements for canonization as a chaste widow to such an extent that such chastity no longer constituted noteworthy behavior at all, and the numbers of women receiving citations exploded accordingly.

Despite the numbers, the routinized remnant of the High Qing chastity cult functioned without the reforming and civilizing zeal of the Yongzheng and Qianlong years. Indeed, the dynasty became

62 See Theiss, "Dealing with Disgrace."

63 Chen Hongmou, comp. *Jiaonü yigui* 教女遺規 in *Wuzhong yigui* 五種遺規 (1742; reprint, Shanghai: Jingwei jiaoyu lianhe chubanshe, 1935), 40.

increasingly unable even to manage the cult administratively or financially. Successive edicts were issued limiting the numbers and types of chaste women who received money to build their own ceremonial arches. What had been an effective state-centered chastity cult in the eighteenth century, forcefully intervening in local society to shape the practice of female suicide and control its interpretation, was still bureaucratized but banal and overstretched. No longer an arbiter of cultural norms, it was subject itself to social pressures. In the eyes of an officialdom increasingly distracted by social and economic crisis, the chastity martyr became, along with the chaste widow, merely a cipher, one of the many hapless victims of society's ills.

Yet the prominent placement of the chastity cult at the heart of Qing political culture during the eighteenth century and its linkage to emerging visions of an interventionist and morally activist state left a significant legacy. Whatever the limits of its effectiveness in influencing behavior at the local level, and that effectiveness no doubt decreased over the last century of Qing rule, the new legislative apparatus for the promotion of a politicized normative agenda systematically associated state legitimacy with its role as moral arbiter and social reformer. The state chastity cult of the mid-Qing thus planted the seeds for what would become, a century later, routine expectations about the potential and responsibility of the state to reform, civilize, and regulate society.

Mid-Qing chastity policies also made chastity-centered gender norms inescapably relevant to evolving notions of the relationship between ruler and subject, so that women's virtue became central to visions of political order and its transformation. Norman Kutcher has recently argued that the dynasty gradually "disengaged" itself from the Confucian system of mourning practices: filial grief was, increasingly, a matter for private expression rather than public display, and filial piety was displaced as the normative heart of a political order based on the parallel conception of the state's relationship to society.[64] One could argue that filial piety was replaced as the relevant paradigm of loyalty and hierarchy in Qing political order by the paradigm of female chastity, not, of course, the passionate, individually focused chastity of the late Ming widow martyr but the duty-bound chastity of obedient service to the family and the Qing political order. For filiality was only rarely at issue in changes to

[64] Kutcher, *Mourning*, 190-94.

ritual regulations or law, or in official discourse on ritual, law, customs, or morals throughout the dynasty. Instead it was the problems of defining, enforcing, and awarding female chastity that dominated such policy discourse in the mid-Qing. Year-end tallies of state honors register filiality awards in single digits, while recording hundreds, if not thousands of chastity canonizations. If chastity was the dominant political metaphor for obedience and social duty, then it is hardly surprising, though not without irony, that for revolutionaries at the end of the nineteenth century and beyond, widow suicide and the chastity cult in general were among the most powerful symbols of the "backward" and "authoritarian" society governed by the Qing state.

# UNTAMED HEARTS: EROS AND SUICIDE IN LATE IMPERIAL CHINESE FICTION

BY

PAOLA ZAMPERINI*
(Institute of Literature and Philosophy, Academia Sinica)

*Abstract*

In Chinese fiction there are heroines who use suicide as a vehicle to convey to eternity the strength of their passions, from love to hatred, from jealousy to thirst for revenge. The present paper is an exploration of late imperial literary representations which depict women's suicide as an act of passion and self-reassertion: this act, rather than being constructed as defeat in the face of adversities, a response to abuse suffered, or as a last resort to preserve chastity, is presented as a path of independence that shows these female characters not as virtuous martyrs or victims of an unjust patriarchal system, but as passionate agents of free will. These sources challenge the assumption that women's suicide in Ming and Qing fictional sources is primarily related to chastity. In this sense, they are useful in furthering understanding of the complex ways in which legal and moral mandates around the issue of women's suicide could be resisted, absorbed, and ignored in late imperial vernacular fiction.

## *Deeper Than Death*

Traditional Chinese fictional and non-fictional texts abound with images of chaste and virtuous women willing to become martyrs and

* I want to thank Katherine Carlitz, Paul Ropp, Janet Theiss, and Harriet Zurndorfer for being such amazing colleagues and such patient and enthusiastic friends. To Paul Ropp and Harriet Zurndorfer I am indebted for their trust, encouragement, and support at one of the most critical junctures of my academic life. I also thank Sara Jenkins for leading me –or at least attempting to– through the maze of the English language. A special thanks to Bryna Goodman for sharing her work with me, and to Maureen Robertson for helping with primary sources difficult to find. I am also grateful to Petros Koumoutsakos for providing me with the hardware necessary to conduct my scholarly work. This article, and, in a way, this whole issue, would have not been published had it not been for the trail-blazing work of scholars such as Grace Fong, Beata Grant, Katherine Carlitz, Maureen Robertson, Paul Ropp, Ellen Widmer, and Harriet Zurndorfer. All that is good in my work I owe to them, because they have inspired me look at Chinese culture and literature with new eyes. I dedicate this work to my students, with the hope that they too may learn not to be afraid to include gender studies among the many tools at the disposal of a sinologist. Naturally, I alone bear responsibility for my mistakes and limited knowledge.

forfeit their lives for the sake of their husbands, fiancés, parents, and children. Indeed, one of the first things one learns about traditional China is that female suicide was common and often became for women and their families a sure way to gain fame and a virtuous reputation.[1] Yet, side by side with these selfless women, who chose sacrifice for the benefit of their (male) kin, there are fictional heroines who can use suicide as a vehicle to convey to eternity the strength of their passions, from love to hatred, from jealousy to thirst for vengeance.

The present paper is an exploration of late imperial literary representations which depict women's suicide as a passionate act of self-assertion, and not as a defeat in the face of adversities, a response to abuse suffered, or a last resort to preserve chastity. On the contrary, it is presented as a path of independence that shows these female characters not as virtuous martyrs or victims of an unjust patriarchal system but as passionate agents of free will.[2] In this sense, they are useful in helping us understand the intricate ways in which legal and moral mandates around the issue of women's suicide could be resisted, absorbed, and ignored in Ming and Qing vernacular fiction. As a matter of fact, regardless of whether it is constructed as an attempt to resist rape, as a way to reiterate the connection between eros, women, and death, or as a diabolical retaliation, in all the cases analyzed here suicide is an act that is "deeper than a simple death,"[3] because it transforms what could be decoded as a surrender into a very empowering gesture with long-lasting consequences.

The sources are drawn from various vernacular Ming and Qing

---

[1] See, for example, Mark Elvin, "Female Virtue and State in China," *Past and Present* 104 (1984): 111-52; T'ien Ju-k'ang, *Male Anxiety and Female Chastity: A Comparative Study of Chinese Ethical Values in Ming-Ch'ing Times* (Leiden: E. J. Brill, 1988); Margery Wolf, "Women and Suicide in China," in Margery Wolf and Roxane Witke, eds., *Women in Chinese Society* (Stanford: Stanford University Press, 1975), 111-41. For the most complete (at present) analysis of the various sources about female suicide in late imperial China, see Paul Ropp's introduction and his bibliography to this volume.

[2] T'ien Ju-k'ang imputes the elevation of women's suicide to an exemplary act of virtue during the latter part of the Ming dynasty and the beginning of the Qing dynasty to the anxiety the literati felt vis-à-vis the historical, political, and social changes going on at their time. One may, unfortunately, add that it was a sad historical fact that women killed themselves to escape rape and abuse by roving soldiers and bandits in times of political turmoil, such as during dynastic transitions.

[3] Jeffrey Eugenides, *The Virgin Suicides* (New York: Warner Books, 1999), 248.

stories and novels. We will first look at those sources that construct suicide as a "good death," in other words, as the result of a positive—albeit morally ambiguous—desire, and then we will explore the complex relationship of suicide, death, and eroticism.[4] The second part of the paper analyzes those representations that construct suicide as a "bad death," one that engenders ghosts and that needs to be "exorcised." It is important to stress that these two categories are not airtight: as we shall see, even a "good suicide," one, in other words, that can be translated into a safe narrative of feminine virtue, always engenders ambiguities. In the final section of the paper, we will compare the rhetoric of male suicides, both in fiction and in real life, with that of women, to bring together the different interpretative strains we have outlined in the two previous sections and to postulate the meanings that late imperial Chinese writers and readers could attach to these representations.

This article is a preliminary investigation of a topic that has been little studied in traditional Chinese fiction, at least to my knowledge. Given the richness and wealth of sources, the present endeavor does not claim to be an exhaustive survey of all representations of female suicide in all available sources. Rather, it aims to be a first step towards a systematic exploration of all vernacular sources and later sources in classical Chinese and towards establishing differences and similarities between the two. The long-term goal of this study will be understanding and unraveling the complex web of meanings evoked by late imperial representations of femininity, the body, and death. For now we wish to show how female suicide can be a narrative device, a negative or positive representation of desire, and how it can be used to eroticize or to exorcise female characters.

From this angle, it is important to remember that, no matter how tempting it may be to view these representations as "protofeminist," the authors and most of the readers were males.[5] Thus their works

---

[4] Clearly, the suicide of the heroine can have a very important role as a narrative device within the overall plot of a story or a novel. It is clear that at the beginning of a story, it propels the narrative forwards, while at the end of a story it concludes and brings together the different strains of the plot. Still, analysis of narrative structure is not the focus of our present endeavor.

[5] We can assume that among the audience for the texts under study were female readers, since we know that there were women who read novels and plays. Still, we also know that the wider reading audience was male. For female responses to fictional texts, see Ellen Widmer, "Xiaoqing's Literary Legacy and the Place of the Woman Writer in Late Imperial China," *Late Imperial China*, 13.1 (1992): 111-55; Kang-i Sun Chang and Ellen Widmer, eds., *Writing Women in Late Imperial China*

confirm the Lacanian view that "femininity becomes the place in which man reads his destiny, just as the woman becomes a symptom for the man." In other words, we should not read in them any attempt to subvert the gender hierarchies existing in China at the time. This is, after all, literature that was meant to entertain, to perhaps admonish Chinese readers, to make sense of but not to overthrow the Chinese moral universe. On the contrary, by stretching its boundaries, these images reinforce the notion of women's role as the ultimate, albeit at times recalcitrant, object of male desire.

*Dying Grandly*

> "Our third daughter has already become an immortal, what are you crying for? She died well, and I only wish I could die for such a good cause myself!" Thus, throwing back his head to laugh, he said: "She died well, she died well!" Then, laughing out loud, he left the room.[6]

This quotation comes from Chapter 48 of *Rulin waishi* 儒林外史 (The unofficial history of the literati), and refers to the conversation of the parents of a young woman who had starved herself to death to follow her husband in death. While her in-laws and her mother Mrs. Wang did try, albeit in vain, to dissuade her from doing so, her father, Wang Yuhui 王玉輝, was actually quite supportive and almost elated by her choice. He even goes so far as wishing for himself the good death his daughter was able to choose. Why would the voluntary death of a young woman be depicted in most late imperial vernacular fiction, as we see here, as *haodesi* 好的死, dying well? Parry and Bloch state that

> [t]he "good" death is thus the one which suggests some degree of mastery over the arbitrariness of the biological occurrence by replicating a prototype to which all such deaths conform, and which can therefore be seen as an instance of a general pattern necessary for the reproduction of life. By contrast, ... those deaths which clearly demonstrate the absence of control are those which are represented as "bad" deaths and which do not result in regeneration.[7]

It is true that the young woman's death, as a suicide, would qualify more as an instance of bad death, one that undermines this very

---

(Stanford; Stanford University Press, 1997); Judith Zeitlin, "Shared Dreams: The Story of the Three Wives Commentary on *The Peony Pavilion*," *Harvard Journal of Asiatic Studies* 54.1 (1994): 127-79.

[6] Wu Jingzi 吳敬梓, *Rulin waishi* 儒林外史 (Changsha: Lulinshushe, 1988), 299.

[7] Maurice Bloch and Jonathan Parry, eds., *Death and the Regeneration of Life* (Cambridge: Cambridge University Press, 1982), "Introduction," 1-44; quote is from p. 15.

pattern necessary for the reproduction of life (the woman is young, she could remarry and have children, or she could—and should devote her life to serve her aging parents-in-law), and that demonstrates lack of control. But from another perspective, it fits quite well within the normalizing (and male) function of tradition, which coded the young woman's act as proper precisely because it did require a degree of mastery over the arbitrary nature of death. Furthermore, the young widow chooses to die for the noblest of reasons, namely to be loyal to her husband and not be a financial burden to either her old parents-in-law or her biological parents.

In this respect, it is important to note the two different behaviors, on the one hand, of the mother and the in-laws, and of the father, on the other. The earlier ones do all they can to change the daughter's mind, while the latter laughingly approves and praises her. This is not to be read as a display of callousness on the father's part; on the contrary. Why? The mother and the in-laws understand the daughter's choice emotionally and personally. The in-laws have just lost their son, and the mother is shocked by her daughter's desire to leave her forever. Wang Yuhui, on the contrary, reads his daughter's suicide as a means his daughter has to make a name for herself and is happy about it. He transcends his personal attachment to his daughter and looks at her decision with the outlook of the man of letters who approves of displays of Confucian values, such as loyalty, regardless of gender.

To Wang Yuhui, his daughter's death is a good death because it is not a source of *luan* 亂, disorder, but a manifestation of the order that should regulate the relationships within society. The woman follows the man, even in death, just as the loyal minister follows his king. The father is almost jealous of his daughter's choice; we will come back to this very important point. Here let us note how this episode immediately reveals the potential complexity of a fictional suicide. Even before it has taken place, as we see in this example, it begs to be read and interpreted by the close of kin—much more so *after* it has happened, when the authorities will invest it with symbolic meanings and reward it with arches and ceremonies.

If death is the most private experience in the life of a person, since it involves, at least physically, exclusively the individual who dies, female suicide appears within the realm of Chinese fiction to make this very private act into a public text for the eyes of all and sundry. Each reading (the father's, the mother's, the in-laws', the state's, and so on) is related to factors such as social status and gender as well as to concrete preoccupations (by killing herself, the daughter is depriving her aging parents and parents-in-law of practical help and support), emotional values, and ethical standards (loyalty, posterity, fame).

It is also just as clear that, between the reading of the father (which resonates with that of the state and that of the community of the men of letters) and that of the mother, namely between rational approval and emotional reproach, there lies the third reading, perhaps the most intriguing of all, namely that of the daughter. Her will is to die, but her real reasons are obscured by the rhetoric that will be ascribed to her act. Others choose to read her act as filial, unfilial, virtuous, or selfish. Yet it is evident that, for all the ambiguities evoked by this case, we are still dealing with female behavior that society at large (within and outside the realm of novels) can construct as positive.

Just to mention a few of the many examples we could find of this type of suicide, in Chapter 32 of the most famous Chinese novel of late imperial times, *Hongloumeng* 紅樓夢, the maid Jin Chuaner 金釧兒, unjustly punished by her mistress, Lady Wang 王夫人, for breaking a small object, jumps in the well, thus dying an "exemplary death," *liesi* 烈死.[8] In the same novel, You Sanjie 尤三姐, a relative of the Jia 賈 family, kills herself out of shame when Liu Xianglian 柳湘蓮, her betrothed, rejects her because he thinks her reputation is tarnished. She slashes her throat in front of him, with the sword he had given as an engagement gift, right after he has gone back on his word to marry her.[9]

Though the examples quoted above involve women from respectable backgrounds, "dying well" was not a class privilege. In Ming and Qing vernacular literature women from tainted backgrounds also could resort to suicide to save face and defend their reputations. For example, in *Luye xianzong* 綠野仙蹤 (Trails of immortals in the green wilds), an eighteenth-century erotic novel, the prostitute Jin Zhonger 金鍾兒 swallows mercury when her parents, who are also her "managers," discover that she has been secretly giving money to her lover to help him pass the civil service examinations. She decides to take the poison because she feels that, after all that had transpired, she would have no face with which to face the world.[10]

---

[8] Cao Xueqin 曹雪芹, *Hongloumeng* 紅樓夢 (Beijing: Renmin wenxue chubanshe, 1988), vol. 1, 449-51.

[9] Cao Xueqin, *Hongloumeng*, vol. 2, 945.

[10] Li Baichuan 李百川, *Lüye xianzong* 綠野仙蹤 (Beijing: Beijing daxue chubanshe,

In other words, the desire to remove the stain from their honor positions all these women under the spotlight: it removes them from the inner quarters and brings them to the attention of men, not only their husbands and siblings but the (male) audience within and outside the novel. From this angle, then, it is important to note that suicide, in its literary representations, is an act that erases the invisibility of women and in particular their death, by forcing women onto the public stage in the role of dramatic heroines. It is not, then, a matter just of the private experience of death made public. It is also the agent of this death, the woman, who breaks the boundary of her socially prescribed sphere of action, the *nei* 內, to get her moment of fame for the very first and very last time of her life. As Emily Martin convincingly states:

> Society transforms the potentially avenging ghost of a suicide into a chaste widow; for her part, the chaste widow, subordinate to her husband even to the point of dying when she dies, becomes not a forgotten ancestor but a goddess in a public realm. The cost for the woman is of course that she must act on the "perverse" dominant male ideology: that immortal life can only be obtained at the cost of forfeiting life through a heroine's death.[11]

We will talk about ghosts later, but now we must illuminate the nexus between death, virtue, and female visibility. The realm of *wai* 外, the outside, is always a dangerous and tricky arena for a woman in the context of Chinese literature.[12]

The extent to which this is so becomes clear when we turn to the cases in which women who intend to kill themselves in order to save their reputation are prevented from doing so. In these episodes we see how the female characters who, willingly or unwillingly, leave their *nei* world, exposing themselves to the predatory male "I"/eye, which can assume total control of them, in death as well as in life. The risks that being seen entailed for a woman of a respectable background are clearly observed in *Yuguihong* 玉閨紅 (The rouge in

---

1985), *j.* 46: 311. See also Keith McMahon, *Misers, Shrews, and Polygamists: Sexuality and Male-Female Relations in Eighteenth-Century Chinese Fiction* (Durham: Duke University Press, 1995), 235.

[11] Emily Martin, "Gender and Ideological Differences in Representations of Life and Death," in James L. Watson and Evelyn S. Rawski, eds., *Death Ritual in Late Imperial and Modern China*, (Berkeley: University of California Press, 1988), 164-79; quote is on p. 177.

[12] It also forces attention to "grotesque" aspects of the body, and in particular of women's bodies, namely mortality, decay, pollution, and death itself. See Paola Zamperini, "Lost Bodies: Images and Representations of Prostitution in Late Qing Fiction." (Ph.D. diss., University of California at Berkeley, 1999), Ch. 4.

the boudoir), a supposedly late Ming pornographic novel "rediscovered" in the twentieth century.[13] In Chapter 8, the heroine Guizhen 閨貞, Boudoir's Chastity, a girl of an upper-class family fallen on hard times, ends up in a brothel because in her grief at her parents' suicide, she left her home and was seen by a disgruntled ex-servant of her father.[14] Guizhen tries to commit suicide every single time she is raped or abused in the brothel but is always prevented from leaving the source of her sufferings.[15] She cannot kill herself by slamming her head against the wall, because the slum in which she is imprisoned is made of mud and does not offer a surface hard enough. She cannot strangle herself, because she is stripped of her clothes, and in any case there would be no beam from which she could hang herself. She cannot starve herself because she is force-fed by the madam and the pimp, who do not want to lose such a valuable asset and keep her under suicide watch all the time. If a woman fails to gain control of her own body, it means she is at the mercy not only of her tormentors in the story of which she is the heroine but of the male readers as well.

Clearly, *Yuguihong*, like other pornographic works, is a voyeuristic novel, in that it offers its readers the view of a girl, who, by virtue of her high social status, should be invisible to the eyes of most men, safely hidden inside the boudoir. Guizhen instead becomes visible completely, in all the splendor of her body, to the eyes of beggars and petty thieves, madams and pimps who crowd the low-class brothel as well as of those of the readers. The acute scopophilia derived by the sight of the young girl raped and attacked is reinforced every time the heroine fails to escape from the male reader's gaze through suicide. Her will to preserve her chastity, to be spared shame and humiliation, is erased. The right to cancel herself from being written as a sexual object—a right that she tries to assert by re-inscribing herself in the history of chaste and virtuous women—is denied to her. The same line of reasoning can be applied to her "sister-in-despair" Cui Qiao 翠翹, the heroine of *Jin Yun Qiao zhuan* 金雲翹傳 (The story of Jin, Yun, and Qiao), a mid-Qing novel: tricked into prostitution, she keeps trying to kill herself, to save her family's honor and her reputation, and she keeps being saved and

[13] Dong Lu Luoluo pingsheng 東魯落落平生, *Yuguihong* 玉閨紅 (Taibei: Tianyi chubanshe, 1995).
[14] Dong Lu Luoluo pingsheng, *Yuguihong*, 388.
[15] Dong Lu Luoluo pingsheng, *Yuguihong*, 388.

rescued, almost invariably by her tormentors, only to fall into more difficult and painful predicaments.[16] These two examples are important because they show how vulnerable women are once they have become visible. Being seen equates, for an upper-class woman, with being socially and almost unavoidably physically/sexually violated. As visibility and its nefarious consequences are so "contaminating," they call for a radical "cure." Unless they manage to embrace death to become "goddesses in a public realm," female characters such as Guizhen immediately fall, without remedy, into the category of public women, who are put forth in society, without veils and protections, as the utmost symbol of social debasement.

We can see how problematic all the stories mentioned so far are; each reading begs another, and each case has to be read against the grain of the other. But there is more. Not only are these literary representations part of the late imperial discourse on women's suicide, so filled with contradictions and anxiety: female suicide as represented in fiction is part and parcel of the multi-faceted feminine death figure that had played a very important role in the erotic imagery of Chinese readers. It is important at this juncture to make visible "the excessively obvious but often non-read figure that crosses femininity with death."[17]

In the West, nineteenth-century literature connected women, eroticism, and death in an unprecedented fashion: because of changed economic and social circumstances, "as death became unfamiliar and as such connected with fear, it was not only put under cover but relegated to the site previously occupied by love—the imaginary."[18] In the context of Chinese culture, death had occupied ever since the Tang dynasty the realm of the imaginary, side by side with love, women, and eroticism.[19] But it is especially during the Ming dynasty that male and female readers appear mesmerized by the titillating

[16] Qingxincairen 青心才人, *Jin Yun Qiao zhuan* 金雲翹傳 (Shenyang: Chunfeng wenyi chubanshe, 1983), 58.

[17] Elisabeth Bronfen, *Over Her Dead Body: Death, Femininity and the Aesthetic* (New York: Routledge, 1992), 35.

[18] Bronfen, *Over Her Dead Body*, 87.

[19] See Paola Zamperini, "A Star is Born: The Fantastic Childhood of a Courtesan To Be," Ch. 1 in "Lost Bodies." See also André Levy, "Le renard, la morte et la courtisane dans la Chine classique," in *Études mongoles* 15 (1984): 111-39. In this article, Levy aims to show, in a very intriguing but not completely convincing manner, that the images of the dead woman in love, the vixen, and the courtesan belong to the same paradigm and are but three different ways of imagining an alternative—perceived as illusory—to the traditional system of matrimonial alliance.

spectacle offered by the death of young, beautiful women.[20] In the *Mudanting* 牡丹亭 (Peony pavilion), Liu Mengmei 柳夢梅 falls deeply in love first with the portrait of the beautiful but by then deceased Du Liniang 杜麗娘 and later with her ghost.[21]

Anthony Yu and Judith Zeitlin have shown how female ghosts were perceived as amorous counterparts of young scholars in the macabre romances of late imperial times.[22] Interestingly enough, whereas in many nineteenth-century Western novels, "the only safe woman is a dead woman. But even she, if young and beautiful, is only half safe .... the only safe, safe female is a preadolescent girl dying or dead,"[23] in the context of late imperial Chinese fiction, as we shall see, not even death makes a woman, or a preadolescent girl, for that matter, safe. Female ghosts could be sexual and sexy, and the allure of the dying beauty captured the imagination of both men and women. A morbid fascination with the spectacle of the marriage between youth, femininity, and death cannot be excluded from these images of female suicide. This view is yet another facet of the late imperial discourse on suicide, which, on the one hand, praised and canonized (with official titles and memorial arches) women who killed themselves, while, on the other hand, strove to contain the "epidemic" of young and older women doing away with themselves.

Not all authors were so smitten with dying beauties. We find some writers who, though viewing female suicide as a way to save one's reputation, appear to encourage women not to lose their heads in

---

[20] See Widmer, "Xiaoqing's Literary Legacy and the Place of the Woman Writer in Late Imperial China," and Zeitlin, "Shared Dreams."

[21] Tang Xianzu, *Mudanting* 牡丹亭, in Xu Shuofang 徐朔方, ed., *Tang Xianzu xiqu ji* 湯顯祖戲曲集 (Shanghai: Shanghai guji, 1982). We find a parallel to this in Edgar Allan Poe's "The Oval Portrait," where the narrator falls under the spell of the portrait of a dead woman (1842, in *Poetry and Tales: Literary Classics of the United States* [New York: Viking Press, 1984]). See also Bronfen, *Over Her Dead Body,* 110, for a reading of Poe's story. In the world of late imperial Chinese literature, for a woman to paint her own portrait is very much like suicide, in the sense that it implies a powerful assertion of one's individual personality and will (interestingly enough, in most literary sources, when a young woman paints her self-portrait, she almost invariably dies, but this is entirely another paper!).

[22] Anthony Yu, "'Rest, Rest, Perturbed Spirit!' Ghosts in Traditional Chinese Prose Fiction," *Harvard Journal of Asiatic Studies*, 47.2 (1987): 397-434; Judith Zeitlin, "Embodying the Disembodied: Representations of Ghosts and the Feminine," in Kang-i Sun Chang and Ellen Widmer, eds., *Writing Women in Late Imperial China*, 242-63.

[23] L. A. Fiedler, *Love and Death in the American Novel* (New York: Stein and Day, 1966), 267.

order to keep their chastity. After all, it could be argued that if Guizhen had not panicked and let her emotions get the better of her judgment, she would have perhaps been able to save herself from her predicament. In Li Yu 李漁 (1611-1680)'s *Opera* 5 in *Wushengxi* 無聲戲 (Silent operas), the female protagonist manages to keep her chastity through ruses and deceit.[24] Li Yu uses her to expose the hypocrisy of his contemporaries, both men and women, who paid lip service to the Confucian moral standards of chastity and honor but failed to live up to them. He does not oppose female suicide when a woman is about to be raped by soldiers or bandits. On the contrary, he sees women who vow martyrdom and keep their vows as the pure sages of his times. But he does provide women with a concrete alternative to doing away with oneself when confronted with the choice between dishonor and death. From this point of view, he seems to follow Lü Kun 呂坤 (1536-1618), a late Ming advocate of women's education, who argued that in order for women to be good mothers and virtuous wives, they had to be taught how to think for themselves.[25]

*Raising Hell*

But women, in much late imperial Chinese fiction, are creatures governed by their often uncontrollable and indomitable *qing* 情, emotions. Charlotte Furth has shown how in the medical and literary tradition of late imperial China women were imagined to be especially vulnerable to strong emotions such as melancholy and anger.[26] Ming and Qing literary heroines are figures of great, and at times, tragic passion (and their passion is not always represented as a negative trait) acted out almost invariably at the level of the body.[27] For these passionate women, suicide, more than the tangible

---

[24] Li Yu 李漁, *Wushengxi* 無聲戲, Vol. 12, in Helmut Martin, ed., *Li Yu quanji* 李漁全集 (Taibei: Chengwen chubanshe, 1970).

[25] See Joanna Handlin, "Lü K'un's New Audience: The Influence of Women's Literacy on Sixteenth-Century Thought," in Margery Wolf and Roxane Witke, eds., *Women in Chinese Society*, 13-38, for an analysis of Lü Kun's work.

[26] See Charlotte Furth, *A Flourishing Yin: Gender in China's Medical History, 960-1665* (Berkeley: University of California Press, 1998).

[27] For an analysis of the relationship between women's bodies, the state, and virtue in the Ming and Qing dynasty, see Katherine Carlitz, "Desire, Danger, and the Body: Stories of Women's Virtue in Late Ming China," in Christina. K. Gilmartin, Gail Hershatter, Lisa Rofel, and Tyrene White, eds., *Engendering China. Women, Culture, and the State* (Cambridge: Harvard University Press, Cambridge, 1993), 101-24.

expression of their desire to save their own or their husband's good name, constitutes the ultimate expression of love, or, more often, it is the only way left to mend their broken hearts.

One could even detect in these Ming and Qing heroines the legacy of Tang characters such as Huo Xiaoyu 霍小玉, the selfless courtesan who lets herself die after being rejected by her beloved, a scholar she loved dearly and had helped financially so that he could pass the examinations and come back to spend three years with her before marrying a woman from a more respectable social background.[28] In Chapter 69 of *Hongloumeng*, You Erjie 尤二姐 the concubine of Jia Lian 賈璉 harassed by his first wife Fengjie 鳳姐 to the point of losing her unborn child, kills herself by swallowing gold. Realizing that her husband Jia Lian's love pales in front of his first wife's hatred, she sees suicide as the only escape from the dreadful horror of a whole existence under the clutches of the cruel first wife.[29] In Chapter 89 of the same novel, Lin Daiyu 林黛玉, one of the two main female protagonists, resolves to starve herself to death when she learns that her beloved Jia Baoyu 賈寶玉 has been betrothed to her cousin and rival Xue Baochai 雪寶釵.[30]

In these three cases, heartbreak is the main drive behind the women's resolution, the only way they seem to have to cope with losing the man they love and on whom they centered their whole existence: the woman who loses her man is perceived to lose herself. The loss of the man fuses with that of life. Since her identity as an individual is built around being loved by a faithless man, once she has lost his love, she has lost also her life-force and her reason to exist. The insistent representation of women, rather than men, who commit suicide for love complements the familiar assumption that woman lives for love, man for himself (or one could say, most women are represented as having a very limited range of vision).[31]

---

[28] "Huo Xiaoyu zhuan" 霍小玉傳, in *Tangren xiaoshuo* 唐人小說 (Xianggang: Zhonghua shuju, 1973).

[29] Cao Xueqin, *Hongloumeng*, vol. 2, 984.

[30] Cao Xueqin, *Hongloumeng*, vol. 3, 1277. Both in real life and fictional texts, women killed themselves with the tools they had at their disposal. Thus, opium seemed to be the choice of many courtesans and prostitutes, while upper-class women often swallowed gold or starved themselves, and servants and maids often hanged or drowned themselves.

[31] Love itself can, of course, be taken as a form of suicide for a woman (especially for a courtesan, who by virtue of her profession, should not expect love; erotic initiative could lead to unwanted pregnancies and abortion of selfhood). See Margaret Higonnet, "Speaking Silences. Women's Suicides," in Susan Suleiman

There are also women, however, whose turbulent hearts lead them consciously to choose suicide as the best way to get back at the men who used and abused their love and affection. Once they die, some of these women become ghosts, who come back and harass their faithless lovers. Huo Xiaoyu haunts her lover so often that he becomes insanely jealous and kills all his concubines and lovers: we can indeed say that in the end she is vindicated. In the late Ming short story "Du Shiniang nu chen baibaoxiang" 杜十娘怒沉百宝箱 (The courtesan's jewel-box), for instance, the beautiful courtesan Du Shiniang 杜十娘, upon discovering that she has been sold by her faithless lover to a greedy and scheming salt merchant, drowns herself in the river, after having shamed both her doltish lover and the merchant in front of a whole audience of people by revealing her (financial and moral) worth. Du Shiniang's lover later becomes insane, and Sun, the salt merchant, dies a month after the woman's suicide.[32]

A broken heart, and not revenge, was the main reason behind these women's gesture, yet their act of purification, suicide, transforms them in *yin* 陰 creatures, ghosts, who, though impure, have the power to exact revenge on those men who wronged them. The idea that vengeful ghosts seeking retribution can cause deaths is quite old in Chinese folklore. Alvin Cohen shows that already in early historical sources we find the belief that the soul of a person unjustly killed can return as an avenging ghost.[33] He argues quite convincingly that

> through a fusion of ancient soul-theory that allowed for the potential presence of a soul-aspect, with the popular Buddhist idea of reincarnation through the cycle of karma, and the desire of ancestor worship for the continued presence of the departed, Chinese popular belief came to regard death as only a transition from one form of existence to another, rather than the beginning of the final termination of life.[34]

---

Rubin, ed., *The Female Body in Western Culture* (Cambridge: Harvard University Press, 1986), 68-83.

[32] "Du Shiniang nu chen baibaoxiang" 杜十娘怒沉百宝箱 in Feng Menglong, 冯梦龙 ed., *Jingshi tongyan* 警世通言 (Peking: Renmin chubanshe, 1959), 585-600.

[33] Alvin P. Cohen, "The Avenging Ghost. Moral Judgement in Chinese Historical Texts." (Ph.D. diss., University of California, Berkeley, 1971), Ch. 2. See also *Tales of Vengeful Souls. A Sixth-Century Collection of Chinese Avenging Ghost Stories*, translated and annotated by Alvin P. Cohen (Taipei: Institut Ricci, 1982).

[34] Alvin P. Cohen, "The Avenging Ghost," 19. See also Yu Ying-shih, "'O Soul, Come Back!' A Study in the Changing Conception of the Soul and the Afterlife in Pre-Buddhist China," *Harvard Journal of Asiatic Studies*, 47.2 (1987): 363-95.

In other words, the native notion of the avenging ghost later came to be amalgamated in popular understanding with the Buddhist concept of retribution and karma. In this respect, J. de Groot saw the belief in vengeful ghosts as an effective tool to keep people from committing injustices, "because the wronged party, thoroughly sure of the avenging power of his spirit when disembodied, will not always shrink from converting himself into a wrathful ghost by committing suicide."[35] Cohen explains that the belief in this type of ghost allowed historians first and then people at large to pass objective moral judgement on individuals who could not be reached by law by virtue of their power or because they had committed their crimes in secret.[36] T'ien Ju-k'ang also argues that "the hope for restitution of right in the underworld by retaliation of ghosts can be said to have resulted from the oppressiveness of traditional Chinese society which left no channel open to meet the social and psychological needs of people while alive in this world."[37]

The presence of avenging ghosts was also seen as a result of the dissolution of the body and of the polluting effects of death and its vapors.[38] As James Watson explains, *sha qi* 殺氣 (killing airs) emanate from the corpse at the moment of death, and the *sha qi* associated with "untimely or inauspicious deaths are particularly virulent. Worst of all are the killing airs that accompany suicide."[39] Zhu Xi's 朱熹 formulation, as recounted by Ji Yun 紀昀 (1724-1805), a scholar with a strong interest in the supernatural, is that *qi* 氣 generally dispersed—returned to Heaven and Earth—when a man died,

---

[35] J. de Groot, *The Religious System of China* (Leiden, 1892; reprint Taipei: Ch'eng-wen Publishing Company, 1972), vol. 4, 451.

[36] Cohen, "The Avenging Ghost. Moral Judgement in Chinese Historical Texts." See also Alvin P. Cohen, "Avenging Ghosts and Moral Judgement in Ancient Chinese Historiography: Three Examples from *Shih-Chi*," in Sarah Allan and Alvin P. Cohen, eds., *Legend, Lore, and Religion in China. Essays in Honor of Wolfram Eberhard on His Seventieth Birthday* (San Francisco: Chinese Material Center, Inc., 1979), 97-108.

[37] T'ien Ju-k'ang. *Male Anxiety and Female Chastity*," 117.

[38] For the pollution of death, see Emily Martin, "Gender and Ideological Differences in Representations of Life and Death;" Emily Ahern, "The Power and Pollution of Chinese Women," in Margery Wolf and Roxane Witke, eds., *Women in Chinese Society*, 193-214; James L. Watson, "Of Flesh and Bones: the Management of Death Pollution in Cantonese Society," in Maurice Bloch and Jonathan Parry, eds., *Death and the Regeneration of Life* (Cambridge: Cambridge University Press, 1982), 155-86.

[39] James L. Watson, "Of Flesh and Bones: the Management of Death Pollution in Cantonese Society," 158.

but that "it does not in the case of three types of people: those who were wronged, Buddhist monks and Daoist priests who practiced spiritual cultivation, and those who died unnatural deaths."[40] For those in the last group, *qi* is not exhausted, so they can return to haunt the living. If in the West the saying *mors ultima linea rerum*, "death is the ultimate boundary of things," horrified centuries of scholars, writers, and readers and kept them grappling for centuries with their *horror vacui* in many of their artistic expressions, for the Chinese this boundary was quite porous.[41]

According to T'ien Ju-k'ang, the belief in the capability of ghosts to retaliate against enemies of the previous life was spread mostly through the theatrical performances of the Song dynasty, such as the dramatic story of Mulian 目蓮.[42] We also know that the first Ming emperor, a man known for his desire to rule both this and the netherworld, divided ghosts into twelve categories and had altars for praying to malicious spirits built throughout the empire, thus reinforcing the notion that the wrongfully dead are dangerous for the living and need to be kept at bay. By the late Ming dynasty, both elite and popular culture concurred to circulate and reinforce the notions about the power of and the threat posed by those who, having committed suicide, would remain in an

> unsettled state after death and so neither receive the regular rites nor have hope of becoming socially immortalized through a tomb or a hall tablet. In fact, because the soul is not in its proper place in the underworld, and can harass the living, making them sick, troubled, and unsuccessful, suicide can be used as an act of aggression against one's kin.[43]

We thus see that many complex factors, from religious beliefs to funerary practices, supported the continuing presence of the avenging ghost motif through the history of Chinese literature, as well as in the belief system of traditional and contemporary Chinese culture. But this continuity should not obscure the changes this motif underwent throughout the centuries. In earlier sources we are deal-

---

[40] See Leo Tak-hung Chan, *The Discourse on Foxes and Ghosts. Ji Yun and Eighteenth-Century Literati Storytelling* (Honolulu: University of Hawaii Press, 1998), 135.

[41] Quotation found on Erasmus's medal showing the likeness of the Roman god Terminus; see Julia Kristeva, "Holbein's Dead Christ," in M. Feher, Ramona Naddaff, and Nadia Tazi, eds., *Fragments for a History of the Human Body* (New York: Zone Books, 1989), vol. 1, 238-69; quote on page 255.

[42] T'ien Ju-k'ang, *Male Anxiety and Female Chastity*, 116.

[43] Emily Martin, "Gender and Ideological Differences in Representations of Life and Death," 177.

ing with historical texts with an explicit moral message: people become ghosts as a result of murder and very seldom kill themselves in order to become ghosts. In this early stage we find more examples of unjust murders than of suicides. Late imperial fictional sources then invest the ghosts of suicides with the power of exacting revenge, because suicides become part of those who have died a *hengsi* 橫死, a wrongful death. The time of the return to earth to exact revenge in these earlier sources can be quite long; in some cases years could go by before revenge was meted out. In Ming and Qing vernacular sources, on the contrary, we find a good number of ghosts who appear in fiction to demand justice right after death. Of course, we are dealing with a different genre and thus with different narrative necessities.[44]

The change that appears most relevant to our present enterprise is that the gender of the avenging ghost becomes a fundamental key in late imperial sources. While in early times the avenging ghost is almost invariably male, in late imperial literature we find a "pronounced taste for female ghosts," which "is part of the widespread fascination with the death of beautiful, talented women in the sentimental culture of the period."[45] Anthony Yu distinguishes three kinds of ghosts in late imperial fiction, the apologetic, the avenging, and the amorous. "It is the wrong suffered at the hands of those expected to be trusted and beloved and the compelling need for the requital of justice that stir the wronged soul's activities in Chinese fiction.[46] I am proposing here a fourth type, or a subcategory, of ghost, the "avenging amorous ghost" who, as we shall see, is stirred once her love turns to hatred.

Once they kill themselves, the women under study here do not become figures of absence and loss: they show, unlike the aestheticized and fragile female ghosts studied by Zeitlin, that instead of mourning for eternity the irretrievable loss of love, a scorned woman can use death to rewrite history according to her own volition and desire. In other words, in this kind of suicide, by virtue of killing her own body, the woman challenges the cultural construction of the feminine as a "dead" image ruled and violated by others. By undo-

---

[44] For a more exhaustive account of the presence of ghosts in Chinese fiction, see Yu, "'Rest, Rest, Perturbed Spirit!' Ghosts in Traditional Chinese Prose Fiction."

[45] Zeitlin, "Embodying the Disembodied," 242.

[46] Yu, "'Rest, Rest, Perturbed Spirit!' Ghosts in Traditional Chinese Prose Fiction," 415-16.

ing her body, she undoes the gender construction that places her in an inferior position, and thus she is able to fulfill those desires which cultural constraints would not let her realize in life.

The ideal text in which to study suicide as retaliation is *Haishang mingji si da jingang qishu* 海上名妓四大金剛奇書 (The strange book of the four guardian gods of the courtesans of Shanghai), written by Wu Jianren 吳趼人 (1867-1910).[47] To show how this amusing novel, full of interesting angles from which to observe and deconstruct the complex dynamics of gender relationships and sexuality in late Qing fiction is relevant to our present inquiry, let us turn to the text:

> [Shen Xiaoqing 沈小青] was quite calm: she went back to her room and wrote the three characters "Jin Hongjun" 金洪均 on her hand. Then she took out many leaves of gold, rolled them up in the necessary fashion, and swallowed them. Finally she changed into a new bright red and green dress and climbed into bed for a restful sleep.[48]

Shen Xiaoqing, a blind fortune-teller's daughter, has become a prostitute after her father's death. She falls in love with Jin Hongjun, a young and promising scholar, and gives him the money necessary for him to travel to the capital to take the metropolitan examinations. Once he receives the coveted *zhuangyuan* 狀元 title, the highest rank attainable through the examination system, he forgets all about her. At first he simply puts her out of his mind and willingly accepts a bride chosen from a well-to-do and respectable family. Later, when Shen Xiaoqing sends a maid to deliver him a letter, he has her beaten up. When she decides to plead with him in person, he has her battered by his servants. Devastated by his rejection, Shen Xiaoqing kills herself, only to be reborn as a Suzhou courtesan, the historical character Sai Jinhua 賽金花.[49] Right after her death, as a ghost, she manages to harass Jin's household by haunting his home. Eventually she is chased away by an exorcist, but not without causing walls to crumble, killing his first wife in the process. In her

---

[47] Published in the middle of 1898, just before the crackdown on the Reformers, it consists of two parts of fifty chapters each; there was a brief gap in time between the composition of the two halves, which were published separately. See Chouxi zhuren 抽細主人, pseud., *Huitu Haishang mingji si da jingang qishu* 繪圖海上名妓四大金剛奇書 (Shanghai: 1898, reprinted in *Shinmatsu shosetsu* 清末小説 15 ([1992]: 97-160; 17 ([1994]: 97-129; 18 [1995]. The page numbers given here refer to this reprint and not to the 1898 original. For more detailed information about this novel, see Zamperini, "Lost Bodies," Ch. 1.

[48] Chouxi zhuren, *Haishang mingji sida jingang qishu*, Ch.16.

[49] See Zamperini, "Lost Bodies," Chapter 5, for biographical references to Sai Jinhua and her life.

second incarnation, she loses her virginity to Jin Buhuan, the rascally son of Jin Hongjun, whom she then proceeds to marry, to cuckold with many different men, and to eventually poison.

Like Du Shiniang and You Sanjie, upon realizing the heartlessness of the man she loves, Shen Xiaoqing is faced with the disintegration of her life and chooses suicide as a revitalizing self-assertion in death against the lethal self-alienation in life, because it reaffirms her autonomy after Jin Hongjun's abandonment. But unlike them, she has a long-term plan, as it were, of vengeance. Once she has made her choice, Shen Xiaoqing finds strength: as long as she had hopes of finding her beloved and his love again, she lingered sick between life and death. As soon as she realizes he does not love her anymore, she makes up her mind to kill herself, and her will and her strength return. She tries to hang herself first but is revived by her mother. Then she convinces her mother to go to the capital, where Jin Hongjun is, to try one last time to talk some sense into him. After she is beaten by him, she fools her mother, telling her that Jin has agreed to marry her. She gets her mother drunk so that she will be out of the way until the morning, and then she proceeds to kill herself. Jin's rejection brings out her will to become an independent agent through death: her staged performance of death signifies a moment of control and power, given that the woman's self-disintegration becomes an act of self-construction.

Suicides like Shen Xiaoqing's make trouble; because they do not fit into the logic of Confucian patriarchy, the state could not integrate them into its propaganda. Such women borrow the rhetoric and the mode of a just suicide for individual (and thus selfish and disorderly) reasons. When the trauma and the reaction produced by the suicide functions exclusively at a personal level, and not as martyrdom, not as a following in death, then female suicide cannot be rewritten in moralizing history and fiction, and it becomes "bad." It does not do what a good death is supposed to do; it does not educate and admonish.

If her treatment at the hands of her ex-lover has caused her to lose face, Shen Xiaoqing reconstructs it in death on two levels. First of all, in death she regains her honor. In his beautiful letter to Ren An 任安 Sima Qian 司馬遷 presents suicide as honorable death, open to the captive slave girl as well as the high official. In trying to explain why he did *not* choose death, but preferred the uppermost shame of castration, he writes something very useful and illuminating for our present inquiry: "Human beings truly have but one death. There are deaths that seem heavier than Mount Tai, but to some death seems lighter than a piece of swansdown. *The difference lies in what is done by dying.*"[50] Sima Qian here points out that death can be a willful, self-signifying act that can achieve something, have an effect on posterity. In his case, he chose writing over suicide, a postponed literary immortality (and indeed he succeeded in his goal) to an immediate liberation through suicide. The fictional heroine Shen Xiaoqing, two thousand years later, still claims the historian's argument as her own, in the sense that she achieves something by dying.[51] But she combines the dying with the writing, without privileging one over the other.

Secondly, her suicide is an act of defiance rather than of defeat. Not only does she get back her face, as it were, she also gets the terrible powers of the avenging ghost. Shen Xiaoqing's act of writing the name "Jin Hongjun" on her hand points out that much: her vengeance spans over two lifetimes and crosses the boundaries between life and death.[52] It is a gesture addressed to two different audiences: to those who will find the girl's body in the morning, it will give a precise explanation of why she decided to take her own life (and as Janet Theiss shows in her contribution in this volume, this could have serious legal consequences in real life). Reading the

---

[50] Sima Qian, "Letter in Reply to Ren An," in Stephen Owen, ed., *An Anthology of Chinese Literature. Beginnings to 1911* (New York: W.W. Norton and Company, 1996), 139.

[51] I hope the reader will not be shocked if, for the sake of my argument, I bring the most famous Chinese historian and a fictional entertainer to the same level. Sima Qian himself suggested the comparison to me when, also in the letter to Ren An, he lamented the fact that the emperor kept historians "on par with singers and acrobats, thus held in contempt by the common opinion" ("Letter in Reply to Ren An," 139).

[52] I am thankful to Luca Stirpe for pointing out to me the fact that the specific choice of the hand as canvas is quite an interesting one. Singling out the hand as the one place in the body to bear witness against the faithless lover is actually quite important. Some possible explanations are that since the woman is dressed in all her finery, she would not want to spoil it with ink, so her hand is a convenient choice. Besides, as a woman would not want to be seen in any indecent position, even on her deathbed (and much more so in the case of the courtesan who is trying to shame a "respectable" member of society) the hand could be displayed for everybody to see, without disgracing the body of the dead woman. No disrobing or nudity would be required. Catherine Yeh has also suggested that where the name was written on the hand could be relevant. The Chinese text, unfortunately, is not clear on that point. Both observations beg further reflection and inquiry than is here possible, and I am thankful to my colleagues for putting me onto a very interesting, albeit yet undeveloped, track.

dead body of Shen Xiaoqing is a hermeneutic task that will force those who survive her to read her death in the way she wants them to. In this way her corpse is immediately reinscribed in textuality.

The second audience is constituted by Shen Xiaoqing herself and those in the underworld; it will be a reminder of the karmic debt that Jin Hongjun owes Shen Xiaoqing. The skin on which she writes the cursed name is a porous surface that allows passions to seep from one level of existence into another. As Kristofer Schipper writes in *The Taoist Body*:

> Chinese writing was used first for communication between men and the gods before it was used among men [and in this case women] themselves .... Even when the use of writing was secularized and extended to all forms of literature, its ritual function was not forgotten.[53]

In other words, the heartbroken maiden is using her skin as a canvas to record her history, so that she and others will not forget it, but also as a ritual vessel to convey a message to the gods. This dramatic act of self-assertion is quite meaningful, since "it depicts a woman using death as a conscious act of setting a mark, as a form of writing with her body, a materialization of the sign, where the sheer material factualness of the dying and dead body lends certainty, authority and realness to this attempt at self-textualisation."[54] While Shen Xiaoqing in life had been unable to get her faithless lover to listen to her (he even has her beaten when she, already sick and desperate, travels to his home to get a sign of acknowledgment from him), by choosing death she can rewrite her story. In this sense her suicide can be seen as a claim to authorship over one's life, a form of writing the self and the rest of the world. Shen Xiaoqing's death reiterates what all these fictional suicides amply illustrate, namely, that one of the main characteristics of female suicide is its textual nature.

## *Putting the Pieces Back Together*

> It didn't matter in the end how old they were, or that they were girls, but only that we had loved them and that they hadn't heard us calling, still do not hear us, calling them out of those rooms where they went to be alone for all time, alone in suicide, which is deeper than death, and where we will never find the pieces to put them back together.[55]

---

53 Kristofer Schipper, *The Taoist Body* (Berkeley: University of California Press, 1993), 90-91.

54 Bronfen, *Over her Dead Body*, 141.

55 Jeffrey Eugenides, *The Virgin Suicides*, 248-49.

"Hell hath no fury like a woman scorned," and Shen Xiaoqing's fury indeed raises hell for Jin Hongjun. But the question remains: what are we to make of these representations? What types of emotion were they supposed to evoke, and in whom? Why were men interested in and almost obsessed with women's suicides? What is the relationship between female death/male authorship? How can we put the pieces back together to make sense of these deaths? And what sense and meanings did these representations hold for late imperial Chinese readers?

Since we know that the majority of readers were males, we could read these representations as an expression of anxiety and, simultaneously, a way to exorcise the anxiety through laughter and trivialization, as a vengeful ghost appears to pose serious problems, even in today's China.[56] Whether deplored or exalted, victimized or victimizing, these passionate women cause the readers to pause and wonder. Admiration, desire, regret, fear, these and many other emotions are invoked by these fictional characters: the interlacing of femininity, death, eroticism, power, and virtue create instability, marking moments of ambivalence, disruption, or duplicity. If for many women to be chaste through suicide implied taking control of and damaging the body, it also involved breaking two of the most important taboos in Confucian morality. First of all, it meant harming the body that one's parents had given to cherish and to hold, as it were, as one's most prized possession. But a perhaps more powerful transgression implied in the act of suicide could be women's subordination to reproductive imperatives: the ambiguity that men felt when a woman took her life in her own hands points clearly to the fear that women could in fact escape the roles of biological and social mothers they were supposed to play within the larger framework of Confucian patriarchy.

At the same time, the fact that they could escape presented them as powerful, erotically charged objects of desire, who could stand to gain more in charm at times by becoming more inaccessible, and thus more tantalizingly appealing, through death. Furthermore, death was not seen as an insurmountable physical barrier for the dead woman: Du Liniang and a whole host of female ghosts proved to be quite attractive sexual partners for many Chinese literary heroes, and, as we have seen in the case of Shen Xiaoqing, she could

[56] James L. Watson, "Of Flesh and Bones: The Management of Death Pollution in Cantonese Society."

come back and harass her faithless lover much more powerfully in death than in life.

Margery Wolf writes that "[l]ike so much Chinese behavior, suicide is not only an individual act, a gesture of personal despair, but also an act that implicates others," and that "for a woman [it] is the most damning accusation she can make of her mother-in-law, her husband, and so on."[57] Perhaps then, writing about female suicide for men was also a way to warn the readers about the calamity such a situation could entail for a man and his family. Indeed we find some late imperial stories in which women could be forced to kill themselves and their dead bodies used as false evidence. [58]

At this juncture it may help to compare suicide as practiced by men and by women in traditional China. Though fictional sources do not include many male suicides, in real life suicide had been constructed as a noble gesture for men in the face of disgrace or when faced with disasters such as turbulent dynastic changes. Certainly this type of event prompted dramatic responses in the people who witnessed the slaughters carried out by soldiers. The horrors of the Mongol conquest, the fall of the Ming, the rise of the Qing all concluded with incredible destruction of human life. Funeral pyres burned for days in 1650 when Canton fell to the Qing.[59] For men of letters, these traumas were quite hard to bear because they also required them to examine whether or not they were willing to serve the new rulers or to follow their former sovereign in death.

Wakeman interestingly groups late Ming men of letters in three groups, romantics, stoics, and martyrs. The romantics were unable to make their feelings prevail and served the new dynasty, shamefully. The male feeling of failure because one had not been able to find nobility in suicide is well expressed by the poet Wu Weiye 吳偉業 (1609-1672). As Wakeman notes, his poetry "consistently reflects a sense of guilt for not having committed suicide when so many of his classmates died."[60] To his very last day Wu Weiye "was pervaded by a profound sense of melancholy that seems to have

---

[57] Wolf, "Women and Suicide in China," 112.

[58] Paola Zamperini, "Body of Evidence: Corpses, Gender, and Retribution in Ming and Qing Fiction." (work in progress).

[59] Frederic Wakeman, Jr., "Romantics, Stoics, and Martyrs in Seventeenth-Century China," *Journal of Asian Studies*, 43.4 (1984): 631-66; reference here is to p. 643.

[60] Wakeman, "Romantics, Stoics, and Martyrs in Seventeenth-Century China," 639.

been associated with his decision not to commit suicide in 1644 when the Chongzhen 崇禎 Emperor (1628-1644) took his life."[61] The stoics remained stuck between the old and the new orders, and they too were often tormented by guilt for having survived the holocaust. Only those who chose suicide were able, by virtue of becoming martyrs, either of the old or of the new order, to "successfully" make the transition. Once more, we see that death means something, and the suicides achieved something with their own deaths.

Qu Yuan 屈原 (340?-278 BC) of course, was the progenitor of late imperial Chinese political martyrs. A misunderstood political hero, he chose death because his ruler, whom he so loved and cherished, did not appreciate him. By the late Ming, Qu Yuan had become *the* loyal minister and a role model for many intellectuals. What made him so valuable for martyrs who chose death with an agenda, a point to prove, was that Qu Yuan provided them with a superb example of noble suicide on which they could model their own demise. As Wakeman observes

> The importance of the audience before which the martyr is to perform is underscored: it is the impact upon that audience—the effect produced by the activity observed—that both affirms the authenticity of the actor and inspires those who watch and listen. Romantics may prefer to express themselves in poetry, and stoics may prefer to express themselves in prose; the genre par excellence of the martyr is drama, where the private is made public at once.[62]

Making public the private is thus the propelling motive behind male political suicides. Choosing suicide, the loyal man of letters gains immortality and saves his honor, just as Qu Yuan did. In the examples from real life, male suicide was always tragically heroic, while the choice not to commit suicide was always problematic. This left those who did not kill themselves in a quandary, but Sima Qian's legacy could come to their rescue. Instead of choosing suicide in the face of humiliation and defeat, the *wenren* 文人 could claim for himself the role of the record-keeper who had the right and the moral duty not to die. West argues, for example, that writing poetry helped Yuan Haowen 元好問 (1190-1257) cope with the death process in which he lived: by writing about the destruction he saw around him he found a way to deal with mortality and the horrors

[61] Wakeman, "Romantics, Stoics, and Martyrs in Seventeenth-Century China," 639.

[62] Wakeman, "Romantics, Stoics, and Martyrs in Seventeenth-Century China," 649.

of violent death.[63] Hoyt Tillman upholds a similar thesis in his forthcoming work, where he argues that writing poetry about death could offer a therapeutic space for the horror-stricken literatus.[64]

In other words, Sima Qian chose life over death because he had to write history, and Song and Ming literati and poets wrote endless poems to explain why they did not kill themselves after the Yuan and Manchu invasions, respectively. Suicide could be seen as a masculine response to trauma: if anything, its omission engendered many doubts as to the moral stamina of the man. When men did kill themselves, they could do it through writing themselves into the rhetoric of Qu Yuan, the loyal subject. But they could also find a positive outlet for their grief, shame, and so on by ascending to the role of record-keepers, by making sure that posterity would know and not forget. An illiterate woman could jump in a well, but a historian or a poet—that was a different matter.

Women often did not have access to the "healing powers" of the Word and could only use their bodies to bear testimony of their story and of history.[65] This does not mean that in real life women did not commit suicide out of a sense of political duty, too. For example, Gu Yanwu 顧炎武's (1613-1682) mother killed herself, enjoining her son not to take office under two surnames. In 1677, the women of Ma Xiongzhen 馬雄鎮's (d. 1672) household, all twenty-five of them, killed themselves in one night to follow Ma Xiongzhen and his two sons in death. They were following the example of other women of their lineage: forty-two of them chose suicide after the Manchus had captured Xiongzhen's grandfather.[66] But these female mass suicides appear to echo the male initiative; they follow in death as they followed in life; they act on principle, not on reckless passion.[67]

---

[63] Stephen H. West, "Chilly Seas and East-Flowing Rivers: Yüan Hao-wen's Poems of Death and Disorder, 1233-35," in Hoyt C. Tillman and Stephen H. West, eds., *China Under Jurchen Rule* (New York: State University of New York Press, 1995), 281-304.

[64] Hoyt Tillman, "Disorder (*luan*) as Trauma: A Case Study of Reactions to the Mongol Conquest." (forthcoming).

[65] Li Qingzhao 李清照 was one of the few women who wrote about her experience during the fall of the Song dynasty, and she expressed the grief she felt in terms of her husband's death and the disintegration of her personal world. For men it is the loss of the nation, for a woman the loss of a man—in both cases a tragic strike at the self and its social, cultural, emotional, and political identity.

[66] Wakeman, "Romantics, Stoics, and Martyrs in Seventeenth-Century China," 654.

[67] Also, female suicide can be constructed in fiction as an act of political de-

We see that in real life, suicide could be constructed as a "good death" for men, too. But in fictional sources, suicide is a feminine act. The only example of (attempted) male suicide I have been able to find so far in late imperial vernacular fiction is that of the merchant Lin Zhiyang 林之洋, in the Qing novel *Jinghua yuan* 鏡花緣 (Flowers in the mirror). He tries to kill himself after he has been kidnapped by the King of the Women's kingdom and is forced to have his feet bound—in other words, after his gender has been forcibly changed from male to female. In the novel suicide was coded as a feminine reaction to misery and as a way to escape the pain and the humiliation of the "sad plight of a beautiful woman."[68]

It is then up to the romantic heroines we find in late imperial fictional sources to follow in Qu Yuan's footsteps. Just like political martyrs, they too stage their death with a specific audience in mind, carefully planning their mode of death, as well as their attire. When Shen Xiaoqing stages her death she constructs it as a performative act that she controls, not one that she passively suffers. Nothing is left to chance. It might seem a little far-fetched to connect female characters' passionate suicides to those of late Ming and Qing political figures, but we must bear in mind that the authors of much Ming and Qing fiction were men of passions, political and otherwise, who could have transposed their passions onto their fictional heroines. The writers and the readers, not unlike Wang Yuhui in the above-mentioned *Rulin waishi* episode, might have felt admiration and envy for those women who, through suicide, found an outlet for their turbulent emotions, a "privilege" that men were socially expected to keep at a distance. These female characters could indeed become a sort of liberated and wilder Other to the male fantasizing self.

The longing for and the sexual attraction toward the female ghost

---

fiance, but we have very few examples of it, especially in novels. One of the most notable examples is to be found in the story of Yu 虞, the beautiful concubine of the Zhou King Xiang Yu 項羽. Her suicide is proof of loyalty and sets an example for the defeated ruler ("Bawang bie ji" 霸王別姬 in Li Bihua 李碧華 *Bawang bie ji* 霸王別姬 [Xianggang: tiandi tushu youxian gongsi, 1992], 355-68). There is also another form of "suicide" that begs further investigation. Cui Qiao, for example, in the already mentioned in the *Jin Yun Qiao zhuan*, chooses monastic life as well, after a lifetime of sorrows and abuse. Renouncing the world of the family and of sexuality equals death. Opting for monastic life or entering a convent, for both men and women, is a sort of suicide, as leaving the family meant social death.

[68] Li Ruzhen 李汝珍, *Huitu jinghua yuan* 繪圖鏡花緣 (Beijing: Beijingshi Zhongguo Shudian, 1985 ), *hui* 33, 1.

bears testimony of the reluctance to let go of this Other, a very important side of the male self. Loving the dying girl, the female suicide, the author can simultaneously recapture his emotions, his fears, his coming to know sex and death (inevitably linked in the male coming of age tale). This coming of age implies being exposed to the helplessness of fluids and to the decay that sex implies. This fact explains perhaps why in so many stories it is the first lover of a male character, the young scholar at his first sojourn in the capital, who becomes the ghost who haunts him and kills him: it is that very first woman with whom he succumbed to power of sexuality, "associated with flesh, decomposition and women."[69] Thus in novels and short stories the female ghost appears as the much desired but much feared abyss of pure and barren female sexuality, devoid of reproductive aims. We could also see in these women's suicidal behavior a male interpretation of "the furious power hunger of the powerless."[70] Hunger is what characterizes many ghosts in late imperial lore; hunger is *yin*, the barred sign of femininity and emptiness.

Is it yet another facet of male perversion that authors created heroines who, in order to become important for their husbands and lovers, had to kill themselves? Or is it the final victory of the patriarchal system that the woman willingly becomes a sign, embodiment of nothingness, which can then be read into "somethingness" by the male and creative pen/eye? Putting the pieces back together is not an easy task. In terms of adopting a feminist viewpoint to read these representations of female suicide, it could be tempting to conclude that "[f]or a 'fallen' woman, trapped in the distorting mirrors of patriarchy, the journey into death is the only way out, and the *Liebestod* is not (as it would be for a male artist, like Keats or Wagner) a mystical but a practical solution."[71] And yet, in these Chinese sources one would have to struggle to read them simply as "masochistic surrenders to the 'savage god' of suicide."[72]

Julia Kristeva argues that a woman without a cause or without fuss for an apparent cause can carry off suicide without tragedy, even without drama, as if she were making an "inevitable, irresistible and self-evident transition."[73] In the Western context, she speculates,

---

69 Maurice Bloch and Jonathan Parry, eds., *Death and the Regeneration of Life*, 21.

70 Sandra M. Gilbert and Susan Gubar, *The Madwoman in the Attic: The Woman Writer and the Nineteenth-Century Literary Imagination* (New Haven: Yale University Press, 1979), 285.

71 Sandra M. Gilbert, and Susan Gubar, *The Madwoman in the Attic.*, 284.

72 Gilbert and Gubar, *The Madwoman in the Attic*, 284.

73 Julia Kristeva, *About Chinese Women* (New York: Marion Boyars, 1986), 41.

men kill themselves *to be*, that is, to be God. The women writers Kristeva considers, Virginia Woolf, Maria Tsetaeva, and Sylvia Plath, kill themselves propelled by the desire *not to be*, to dissolve being. They should not then be seen as victims of an unjust patriarchal order or as farcical emulators of male sacrificial heroism but rather, perhaps, as "the most radical atheists, the most committed anarchists."[74] Here lies the fallacy of the feminist thinker who, by addressing and trying to elevate women's difference, manages to erase the voice spoken by the gesture. If women sink into death in silence in a culture dominated by the Word (*logos/wen* 文), as both the Western and the Chinese were, then their suicides will remain unread and thus meaningless. The anarchy, the atheism is precisely in the fact that in killing herself the woman can trespass into the realm of textuality.

It is impossible at this point not ask oneself how women in late imperial China viewed and experienced female suicide. Grace Fong's essay in this volume is a fundamental contribution in this sense. Male representations of women's suicides, be they fictional, fictionalized, or historicized, must be read against the grain of women's voices and acts.[75] Fan Huzhen 范壺貞 (fl. 1800), a nineteenth-century female poet, wrote on the occasion of the death of Daughter Yang, a young woman who had committed suicide after the premature death of her fiancée, thus acquiring the status of *zhennü* 貞女 (chaste woman):

> At her throat was a white silk sash
> like a white rainbow suspended;
> it lifted up those dark and moth-like brows
> onto the pages of history.[76]

Killing herself, Daughter Yang has left her mark in history. Death is the threshold the woman has to cross to gain a pure fame and public recognition, just as prestigious as the one a man would gain by passing the civil service examinations. As Maureen Robertson suggests, the shift in registers of language that takes place in the last

[74] Kristeva, *About Chinese Women*, 40-41.

[75] From this perspective, Bryna Goodman's on-going work on female suicide illuminates intriguing continuities and fractures in the discourse about female suicide between late imperial times and the Republican era. See Bryna Goodman, "The New Woman and the Vengeful Ghost. Reflections on Gender in the Public Culture of Early Republican Shanghai." (work in progress).

[76] Maureen Robertson, "Changing the Subject: Gender and Self-inscription in Authors' Prefaces and *Shi* Poetry," in Kang-i Sun Chang and Ellen Widmer, eds., *Writing Women in Late Imperial China*, 171-217; quote is from p. 213.

stanza, from vernacular to "high-brow" literary Chinese, at once erases the dead body and introduces the possibility of irony on the part of Fan Huzhen.[77] But the point that interests me here is the fact that the poet illustrates how by dying the young woman can get attention and public visibility in a socially approved way. The choice of death emerges here, just as in the novels I have analyzed, as a "feminine strategy within which writing with the body is a way of getting rid of the oppression connected with the feminine body."[78] Fan Huzhen's ironic reconstruction of Daughter Yang's suicide confirms the fact that the male patriarchal view of women's suicide was that it was the one acceptable way for women to inscribe the social landscape of late imperial society, the one form of self-inscription that, though at times represented in an haunting way in the pages of novels and short stories, was given by men to women to save and immortalize their untamed hearts.

---

[77] Robertson, "Changing the Subject," 214.
[78] Elisabeth Bronfen, *Over Her Dead Body*, 142.

# SIGNIFYING BODIES: THE CULTURAL SIGNIFICANCE OF SUICIDE WRITINGS BY WOMEN IN MING-QING CHINA

BY

GRACE S. FONG
(McGill University)

*Abstract*

This paper examines the form, content, and cultural significance of poems written by a number of otherwise unknown women before they committed suicide. The specific conditions under which these inscriptions are produced are disorder or violence in various forms, whether cultural, social, or familial, that threaten the integrity of the female body. The suicide poems are often accompanied by a short autobiographical preface. The author argues that this act of self-inscription at the moment of death is an act of agency. Through this textual production, the women reproduce a peculiarly Chinese sense of embodiment in inscription, and as self-recorders, they write themselves into history. These women construct the integrity of their bodies in/out of disorder by textualizing and transforming them into cultural bodies inscribed with value and order.

In the Ming-Qing period, the gendered agency of women became visibly self-scripted for the first time in Chinese history. This is the effect of a significant cultural phenomenon—the emergence of writing women as a critical mass among the scholar-gentry class. Many gentry families gave their daughters literary training often as cultural or symbolic capital—an asset to the family and future marriage prospects. This widespread female literacy relative to previous historical periods brought about an unprecedented level of textual production by women. As recent studies of women's culture of this period have shown, many of these texts are poetry collections, which were printed and circulated, and in which women inscribed their self-representations in their own voices. Women developed a growing self-consciousness in relation to writing, and, despite the rhetoric of modesty they often employed, a self-confidence about their literary performance also emerged. Regarding this change in attitude, Susan Mann has stated with insight that "we may imagine poetry as a constant personal resource available to learned women whenever they were moved to use it .... Poems on silk and paper...entered the arena of literati discourse where the sentiments they celebrated were dignified, appreciated, and accepted as normative by elite men and women alike."[1] In the sense of a regularly employed technology of self-expression and self-representation, women's literary practices indeed gained entry into a discursive field shared with their male counterparts.

Within this broader context of female literacy, this paper will examine the intersection of gender, literacy, and agency in contexts of violence and disorder by focusing on women's suicide writings from this period. What social or cultural meanings does the female body have that acts of violence render intelligible? What are the content and form of suicide writings by women and the agitated and brutal contexts of their production? In other words, what motivated women to write, and what did they write before they took their own lives? What did women hope to achieve by their actions and their words? What cultural significance can we draw from this body of writings? By attempting to seek answers to these questions, I hope to articulate the relationship between the female embodiment of violence and the agency of self-inscription. Through analyses of these texts my paper thus emphasizes as much as possible the perspectives of the women involved. The cultural contexts of the production of these writings and their circulation are inevitably implicated, and thus this inquiry also addresses issues that pertain to context.

### *Signifying Bodies and Female Agency*

Recent historical studies have shown that the female body was a potent site of meaning production in imperial China, the body/site on which cultural values were inscribed. From early biographies of exemplary women, we find examples of the self-mutilated face of resistance: cases of beautiful widows who embodied the female virtue of faithfulness literally by applying a sign on their visage. In order to prevent themselves from being forced to remarry, young widows would disfigure their faces by slashing them or cutting off nose or ears—the most visible signs of feminine beauty. Such self-mutilation also rendered them ritually incapable of serving the ancestors of any future proposed husband, because they could not

---

[1] Susan Mann, *Precious Records: Women in China's Long Eighteenth Century* (Stanford: Stanford University Press, 1997), 217.

perform the sacrifices with "unwhole" bodies. In late imperial times, the flesh sliced off from the young female body and cooked as medicine (*gegu* 割股) for parents and parents-in-law materialized filiality, particularly the giving back of nourishment in a condensed form in return for that received in the womb and in infancy. The "disciplined" bound feet manifested by their shrinkage and concealment multiple and contradictory significations of femininity.[2] In erotic art, the bound feet were the part of the body that was most apparent to the observer by being decorated and covered, controlled and cultured (tamed). From an anthropological perspective, C. Fred Blake argues powerfully that the painful and protracted process of binding the feet that the mother performed on and trained the young girl to do produced a "mindful body" informed "of its fate in patriarchal society and armed it with an effective discipline, not only...to maintain the strict rule of chastity, but also to deal with the travails of becoming a wife, daughter-in-law, and mother."[3] In times of "national" crisis, such as the disorder following the dynastic conquest by the Manchus and during the many local rebellions and banditry that wracked the late Qing, women's bodies furthermore embodied through violent acts normative social values and cultural meanings.[4]

---

[2] For the locus classicus of mutilating the face by cutting off the nose, see Liu Xiang 劉向, "Liang gua Gaoxing 梁寡高行," *Lienü zhuan* 列女傳 (reprint, Taipei: Guangwen shuju, 1987), 4.7b-8a. Examples from later periods include disfiguring the face and cutting off other compromising or compromised parts of the body such as ears and arms. For the prevalent practice of *gegu* among women in Shexian 歙縣, Anhui, see T'ien Ju-k'ang, *Male Anxiety and Female Chastity* (Leiden: E.J. Brill, 1988), 161. For the multiple meanings of bound feet as a gender, cultural, and ethnic marker, see Dorothy Ko, "The Body as Attire: The Shifting Meanings of Footbinding in Seventeenth-Century China," *Journal of Women's History* 8.4 (1997): 8-27. For the commodification and eroticization of the virtuous female body in the commercial print culture of the late Ming, see Katherine Carlitz, "The Social Uses of Female Virtue in Late Ming Editions of *Lienü Zhuan*," *Late Imperial China* 12.2 (1991): 117-48.

[3] C. Fred Blake, "Footbinding in Neo-Confucian China and the Appropriation of Female Labor," *Signs* 19.3 (1994): 676-712, quote is on p. 685. Blake points out that "footbinding violated an ironclad dogma that pervaded the whole of the Confucian doctrine—the rule that prohibits the physical abuse of the body" (695). Furthermore, he also notes that women performed significantly many more acts of physical abuse on their own bodies. His explanation, originating out of an anthropological perspective, is that "the rule against self-mutilation applied less to women because they did not constitute, in the dominant discourse, a formal link in the agnatic chain of descent through fathers and sons. They constituted instead a formal 'break' in that linkage" (696), that is, through exogamy.

[4] Dorothy Ko argues for women's supportive role in producing the female virtue

We may consider further the link between the various modes of disciplining the female body and the potential for female agency. The specific conditions under which women's suicide writings were produced were disorder and/or violence in various forms—cultural, social, and familial—that threatened the integrity of the female body. On a public scale, during the two major traumatic periods of social and political disorder—the Manchu conquest of China (mid-seventeenth century) and the Taiping Rebellion (mid-nineteenth century), countless women took their own lives in order to preserve their integrity and chastity, to preserve the cultural value inscribed on their bodies. Before they committed suicide, a not negligible number of these otherwise unknown women wrote poems, often accompanied by a short autobiographical preface. These writings provide details concerning the circumstances in which the writing was produced; the material medium of inscription—paper, cloth, ink, blood; and the site of the inscription—wall, cliff, and often the body which carried the inscribed cloth or paper. These writings point back to the conscious and deliberate actions that these women carefully planned and executed under extremely difficult and stressful conditions. Similarly, ordinary women—usually young widows—caught in predicaments arising from private contexts of family conflicts and pressures to remarry also often inscribed their personal history, feelings, and self-determination in prose and poems before they committed suicide. This paper examines suicide writings by women produced within both public and private, or personal, domains.

Women who wrote before they took their own lives create another signifying body, another medium of embodiment: the text. The physical body of the woman and the material body of the text are both inscribed with social and cultural values that the writing subject—the woman about to commit suicide—brings together in the ultimate moment of disembodiment that threatens disappearance and oblivion. Through this act of self-inscription on body and text, women (re)produce the ethical values of female virtue and the social values of order and integrity in moments when their bodies threaten to become abject—objects out of place, outside the social and cultural space in which they should properly be located.[5] The exposure

of chastity, "The Complicity of Women in the Qing Good Woman Cult," in *Family Process and Political Process in Modern Chinese History*, Part 1 (Taipei: Institute of Modern History, Academia Sinica, 1992), 451-487.

[5] I draw on Judith Butler's elaboration of the abject in *Bodies That Matter* (London:

of these women, beyond the normative physical and moral boundaries, turns their bodies into transgressive bodies, "matter out of place," to use Mary Douglas's term,[6] or potentially objects of defilement. In this light, their writings and suicides can be read as at once discursive and material attempts to reverse this ethically and ritually polluted status of abjection and reincorporate themselves into the dominant discourse.

By the combined acts of writing and self-immolation, these women assert their agency and appeal to future generations for their right to be remembered; they also insist that they had acted correctly. They claim to have a history and write themselves into history. My theoretical emphasis on public significance is not meant to underestimate the personal meaning that acts of suicide would give to these women's lives and deaths, or to suggest that their suicides might not be psychologically fulfilling. As a matter of fact, we will see from the specific texts examined below that this process of textual embodiment at death is a strong instance of gendered subject and identity construction. The texts are death inscriptions produced by, significantly, more or less "anonymous" women, that is, women about whom we know little, if anything, other than what they themselves tell us in their writing. These women resisted or preempted violence by committing violence on themselves—suicide. The perpetrators of violence and disorder are usually marauding soldiers during invasions and suppressions, rebels and bandits in raids and attacks, cruel and opportunistic relatives, who would commit slander, rape, and other forms of defilement on women. Women caught in such circumstances were expected by parents, husbands, brothers, in short, by representatives of Confucian ideology and themselves as interpellated subjects, to resist the marauders and preserve their virtue, their chastity.

By bringing critical attention to bear on these texts of self-inscription written on the point of death, I want to question and oppose the

---

Routledge, 1993): "The abject designates here precisely those 'unlivable' and 'uninhabitable' zones of social life which are nevertheless densely populated by those who do not enjoy the status of the subject, but whose living under the sign of the 'unlivable' is required to circumscribe the domain of the subject" (3). She explains the concept further in a footnote: "Abjection (in latin, *ab-jicere*) literally means to cast off, away, or out and, hence, presupposes a domain of agency from which it is differentiated.... [T]he notion of *abjection* designates a degraded or cast out status within the terms of sociality" (243, n. 2).

[6] This is developed in her influential work *Purity and Danger: An Analysis of the Concepts of Pollution and Taboo* (London: Ark Paperbacks, 1984), 40.

common biographical motif of women who burn their manuscripts just before death, thereby destroying the symbolic embodiment or extension of themselves when they die. This is the familiar trope of female self-effacement, which expresses women's real or supposed acquiescence to the cultural ambivalence towards or disapproval of women writing and their self-expressiveness. This is one type of embodiment, to which I oppose its paradigmatic negation with the self-inscriptions at death examined in this paper. To the trope of effacement and obliteration are opposed those of visibility and continuity.[7] At the same time, these writings also show that female suicides were neither impulsive and facile nor indicative of "an unhealthy craving for posthumous glory by unfortunate women," which may have been encouraged by the progressive severity of the law in the Ming and Qing regarding female chastity, at least as suggested by repeated examples from legal case histories.[8]

Secondly, I want to reconstruct a female perspective on the significance of this writing. In other words, I hope to show from the writers' own perspectives, their conceptions, as they express them, of women's relationship to the act of writing as self-construction and self-representation, in a symbolic *and* material sense. In extreme conditions of violence and violation of social order and cultural norms, in a word, *luan* 亂 or disorder, ordinary women will assert not only their position but also their voice, or so it would appear from these texts of death inscriptions. What we have in these cases is the creation and/or preservation of their manuscripts at the conjunction of writing and dying. At the point of disappearance a material and

[7] Judith Zeitlin examines the element of visibility and perceived ephemerality in verses written on walls (*tibishi* 題壁詩), many by women, and the relation to loss in her paper "*Tibishi* and the Collecting of Women's Verse in the late Ming and early Qing" (paper presented at the Conference on Gender and Literature in Ming-Qing China, Nanjing, May 16-19, 2000). While this line of inquiry is also germane to a reading of the death inscriptions by women, Zeitlin's study restricts itself to poems on walls—many of which are not suicide poems—from the late Ming and the Ming-Qing transition in the seventeenth century. Furthermore, the focus of her paper is on the role of the male literati who were interested in collecting these poems on walls by women and writing poems to match them.

[8] M. J. Meijer, "The Price of a P'ai-lou," *T'oung Pao* 67.3-5 (1981): 288-304. Though studies in case law bring out perspectives, practices, and voices, especially in relation to the lower social classes absent in other discursive modes, by the very nature of dealing only with transgressions, such cases when read cumulatively can also skew the picture. The recent spate of legal studies by scholars such as Matthew Sommer and Paola Paderni that draw on case history archival materials previously unavailable are giving us a more complex picture.

discursive presence is (re)produced, a body of inscriptions, an autobiographical voice. The women clearly intend their death inscriptions, materially inscribed with ink and brush, on cloth or paper, to continue the existence denied them, to be their symbolic bodies. They arrogate to themselves the act of writing their own lives, producing self-epitaphs and self-memorials.[9]

*Suicide Inscriptions*

Unnatural death and writing have been linked in Chinese culture from early times in the practice of composing a "verse on cutting off/ending life" (*jueming ci* 絕命詞). As early as the Western Han (206 BCE-8 CE), the imperial advisor to Emperor Ai (r. 6-1 BCE) Xifu Gong 息夫躬 wrote a "Verse on Ending Life" when he was Expectant Official, fearing that he would meet with an untimely end, even though, as it turned out, he did not die until a few years later.[10] This act of self-inscription, performed at the point just before dying, constructs a sense of agency in death. With the imminent destruction of the body or the embodied self, writing constitutes an attempt at continuity or vindication of the to-be-disembodied self in a textual body. Ironically, the significance of self-inscription at death is predicated on the notion of the immortality attainable through one's words canonized in the *Zuozhuan* 左傳.[11] The sense of urgency at the moment when a person faces imminent extinction, I believe, is manifested in the common shorthand form that most suicide writings took, an idea which will be examined in the next section.

In general, examples by male suicides demonstrate that a heroic dimension and sense of personal integrity surround the production of self-inscription at death. The classic example cited for *jueming ci* is the martyred official Fang Xiaoru 方孝孺 (1357-1402), who wrote a death poem before he was dismembered as a consequence of disobeying the Yongle 永樂 Emperor (r. 1403-24) who had usurped the throne.[12] Loyalty (*zhong* 忠) to sovereign, state, or moral ideal is the

[9] Men produce self-writings in a number of different genres often as self-conscious literary self-projections or inventions in times of peace, see the numerous examples collected in Guo Dengfeng 郭登峰, *Lidai zixu zhuanwen chao* 歷代自敍傳文鈔 (Shanghai: Shangwu yinshuguan, 1936).

[10] The poem is recorded in his biography in the *Hanshu* 漢書 (Beijing: Zhonghua shuju, 1962), 45.2187-88.

[11] *Zuozhuan*, "Xiang gong 襄公" 24. 1.

[12] Cited by *Dai Kanwa jiten* 大漢和辭典 (Tokyo: Taishukan shoten, 1976), 8.9182; *Hanyu da cidian* 漢語大詞典 (Shanghai: Hanyu da cidian chubanshe, 1994), 9.836.

virtue exemplified by male suicides. The foremost virtue embodied by female suicides is chastity (*zhenjie* 貞節). Here I wish to emphasize again that to perform this act of inscription before death by a woman requires cultural and social disciplining on several levels, disciplines that used to be the prerogatives of elite men. In addition to the moral discipline that produces the appropriate sense of virtue and ideological commitment, the literary disciplines of prose writing and versification and the practice of calligraphy that materializes the script are also necessary skills.

What are the implications of this practice when it was performed by women, in particular ordinary, even "anonymous" women, in the late imperial period? That women could or would write self-inscriptions at death presupposes the moral, literary, and technical disciplines and training described above. Such disciplinary attainments usually belong to women from the elite class. It is thus not so surprising to come across the case of Empress Xiao 蕭后 of the Khitan Liao dynasty (925-1125), who was implicated in a palace intrigue and accused of a sexual liaison with a palace musician through a series of erotic poems she had unwittingly copied in her own hand. When she was ordered to commit suicide by the emperor, she wrote a *jueming ci*, "verse on ending my life," an autobiographical record of her life that proclaims her innocence before she hanged herself with a white silk cord.[13]

That there was an increased incidence of the practice of writing self-inscriptions at death among women correlates with the spread of education among women in the Ming and Qing, the latter a phenomenon quite well mapped by a number of recent studies.[14] The women who wrote these self-inscriptions at death, however, were

---

His suicide poem is recorded in his biography in the *Mingshi* 明史 (Beijing: Zhonghua shuju, 1974), 141.4017-19.

[13] For a translation and discussion of this poem, see Aidong Zhang and Wayne Schlepp, "Xiao Guanyin: Her Tragic Life and Melancholy Poems," *Journal of Song-Yuan Studies* 28 (1998): 219-21.

[14] There are roughly twenty examples of "poems on ending my life" by women in Volume 22 of Qian Zhonglian 錢仲聯, ed., *Qingshi jishi* 清詩紀事, 22 vols. (n.p.: Jiangsu guji chubanshe, 1987). Consecutive examples appear on 22.15526-32, 15536, 15677-84. For recent studies on women's education in late imperial China, see Dorothy Ko, *Teachers of the Inner Chamber: Women and Culture in Seventeenth Century China* (Stanford: Stanford University Press, 1994); Susan Mann, *Precious Records: Women in China's Long Eighteenth Century* (Stanford: Stanford University Press, 1998), ch. 4; Clara Wing-chung Ho, "The Cultivation of Female Talent: Views on Women's Education in China during the Early and High Qing Periods," *Journal of the Economic and Social History of the Orient* 38.2 (1995): 191-223.

not ordered to commit suicide as in the case of Empress Xiao, but chose to do so themselves. I want to argue that, through the choice of suicide and self-inscription, women assume or even construct positions of agency and power on the grounds of normative values of female virtue, both literally and discursively. In this sense, agency, as the cultural theorist Judith Butler puts it, is "a reiterative or rearticulatory practice, immanent to power, and not a relation of external opposition to power." She further observes in her discussion of both the constructedness and materiality of sex and body that "if there is *agency*, it is to be found, paradoxically, in the possibilities opened up in and by that constrained appropriation of the regulatory law, by the materialization of that law, the compulsory appropriation of and identification with those normative demands."[15] In other words, though these women are inscribed in ideology, I believe we can try to think through the possibilities of agency as it might apply in the contexts of their suicide writings. Even though agency is located within a set of cultural constraints or determinants, the act of writing imparts to the women a sense of meaning and gave the suicide increased significance even as the women still were limited in the forms of action or resistance that were available or conceivable.

I would suggest that, ironically, death inscriptions are textual sites in which "ordinary" women attempt to construct their identities (as agents of their own action), and in which they work out their relationship with the perceived and perceiving "public." The message inscribes an individualized identity (the woman who is writing about herself) and a collective target audience—the public who will witness, assess, and take action as a result of coming into contact with this inscription. Some inscriptions explicitly give instruction for specific actions to be taken, such as burial of the body.[16] Most often, they are rhetorically structured to elicit from the readers reflection, sympathy, or admiration. The text is thus constructed as a gendered individual voice addressed to a collective readership. In this process, the disorder inflicted on the physical body is transformed by female agency into order inscribed on the textual body. That order is first and foremost articulated in the formal prose and poetic structures of the writing. The resulting text embodies not only social virtue and integrity, but also individual history and memory. The act of writing, if you will, provides the possibility of self-transformation from within the social system and gender ideology.

---

[15] Judith Butler, *Bodies that Matter* (London: Routledge, 1993), 12-15.
[16] *Qingshi jishi* 22.15529.

*Textual Bodies: Form and Meaning*

When we examine the suicide writings themselves, we are at once struck by the similarity of form they take, to such an extent that we can say that their formal characteristics are culturally determined. A surprising number of these texts consist of a self-preface—a short essay in literary prose—followed by a series of poems, most commonly the five- or seven-character quatrain (*jueju* 絕句). One is tempted to make the link between the "cut-off poem" (*jueju*) and the "cut-off life" (*jueming* 絕命). This combination of preface-cum-poems is very much conceptualized along the lines of a collection of poetry by an individual author, that is, the *bieji* 別集, except in extremely abbreviated form, which recalls my comment earlier about suicide notes as shorthand writing. The form adopted also suggests the perceived authority of poetry as the canonical medium of self-expression, and of the collected work (*bieji*) as a statement and extension of the person. The prefaces are, almost invariably, autobiographical, providing some or all of the following elements: her identity (name and native place), family background, upbringing, the circumstances leading to the decision to kill herself, her action in the last moments, a strong wish to be remembered, and injunctions to the reader. The poems tend to include nostalgic memories of a peaceful and contented life, recount dramatic moments of the self-narrative, and highlight the moral character, determination, and heroism of the author.

To illustrate these textual practices by women, I will discuss three exemplary cases of suicide inscriptions by women: the first two were written by adolescents caught during periods of "national" disorder and the third by a young widow in a difficult family situation. My first example Du Xiaoying 杜小英 (1638-1654), is a sixteen-year-old who was captured by Manchu troops in 1654 and before committing suicide wrote ten poems framed by a preface. Through her suicide writing, which circulated widely and was recorded in a number of contemporary accounts, Du Xiaoying became a celebrated chaste heroine of the Ming-Qing transition. The second example is Huang Shuhua 黃淑華 (1847-64), a seventeen-year-old who was captured by Qing soldiers when they had retaken Nanjing (Huang's hometown) from the Taiping rebels in 1864. Before she committed suicide by hanging herself in a hostel in Xiangtan 湘潭 (in Hunan), Huang Shuhua also wrote a series of ten "poems on ending life" with a self-preface in which she identified herself and her family. She recounted how they had lived under the rebel government in Shangyuan 上元 (Nanjing) and how she was abducted by a Qing soldier who killed most of her family members and carried her off to Xiangtan by boat. The third example is Ling Zhinü 凌帙女 (1806-27), a twenty-one-year-old widow who committed suicide by starvation. In preparation she wrote on the night of the Mid-Autumn Festival in 1827 an autobiographical postscript to her collection of more than three hundred poems, which she had kept hidden in a bamboo satchel. She detailed her family background, marriage, widowhood, and the pressure on her to remarry which brought about a maligning of her virtue and a lawsuit by her husband's family.

The first two texts have obvious similarities in form and meaning, as structured by similar situations and experiences in periods of social disorder. But there are also marked differences in poetic style and the motivation for suicide. Though like Du Xiaoying, Huang Shuhua did not kill herself immediately, her reasons for postponing her death are very different. The text expresses a passionate, even obsessive, desire to take revenge on her captor, who in front of her had murdered in cold blood her mother, little brother, and a sister-in-law. Huang committed suicide only after she had succeeded in exacting the life of her captor in return for the violence he had perpetrated on her family. The example of Ling Zhinü is different from the other two. She had preserved a substantial collection of unpublished poems that she had written over a number of years. She does not have a series of "poems on ending life." Her suicide writing is the long autobiographical postscript, which also has a practical purpose—to clear her name socially and legally. These three texts all bear significant points for comparison with each other and with this genre of writing as a whole. They offer possibilities for reading female agency in a culture that tends to obscure it.

Finally, these textual bodies are also significant in a material sense. The recurring act of careful concealment of the piece of writing on the body in so many cases of female suicide is paradoxically intended to effect disclosure and revelation. The suicide notes are hidden/carried on the body to be found. These women seemed to have tacit knowledge of the mandatory forensic examination by a coroner in cases of homicide and suicide and they manipulate this practice to get their word out. This self-inscription, then, embodies not only moral and social values but also individual agency. When death and silence rule, this is the body that speaks, that remains to tell the tale.[17]

### *Du Xiaoying (1638-54): The Girl from Hunan*

In 1654, sixteen-year-old Du Xiaoying wrote a self-preface to her series of ten "poems on ending life." It is among the most detailed self-prefaces to suicide poems I have found.[18] Right at the beginning, she identifies herself as the daughter of a respectable family in Chen 辰 City (Yuanling 沅陵) in western Hunan. Her desire to distinguish herself as an exceptional woman is indicated by her including the unusual account of her birth told her by her mother: " On the night my mother conceived me, she dreamed of a girl with a beautiful voice like jingling jades who bowed to her and said that her name was Miss Yingtai 英台, and that she wished to rent a place to live in for a few years. Mother woke up and was pregnant. When I was born, she thus named me Xiaoying (Little Ying). My parents both loved me." This story with the unusual dream hinting at the supernatural background of Du Xiaoying no doubt also had an impact on the girl's perception of her own identity and character. Du Xiaoying was also meticulous about naming the male members of her family who had achieved distinction by passing the first level of the civil service examinations. It is a way of emphasizing that she came from a family of moral standing and cultivation. She also located her own education within this cultured family setting. It is interesting that her feminine training and education all came from her maternal relatives: she developed her skill in embroidery by going to learn from her maternal aunt who was married into a powerful lineage in the same city but had been widowed early. Impressed by Du Xiaoying's

---

[17] Janet Theiss discusses in detail the procedures of the examination and the experts, including midwives, involved in "Medicine, Law and Propriety in the Forensic Examination of Women in 18th Century China" (paper presented at the Annual Convention of the Association for Asian Studies, Boston, March 11-14, 1999). It would seem that literate women's practice of carrying a suicide note on the body, creating expectation of discovery, had become a normative practice in the late imperial period. In 1922 Shanghai, the sensational modern case of a secretary who hanged herself in a newspaper office generated endless speculation in the press concerning the missing suicide note, because people expected to find it on her body. I am grateful to Bryna Goodman for sharing with me her draft of a paper on this case, "The New Woman and the Vengeful Ghost: Reflections on Gender in the Public Culture of Early Republican Shanghai."

[18] *Qingshi jishi*, 22.15534-35.

intelligence, her maternal uncle offered to tutor her. In concluding the passage on her family and education, Du Xiaoying significantly stated that her models for ancient prose and poetry were only those of the recorded discourse of virtuous daughters and chaste widows. She goes further by dismissing the popular heroines Mulan 木蘭 and Huang Chonggu 黃崇嘏, whose accomplishments were attained by cross-dressing and venturing into the male public domain and mixing in male company. Her self-presentation and her evaluation of other women in Chinese history establish her own high moral and ethical standards, which enables the reader to understand her choice of actions later.

Du's narrative continues with the disorder that beset her area in 1654 when the Qing army took Chen City. This forced her mother to take her into hiding in the mountains, but she was subsequently captured by the soldiers and presented to the general, surnamed Cao 曹. Explaining that she was two months from the end of a three-year period of (sexual) abstinence taken for the sake of her mother's sickness, she records how she appealed to the general's sense of filial piety as a ruse to postpone her defilement. She declares her real reason for not killing herself at this time: "In the vastness of Lake Dongting 洞庭, it isn't that I could not die. But I could not bear to throw my sincere heart into the desolate mist and wild waters; then no one would know." The need and desire for her life and action to be known are inscribed here explicitly, and it is through the medium of this inscription that her desire could be fulfilled.

Du's narrative mentions that it was the year of the triennial examinations, expressing the hope that "there might be people from my native city who are here to take the examinations," and she indicates precisely that "this is the twenty-fourth day of the sixth month." In analyzing the function of Du Xiaoying's self-narrative, which had been inserted into the eighteenth century erotic novel *Gu wang yan* 姑妄言 (Words said just for the sake of speaking), Martin Huang has noted astutely that "Du Xiaoying seemed convinced that those literati were the most likely people who would appreciate her heroic act of chastity and they were sure to spread around her good name."[19] Knowing that she will be unable to resist the general's

[19] Martin Huang, "The Polarization of *Qing* and *Yu* in the Eighteenth-Century Erotic Novel" (paper presented at the Annual Convention of the Association for Asian Studies, Boston, March 11-14, 1999). Surely Du Xiaoying never anticipated the spread of her fame, even ironically, to the most unlikely place—the heart of an erotic novel, even though it is meant as a didactic biography, a virtuous model

desires much longer, she sees the present as offering the opportune time and place to die. Her strategy is to manipulate the general's empathy with filial conduct. She tells him that her mother had in fact been thrown into the lake by the rival army. She reveals that she is able to write and asks permission to compose an elegy mourning her mother before she acquiesces to the general's wishes. This then was the opportunity she created for herself to write the self-preface and the ten poems. The ending of the preface is significant in that it takes the self-narrative almost right up to the last moment, in which she states her desire to be known to posterity: "If the river spirit has efficacy, escort me in the roaring waves so I can transmit my immortality." If she should die, she would not die in vain. Her penultimate action was to produce the poems and to carefully preserve them on her body: "Thus I write ten quatrains, and with a piece of oiled cloth I insert them inside my bosom." I provide translations of Du Xiaoying's ten suicide poems below:

(1) Once parted from my home town, I can't overcome my feelings.
Today in shame I come to Hancheng 漢城.
Suddenly I hear the general's order to search all,
How can I dare to cherish any remaining days?

(2) The journeying sail they say is passing the Double Gu Peaks 雙孤.
Only the cawing of the ravens at night conceals my crying.
I'd rather be buried among the river fish, going with the thick waves,
Than to leave behind a green mound among the Tartars.

(3) I bid farewell to my brothers and close kin,
But they follow me a thousand *li*,
always startling me in my dreams.
My soul wants to return on the homeward road,
But when I arrive my parents are no longer living.

(4) I hate listening to the songs and laughter of the Tartar youths.
How many times my heart breaks—so many gibbons on the ridge.
The blue bird intends to follow the Queen Mother,
So in vain nets are set up in the human realm.

(5) Covering my body is still my old silk robe.
In dream reaching the Xiao 瀟 and Xiang 湘 Rivers—when will I return there?
Crossing distant wind and waves—who will be my companion?
Deeply I pray from afar to the spirits of the two ladies.

---

which inspires other women, read from a *lienü zhuan* within the novel's narrative. This intertextual borrowing also points to the wide and continuing circulation of new or newer *lienü* stories.

(6) When I was a small girl, alone in the painted pavilion,
I had paid respects to my mother's brother as my teacher.
When night after night the sound of waves bring utter grief
I still remember studying the *Chuci* 楚辭 (Songs of the South) in lamplight.

(7) I cherish the times of leisure in the boudoir.
For what reason am I dragged by my skirt to follow the shore?
I send word to my parents not to worry about me,
When I descend into the river, I am still the body of a daughter.

(8) In life I have not yet pinned up my hair,
My body drowned in the river's waves—I sigh at the incompleteness!
If the river god has a heart and pities my ill fate,
Let me flow directly east to the west of Lake Dongting.[20]

(9) How sad to see my reflection in the river!
Taking leave of the mirror I knit my eyebrows.
By the vermilion gate, in vain it becomes Qin 秦 and Jin 晉.
In death we meet but would never recognize each other.

(10) In years past, my parents explained firmly to me the illustrated histories.
Since ancient times to kill oneself is to desire to become humane.
Though for [lack of] official hat and pin,
I might feel ashamed before an outstanding man,
Still I far surpass those ministers who serve at court.

Du's ten poems highlight her emotional experience and strong resolve on the journey on boat after being taken captive. The poetic narrative begins with their arrival in Hancheng, when the captain's order to round up all the captives precipitated her resolve to die (Poem 1). In Poem 2 she compares her predicament to Wang Zhaojun 王昭君 of the Han, journeying away from her homeland to marry the chief of the Tartars. However, she rejects Wang Zhaojun's narrative—she will not become "a green mound among the Tartars," that is to say, she would rather preserve her purity by drowning rather than going on to live out her life in shame as Wang Zhaojun did and be buried in foreign soil. The negation of Wang Zhaojun's choice is commonly found in suicide poems by women in captivity. By rejecting Wang's choice, these women demonstrate their uncompromising loyalty to nation and family. In other words, they repudiate a model of self-sacrifice who had compromised her chastity, even though historically Wang had elicited sympathy from countless male poets. The allusion to Wang Zhaojun and the refer-

[20] The direction appears to be reversed. As Lake Dongting is southwest of Hancheng (i.e., Hanyang 漢陽 and Wuchang 武昌), she should flow (south)westward to reach first the east side of Lake Dongting. The idea is that her body would flow back in the direction of home, which is further west of Lake Dongting.

ence to Tartar youths in Poem 4 points to Du's captors as Manchu troops. This poem also contrasts the indigenous element of the gibbons' cries on the shore, long a poetic motif for denoting a Chinese traveler's homesickness along the Yangzi, with the uncouth songs and laughter of the Tartars.

By midpoint, the series is poised between Du's nostalgia for her girlhood and her family and, recognizing the impossibility of reunion, her resolve to die. The images begin to take on double meanings. For example, the blue bird in Poem 4 is a metaphor for herself, hinting at the divine origins suggested by her mother's dream before her birth. It also constitutes a metaphor for death when it "intends to follow the Queen Mother of the West," thus eluding the traps set by men.[21] The two goddesses of the Xiao and Xiang also point to suicide, as these two wives of the legendary sage ruler Shun had drowned themselves in the river out of wifely loyalty when they found out Shun had died on his tour of the south (Poem 5). But the two rivers also stand for Du Xiaoying's native home in Hunan, as does the *Chuci* (Songs of the South), named in Poem 6 as the text she had studied as a girl. Etched in her memory is her girlhood and study, the process of the inculcation of cultural values—loyalty, purity, uncompromising integrity, embodied in the text and its author Qu Yuan 屈原, who also drowned himself for these values. Caught in the turmoil of the Ming-Qing transition, Du Xiaoying clearly states that she will preserve her virginity in death (Poem 7): "When I descend into the river, I am still the body of a daughter." However, she also contemplates and regrets her unfulfilled role as a woman. To die not having been betrothed or married, she realizes she has not achieved complete social and ritual status as a woman.[22] Yet in the penultimate poem she rejects the idea of union with the general by leaving the mirror behind—the token of union he has given her, mentioned in the preface.

The last poem seeks self-fulfillment in Du's resolve to die for the

---

[21] Xiwangmu 西王母, the Queen Mother of the West, is a powerful female deity worshipped by women especially in the Tang. See Suzanne Cahill, *Transcendence and Divine Passion: The Queen Mother of the West in Medieval China* (Stanford: Stanford University Press, 1993). Xiwangmu's mythical domain in the Kunlun mountains in the west also suggests the realm of life after death, similar to the Western Paradise of Amida Buddha where good souls are reborn.

[22] For an anthropological study of the ambiguous status of the souls of daughters who die unmarried in Taiwan, see Arthur Wolf, "Gods, Ghosts, Ancestors," in Arthur Wolf, ed., *Religion and Ritual in Chinese Society* (Stanford: Stanford University Press, 1974), 148-53.

right cause. She turns to identify with history and tradition: "Since ancient times to kill oneself is to desire to become humane (*ren* 仁)." She cites the famous passage from the *Analects*, which the Southern Song martyr Wen Tianxiang 文天祥 (1236-82) and other heroic men had also cited in their suicide poems when they committed suicide for a worthy cause.[23] Confucius had said: "For gentlemen of purpose and men of benevolence while it is inconceivable that they should seek to stay alive at the expense of benevolence [*ren*], it may happen that they have to accept death in order to have benevolence accomplished." (15.9)[24] Women began to allude to this canonical passage to inscribe a sense of righteousness and heroism through death, as my second example Huang Shuhua also did in her last poem, discussed below. In upholding the cultural values she believed in by taking her own life, Du Xiaoying ultimately realizes herself in the larger cultural context in which she sees herself, standing above many scholar-officials who have compromised their integrity as former subjects of the Ming.

### *The Girl Avenger Huang Shuhua (1847-64)*

The thematic focus and narrative content of Huang Shuhua's autobiographical preface resemble those of Du Xiaoying's text, such that it might suggest the one is modeled on the other.[25] I do not believe there is a direct relationship between these two texts, with one consciously imitating the other. Rather, as I argued above, the exigencies of suicide may have dictated certain parameters of the writing, and cultural conventions also may have played a determining role. Gender difference offers yet another perspective on the issue of form and content. Men who wrote suicide poems tend to be well-known, whereas the women are unknown to the public outside of their families, and they are conscious of themselves as such.[26] Thus, women's

---

[23] For Wen Tianxiang's death inscription in the form of a *zan* 贊 in four-character lines, see *Songshi* 宋史 (Beijing: Zhonghua shuju, 1977), 418.12540. It was placed in his sash.

[24] *Lunyu* 15.9, in *Harvard-Yenching Institute Sinological Index Series, Supplement No. 16: A Concordance to the Analects of Confucius* (reprint, Taipei: Chinese Materials and Research Aids Service Center, 1972), 31; trans. D. C. Lau, *The Analects* (New York: Dorset Press, 1986), 133.

[25] For the text of Huang Shuhua's preface and poems, see *Qingshi jishi*, 22.15931-32.

[26] For a small collection of suicide poems by both men and women through the ages, see Yang Guangzhi 楊光治, *Lidai juemingshi* 歷代絕命詩 (Tianjin: Baihua wenyi chubanshe, 1996).

strong impulse to self-identify and the various means they take to make "public" their suicide writings evolve into a common practice. Simply to die, to sacrifice oneself in silence is not enough—these women desire to *tell*, to *state*, to *enunciate* the particulars of their identities, life circumstances, motivation, and moral and individual values. If chastity is emphasized in both their own self-records and in their biographical narratives by male scholars, it only demonstrates how a "private" virtue has acquired broader public and cultural significance.

Though we may not be able to pinpoint the precise beginning of this gendered practice, the section of "Biographies of Virtuous Women" in the *Songshi* 宋史 may contain some of the earliest examples from the Mongol conquest. Before she leapt to her death, one woman, simply identified as Wang the Chaste Wife 王貞婦, wrote a poem on a cliff with blood from her own bitten finger. The suicide poem of another woman, Han Ximeng 韓希孟, was found in her sash after her corpse was retrieved from the river. Both these women were captured by the Mongols during the conquest of the Southern Song.[27] They became paragons of virtue, courage, and literary talent enshrined in the official history, belonging to the model biographies Du Xiaoying studied under her uncle's tutelage. The autobiographical strain becomes more apparent and elaborate in suicide poems by women in the sixteenth and seventeenth centuries.[28]

---

27 The biography of Wang the Chaste Wife does not include the text of her suicide poem (*Songshi* 460.13489-90), which is provided in Yang Guangzhi, *Lidai juemingshi*, with no indication of the source (80). Richard Davis discusses the element in this narrative of female suicide as an example which deconstructs the male historians' representation of women as not capable of political consciousness. Before leaping off the cliff, Wang Zhenfu "faced south" and wept bitterly, an action which Davis correctly identifies as "ritualistic" and a sign "of some greater social and political consciousness." He interprets Wang's "wish to leave a written message" as indication that "she intuited her actions as having some historical import." See Richard Davis, *Wind Against the Mountain: The Crisis of Politics and Culture in Thirteenth-Century China* (Cambridge: Council on East Asian Studies, Harvard University, 1996), 185-86. The second example, Han Ximeng, is thought by some to be a descendant of the Northern Song prime minister Han Qi 韓琦; her suicide poem is included in her biography (*Songshi* 460.13492). In her study, Judith Zeitlin highlights the three quatrains with preface by the Girl from Kuaiji 會稽, discovered around 1618, that set off a trend among male literati in collecting and matching poems written on walls by women in the early Qing ("Tibishi," 9). I believe this "collecting" is both broader in scope and a more persistent cultural phenomenon than the focus of Zeitlin's paper (see discussion in the conclusion).

28 See for example "Song of Everlasting Resentment," the long autobiographical

Huang Shuhua began her preface by naming herself, her native place, and the achievements of the male members of her family. She understood precisely her role and status within the Chinese social and moral universe in which she and her readers were located. Thus, she knew well that, as an unmarried young woman, her own identity, character, and credibility were founded on the status and scholarly credentials of her family before Shangyuan County (part of Nanjing) fell to the Taiping rebels when she was four.[29] As the Taiping Heavenly Kingdom established its capital there until its defeat by Qing forces more than ten years later, Huang Shuhua essentially grew up under their regime. This raises the possibility that Huang did not have her feet bound, as the Taiping government prohibited this practice and Huang was too small to have started the process when Nanjing fell. Vincent Shih in his study of Taiping ideology quotes this passage from the 1855 source of information on the Taipings, the *Zeiqing huizuan* 賊情彙纂, compiled by Zhang Dejian 張德堅: "When the rebels reached Nanking, all women were prohibited from practicing foot-binding. Violators were to be executed. Those whose feet were already bound were unable to walk when they were suddenly ordered to unbind them."[30]

Of their life under Taiping rule, Huang Shuhua drew a discreet veil. She only mentions that her two older brothers who were at home turned to farming for subsistence.[31] They continued to edu-

poem by Wang Jiaoluan 王嬌鸞 (sixteenth century) detailing her family background and her long passionate affair with her lover who eventually abandoned her to marry someone else back in his hometown, in Kang-i Sun Chang and Haun Saussy, eds., *Women Writers of Traditional China: An Anthology of Poetry and Criticism* (Stanford: Stanford University Press, 1999), 188-94.

[29] If the year of her birth, based on the reference in the first poem (see below), is 1847, then the year when she was four, when her family came under the rule of the Taiping Heavenly Kingdom, would be 1851. Could it be that her family did not reside within the walled city of Nanjing, the county seat of both Jiangning 江甯 and Shangyuan 上元, but in the surrounding county which would have come under Taiping control earlier? Her brother's words seem to indicate that they lived in the city. Nanjing's walls were finally breached on March 19, 1853. On the Taiping rebellion, which devastated half the Qing Empire for over a decade, see John K. Fairbank, ed., *Cambridge History of China,* Vol. 10, Part I, 264-317. There appears to be some discrepancy in Huang Shuhua's recollection of the dates in her childhood if by the fall of her family to the bandits she means also the fall of Nanjing.

[30] Vincent Shih, *The Taiping Ideology: Its Sources, Interpretations, and Influences* (Seattle: University of Washington Press, 1967), 77. See also the chapter on women in the Taiping Rebellion in Ono Kazuko, *Chinese Women in a Century of Revolution, 1850-1950* (Stanford: Stanford University Press, 1989), 1-22.

[31] This is consistent with the Taiping program for an ideal society based on

cate her and her little brother with materials from the family book collection and instill in them an appropriate sense of cultural integrity and courage in adversity. She quotes her brothers' words to her: "We are forced to stay in the city. If the city is conquered [i.e., retaken by the Qing], we will inevitably meet with calamity. You must be careful not to save your life by ignoble means and disgrace our ancestors' virtue." On her part, she dissuaded her brothers from arranging her marriage when she came of age.[32] By recording her view on the matter, Huang shows she had her own mind and discernment regarding what should be done with her life.

In the beleaguered history of Nanjing 1864 was another bloody page. The Qing army under the command of Zeng Guoquan 曾國荃 (1824-90), brother of the eminent official Zeng Guofan 曾國藩 (1811-75), besieged Nanjing and breached its walls on July 19. As Huang Shuhua noted in her preface, when the imperial army succeeded in retaking the city, they did not bring peace; they burnt it and massacred its inhabitants. Huang's suicide writing is an individual woman's indictment of the ruthless and lawless behavior of the military in general and of her captor in particular. She recounts how almost her entire family—two elder brothers, one sister-in-law, mother, and little brother—were all butchered, the latter three in plain sight before she was abducted and taken on a boat south along the Yangzi River. The note to Poem 4 tells the reader that her captor is surnamed Shen 申 and a native of Baoqing 寶慶 in Hunan; the last line of the poem indicates that he traffics in women and intends to sell her: "I am glad that the slave of fortune only wants merchandise." He has taken his loot back to his home province Hunan. In the note to Poem 8, which tells that they have reached Changsha 長沙, Huang Shuhua also records, "Arriving here, he plans to turn me over to a broker." Certainly, if Shen was interested in money, he could fetch a higher price in the sale if he refrained from deflowering her and she could be sold as a virgin.

Like Du Xiaoying, Huang Shuhua did not kill herself at the first available opportunity. It was three months after her capture when she wrote in the preface to her suicide poems: "It is not that I could

---

equal land distribution to families to farm. Huang may also be implying that her brothers rejected participation in the Taiping civil service examination and recruitment, which began after Nanjing was established as the capital, and chose to live as peasants instead. Shih, *The Taiping Ideology*, 81-84; Fairbank, ed., *Cambridge History*, vol. 9, Pt. I, 278-79, 291-92.

[32] Usually at fifteen *sui*, or fourteen years old.

not find a place to die on the vast river, it is just that I regret having involved my aged mother, my sister-in-law, and my little brother [the three who were killed in front of her]. Now that I have come with him, if I did not think of how to avenge them, what good would it do to die?" Her motivation was clearly to take revenge on her captor, the cold-blooded murderer of her family. Huang Shuhua's preface and poems were written in an inn in Xiangtan, Hunan, where her captor, after disembarking and meeting up with an acquaintance, had checked in for the night. She had decided this was the moment to carry out her action—revenge and suicide. There are signs that the preface and poems were written hastily and under stress: "Even though I have decided to die, I do not know what method to use to die or where to die." On the one hand, they are less elegantly composed than Du Xiaoying's, whether due to differences in literary training, or talent, or the intense hatred Huang felt towards her abductor. Huang's poems employ almost no turns of metaphor, no textual allusions save the most important passage from the *Analects* on the necessity for moral suicide. On the other hand, Huang's prose and especially her poetic style convey an urgent need to provide information. She supplies additional details in the form of annotations that supplement her self-preface in five of the ten poems, as can be seen in the translations below:[33]

(1) I feel sorry for myself—born to meet with strange adversity,
So very pitiful to have encountered the calamity of the red sheep.
If I go against my true conscience and follow the wastrel,
Though I get to preserve my life, my name should be cursed.

(2) In recent years banished to live in the dusty cage,
I've been ungrateful to my parents' kindness in giving birth to me.
A grave cannot bring peace to their bodies and souls,
Trimming the lampwick I'm overwhelmed by memories.

(3) Unfortunately my family had to be in this city,
Twice meeting with destruction we resent war.
Why does hoary Heaven have to hate goodness?
Half of us are dead, but those of us living are scattered.
*Author's note*: The ones alive are myself, second brother and his wife and my niece. But we are in different corners of the world. What sorrow! What grief!

---

[33] I discuss this practice of annotating one's own poems in the poetry collection of Shen Shanbao 沈善寶, an older contemporary woman poet. See "Writing Self and Writing Lives: Shen Shanbao's (1808-1862) Gendered Auto/Biographical Practices," *Nan Nü: Men, Women and Gender in Early and Imperial China* 2.2 (2000): 259-303. The stylistic differences between Du Xiaoying and Huang Shuhua may also reflect broader trends and tendencies in the late Ming and late Qing periods.

(4) Since they came to our gate and I was seized,
Daily I've been in violent waters but I can't yet die.
I am glad that the slave of fortune only wants merchandise,
Heaven let my white jade not be blemished by a fly.
*Author's note*: The one who seized me is surnamed Shen, a native of Baoqing (Hunan). Fearful of being defiled by him, I have already sewn up my garment.

(5) Shortly after we saw the crescent moon again,
He forced us to board the boat on the river.
The boatman hoisted the sail with good wishes—
Do you know that I do not want to keep on living?

(6) Who among our female companions were not dishonored?
Myself, Madam Zhang, and Aunt Jin.
I admire Jin Meishou who rises above the group—
Her death can yet give protection to her friends.
*Author's note*: Jin Meishou 金媚壽 was an old friend of mine. When one of the men wanted to dishonor her, she would not obey. As the boat window was open, she jumped into the river and drowned. After Aunt Jin died, they did not dare to force me. I really respect her high principles. Therefore I say this.

(7) I remember following my female companion to the shore,
Swearing that my body will become immortal in the world.
Traversing the turbulent waves, who is my companion?
Relying on each other, there are only my shadow and form.

(8) They say the traveling sail has arrived at Changsha.
Gazing afar at the Temple of the Xiang Goddess 湘靈廟 I pray for blessing.
I beg her to cut the red thread into pieces,
So I do not have to tell my sadness and anger to the Tartar's pipe.
*Author's note*: Arriving here, he plans to turn me over to a marriage broker. So I silently implore the goddess.

(9) On land the storm subsides then rises again.
Where can my body seek safety?
With entreaties I avoid being sold into marriage,
Though I want to avenge this unique wrong, I fear I won't succeed.
*Author's note*: Here he met up and traveled with a man with the surname of Fu.

(10) Since ancient times to become humane one always kills oneself.
Why should I myself shrink back from this?
I will return the boundless breath to Heaven and Earth,
And keep company with the chaste spirits at Heaven's gate.

The power of the self-preface and the poetic narrative is achieved through a combination of mimetic realism and the violence of representation enunciated in a strong first-person female voice. Huang Shuhua repeatedly uses the first-person pronouns in the poems: *nong*

儂, *wo* 我, *yu* 余, *wu* 吾. In her preface, she had recorded the butchering of her family in a few swift strokes that projected the suddenness and senselessness of the brutality:

> They killed my two elder brothers in the courtyard, went inside and surrounded all the rooms. A sturdy fellow found and carried me out. My little brother held onto his clothes while my mother knelt and pleaded with the soldier. He said irately, 'Those who surrendered to the bandits are to be killed without pardon. This is the commander's order.' He then killed my mother and little brother. When eldest sister-in-law came, he also killed her.

Poem 1 begins with "I feel sorry for myself"—the individual caught powerless within what is perceived as a cosmic scheme beyond her comprehension. Poems 1 to 3 reflect on being born in the wrong place at the wrong time. The term employed, *hongyang jie* 紅羊劫, "the calamity of the red sheep," stands for national calamity. In the hexagenary system of calendrical calculation, the years *bingwu* 丙午 and *dingwei* 丁未 in the cycle were believed to be years in which national disasters would occur. In the ten heavenly stems (*tiangan* 天干) *bing* and *ding*, the first character in each combination, belong to the element fire, and their color is red; furthermore, of the zodiac animal signs for the twelve earthly branches (*dizhi* 地枝), the sheep stands for *wei*. Hence, the "calamity of the red sheep."[34] In the mid-nineteenth century, the year 1847 is *dingwei* in the cycle, a most inauspicious year. Huang sees herself born into a disastrous period, her life coinciding with the temporal beginning and end of the Taiping Rebellion. Geographically, as a native of Nanjing, she was confined to their "dusty cage" since the Taipings established their capital there in 1853.

While she is overwhelmed by a sense of powerlessness in the unfolding of history, paradoxically a sense of personal agency is generated as she contemplates taking action to right the injustice perpetrated on her family members. She cannot live or die in peace until she can "avenge this unique wrong" (Poem 9). But while she waits for an opportunity to carry out her revenge, the overwhelming cultural and personal imperative is to prevent herself from being defiled. In the note to Poem 4, she states that she has taken the precaution of sewing up her garment. This attempt to protect their chastity was a common and apparently effective measure taken by women who were captured or about to be captured.

[34] *Hanyu da cidian* 9.705.

As Huang Shuhua contemplates her life and tragedy shortly before suicide, she goes beyond her personal grievance to embrace other women in her writing—her female companions who were also captured and brought on board the boat. She records the two who stood out in courage with her, forming a kind of sisterhood in resistance. In particular, she declares that her friend Jin Meishou, by jumping into the river when she was threatened with rape, offered protection to the other women. Her suicide acted as a deterrent on the soldiers' lust. Through her self-inscription, Huang commemorates the firm courage and principle of the other women and writes them into history. But she also mourns the loss of Jin Meishou, which left her feeling utterly alone. Coming to Changsha, the ancient land of Chu 楚, Huang Shuhua also prays to the goddesses of the Xiang River for prevention from being sold into bondage. She begs the goddesses to "cut to pieces" the "red thread" that the legendary Old Man in the Moon uses to tie together the man and woman destined to be husband and wife (Poem 8). Line 3 in the penultimate poem seems to indicate that Huang purposely sought not to be sold into marriage right away after they disembarked in Changsha, in which case she would lose track of her enemy, but to travel on with him watching for an opportune moment to carry out her revenge. Huang writes the final poem as a summation of her resolve to die despite the uncertainty of success. It is again the principle enunciated by Confucius that is cited: "Since ancient times to become humane one always kills oneself." In death, Huang Shuhua also seeks a larger cosmological frame for the meaning of her selfhood above the physical and mundane.

When Huang Shuhua wrote her preface and series of poems, she was unable to predict the outcome of her action. The writing was done just before she attempted her revenge. The reader only knows her intention but not the result.

### *A Widow's Own Defense: Ling Zhinü's (1806-27) Suicide and Written Testimony*

Examining Ling Zhinü's text and context, we encounter an entirely different category and context of violence against women. Ling Zhinü is a classic representative of the now much studied familiar figure of the young widow driven into difficult and untenable circumstances by unscrupulous relatives who want to force her into remarriage. As a young widow, the subordinate junior female in the family, Ling Zhinü's subject position was constructed within the powerful discourse and practice of the official ideal of fidelity to the dead husband, or widow chastity, which are predicated on a grid of interlocking patriarchal, patrilineal, and political concerns. Matthew Sommer has discussed how issues of property and descent line are inextricably bound up with the sexuality of widows in the social and legal domain. In order to inherit from her husband—to possess or even just be the custodian of his property, the widow has to safeguard her sexuality for him after his death.[35] Male and official vested interest in the cult of widow chastity also underscores how the ideal virtue of wifely loyalty to a single man has long been appropriated as the principal analogy undergirding the steadfast political loyalty of the male subject to his sovereign. Susan Mann suggests that the "ideology of chaste widowhood" is both symbol and practice of one of the highest Han ethical and ethnic virtues, the maintenance and perpetuation of which express symbolic capital for both local elites and the Manchu state.[36] In social reality, the lives and experiences of widows encompass the whole contradictory range between the extremes of destitution, despair, and self-determination leading to suicide on the one end and empowered freedom and independence leading to successful fulfillment of maternal roles within patriarchy on the other. Current research has further articulated historical, class, regional, and individual differences that might have been obscured by official discourse and seemingly normative patterns of behavior. A complex picture emerges from critical studies that draw on and analyze previously un- or under-explored materials that contain biographies and writings on widows from sources as varied as local gazetteers and fiction, family genealogies, legal archives, legal codes and statutes, challenging any easy conclusion or monolithic representation on the issues of widowhood.[37]

A major difference marking Ling Zhinü's "case" is that she has produced her own written self-defense in the form of a collection of

---

[35] Matthew Sommer, "The Uses of Chastity: Sex, Law, and the Property of Widows in Qing China," *Late Imperial China* 17.2 (1996): 77-130.

[36] Susan Mann, "Widows in the Kinship, Class, and Community Structures of Qing Dynasty China," *Journal of Asian Studies* 46.1 (1987): 37-56.

[37] In addition to the works of Susan Mann and Matthew Sommer, see also Ann Waltner, "Widows and Remarriage in Ming and Early Qing China," in Richard Guisso and Stanley Johannesen, eds., *Women in China: Current Directions in Historical Scholarship* (Youngstown, N.Y.: Philo Press, 1981), 129-46; Kathryn Bernhardt, *Women and Property in China, 960-1949* (Stanford: Stanford University Press, 1999), Ch. 2, 47-72.

poetry framed by a self-postscript, when legal investigation left her in a vulnerable position for several years. The detailed self-postscript, which accompanies her unpublished poetry collection, is also her suicide note. In it she begins by discoursing on and thus showing her knowledge of the fundamental significance of poetry for self-cultivation; she asserts authoritatively the canonical tenet that "[poetry] is that by means of which one keeps hold of one's nature and emotion in order to return to the correct." By demonstrating her correct understanding of the function of poetry, Ling with one stroke upholds her engagement in poetic composition and sets up her poetry as proof of her character and innocence. She states that she began to study under her grandfather's tutelage at six and practiced poetry writing for ten years. She inserts a note of fitting modesty regarding the place of feminine writing, which should not cross beyond the boundaries of the home: "I dare not show even a scrap of paper or a word to people." As we will see, all this is being transformed by her action now of attempting to make her life and writing visible. She next recounts her life after marrying into the Tan family at eighteen in 1824. Though her husband's family was poverty-stricken, her natal family was able to lend a helping hand. Specifically, she mentioned that her grandmother and mother could not stand the state of poverty she lived in when they discovered it during her visit home. Maternal concern prompted them to borrow money to lease some land from her brother's father-in-law for her and her husband to farm for a living. The kinship network is tapped.

As soon as the problem of livelihood seemed to have been solved, the family was hit by an epidemic that killed all the male members. Ling Zhinü became a childless young widow at nineteen, resolved to serve her surviving mother-in-law and adopt a son for patrilineal succession. However, within a year she was forced to remarry by members of her husband's lineage, who saw her as a "rare merchandise." The problem of widows being forced to remarry had become a serious problem, and the Qing code instituted graded punishments for those responsible for the coercion, including the widow's own parents and in-laws.[38] Often the motive was greed on the part of in-laws, who stood to gain possession of the widow's property inherited from her husband and even her own dowry she brought with her if she remarried. In the case of poor families, when there was no property to speak of, they could gain a bride price by selling her in

[38] Waltner, "Widows," 136-38; and Sommer, "The Uses of Chastity," 86-87.

marriage. This seems to be the situation in which Ling Zhinü found herself. When she resolutely refused to remarry, she tells us that her mother-in-law was induced to "file an accusation against me to involve me in a serious crime." When she wrote the postscript in preparation for her suicide, she had already returned to live in her natal home for two years, with her name darkened under a cloud of legal investigation.[39] It appears that what could have been an alternative solution was denied her when her brother's father-in-law refused to give back the money for the leased field, which she said she could have used for supporting her mother-in-law.[40] She felt trapped with no viable alternatives: "At this time I find it difficult to make any move. If I wish to serve my mother-in-law as a widow, my husband's family has no sympathy for me, and neither would my grandmother consent. If I wish to depend on my mother as a widowed daughter, then what concerns my heart would never be cleared, and the gravity of my offence would be increased." She decides death is the only way she can clear her name, even though she says she is aware that Confucius had criticized the shallow meaning of the suicides of the ordinary man and woman who kill themselves out of petty fidelity.[41] Even worse, her suicide could be interpreted as resulting from her guilt and thus evidence of her culpability. She strongly anticipates that possibility by noting: "I only think that after I die it will be unavoidable that my mother-in-law's family will file suit." Thus, merely taking her own life does not suffice to serve her purpose; self-inscription becomes the space where she enacts a self-transformation from simply being a helpless victim to a woman using her literary

---

[39] From Ling's postscript, we cannot tell what crime she was accused of. Nowhere does she spell out the precise nature of her alleged offense. According to Matthew Sommer, whose investigation focuses on issues around chastity, "expelling or selling off an adulteress became a legitimate act of patriarchal self-defense." He also suggests that magistrates commonly ordered "an adulterous widow 'returned to her natal lineage' (*guizong* 歸宗). She would become the responsibility of her natal family, to support or to marry off a second time" ("The Uses of Chastity," 87 and 84 respectively). Does conviction of offenses other than adultery lead to similar legal settlements? Regardless of what they accused her of, Ling's in-laws would appear to be acting with a view to the type of legal outcome similar to the conviction of adultery, which would give them the right to sell her in remarriage. Her actual situation after the lawsuit—going back to live in her natal home—seems to reflect the second type of judicial outcome reported by Sommer.

[40] Presumably, since the lease was terminated early after her husband's death, there was money left.

[41] She cites the last part of *Analects* 14.17, trans. D. C. Lau, 127, in which Confucius defends Guan Zhong 管仲 for not committing suicide.

ability to stand up to and resist the family and legal entrapment. Neither act is sufficient by itself—she conjoins her death and writing as the most potent weapon she can conceive of, a voice of resistance set ambiguously within the dominant ideology, at once conforming to and defying its logic of compulsory submission.

Ling Zhinü concludes her self-postscript by returning to a discourse on poetry *in widowhood*. In recording her thoughts about her person and her poetry, she indicates that she has stopped using any form of adornment on her person and sequesters herself in her quarters with needlework and poetry. She treats her poetry in a parallel manner by keeping it concealed in a trunk. She emphasizes that she writes in the most serious subgenres for historical reflection (*huaigu* 懷古) and self-expression (*ganhuai* 感懷); but she does not see her writing in the same light as the poetry collections of famous gentry women. She believes her poems are probably inferior literary products, but for her, that is not where their value lies. They are what she has "scribbled with her blood and tears;" they *are* her. After her death, she intends them to come to light, to exonerate her person as she could not do during her lifetime. She expressly enjoins her brother to clear her from the false charges laid against her.

Much of the corpus of the more than three hundred poems was likely written during her two years of unhappy widowhood when she in fact had much time on her hands. Accused of some crime, she had returned to cloister herself at her natal home. She wrote that she has not "stepped outside" the door, and besides needlework, she just wrote poems to "manifest her intent" (*shifu jianzhi* 詩賦見志). Indeed, of the extant eighteen titles in *Qingxianglou shixuan* 清湘樓詩選 (Selected poems from the Clear Xiang Pavilion), all but four are plainly written after her husband's death.[42] Of the four exceptions, the first title with two poems celebrates the bucolic life shared by husband and wife:

*I Go With My Husband to Plough the Field at the Wei* 魏 *Family Land*

Keeping each other company we go together to the Wei Family,
A few acres of poor land are our means of living.
My husband—how hard he toils with his strength,
I almost want to change my attire to help him tread the wheel.

You plant mulberries and hemp, I plant flowers,
The flowers have not yet bloomed and we are ready to harvest the hemp.

[42] *Qingxianglou shixuan*, 1832, Fan Baifang suokan shu edition, copy in Jinbun Kagaku Kenkyūjō. See discussion in conclusion.

Work on the hemp just finished, the flowers quickly bloomed,
Flowers, hemp and mulberry—all are equally fine.
(1a)

Though unsophisticated, these lines inscribe the simple delight of a woman able to share her days and activities with her husband in an open rural setting. There is another idyllic poem describing an evening scene entitled "Gazing at Dusk by the River" (1a). Such pastoral romance disappeared quickly in her poetry as it did in her life, a reminder of the close relationship poetry in the Chinese tradition so often bears to personal lived experience. Even as she was enjoying this brief period of happiness with her husband, she notes under the poem "Song of a Phoenix" that, because she went to work in the fields with her husband, vulgar men often came to jeer at her (1a-b). This is the price for showing herself and their conjugal affection in public. The lofty phoenix, which alighted on the fields and was harassed by hunters, is a metaphor for her self and her move downward in marriage.

Replacing the short-lived gaiety is a lifetime of loneliness and sorrow, which she pours into long series of poems reflecting on historical figures (*huaigu*, 1b-2b) and poems "stirred by emotions" (*ganhuai*, 2b-5a), designated as written in the "widow's apartment" (*shuanggui* 孀閨). The emotional condition of grief, mourning, unfulfilled desire and longing dovetail with the poetic tradition's preferred seasons: spring and autumn recur as temporal settings.

*Spring Day in the Widow's Apartment: Stirred by Feelings*

[First in a series of sixteen quatrains]
Playing "Parting from the Crane" on the zither, so much dolor gathers,
Desolate the empty chamber, but what can I do?
Idly let me borrow the blue sky for white paper,
And write out my song of the broken heart from the beginning.
(2a)

She continues in this series about her sleepless nights in spring as she mourns the loss of her husband. She envies the imagined merrymaking of the other girls in their spring outings and activities, while she has no companion except "the person in the mirror"—herself (3b). But she confesses that she cannot bring herself to be more of a burden to her mother:

Endless sorrow and anxiety—to whom can I tell?
Forcing myself to smile in front of mother I grieve behind her back.
Afraid that I would only bring distress to her kindness,
I shed tears in secret as anguish churns in my breast.
(3b)

Emotional experiences or at least their inscriptions in poetry are often culturally constructed. Sentiment and its representation meld to form variations in a common repertoire through practice. In this convention, spring is an effective signifier because the sense of joy and renewal in the season of love and desire can be deployed to contrast with and thus foreground the opposite—sadness, loss, and loneliness:

[Ninth in the series of sixteen quatrains]
The Primal Breath flows, the myriad things flourish.
In gardens they fight to watch the rare buds bloom.
Now I have taken leave forever from the path of spring breeze,
I will not join the ladies of Wu treading on fallen petals.
(3b)

Again and again Ling's writing shows her caught in the vortex of unrelieved contemplation of her tragedy and constant denial of pleasure and distraction, surely a depressed state: "A bamboo curtain has long locked out spring/The east-facing window has not been open" (4b). When her thoughts go beyond the boundary of her sequestered quarter, the path of filiality and fidelity leads them towards her mother-in-law and her husband's home:

*Under the Moon I Think of My Mother-in-law*

Weeping blood I inscribe a poem to send to my mother-in-law;
Though I am lonely, I worry about her being alone.
Moon at night over the empty mountain—who would be her companion?
She sees the full moon but she does not see me.
(5b)

*On a Spring Day I Long for My Husband's Home*

[Second of two poems]
Moving shadows of the banana tree brush against the gauze window.
In utmost sorrow I remember our home.
Are you there by the thatched hut and bamboo fence?
In vain you've left a branch of flowers by the courtyard.
(5b)

In the last line, the metaphor for the bereft woman is all too apparent. Widowhood becomes the veil through which every season and every festival is perceived, screening out all temptations:

*The Lantern Festival*

Night of the Lantern Festival—lights shine on buildings and terraces.
I open all the windows facing the street.
Just about to roll up the pearl curtains—I stop myself,

Afraid that I'll bring the flowers' shadows onto my body.
(5b)

When intrusions take on human form, Ling Zhinü also writes poems to block them. She prefaced two poems suggestively: "I was called beautiful. A certain nouveau riche person tried to persuade me to marry him; I write these poems to reject him." These poems raise intriguing questions with no definite answers: Are these poems a gesture to herself of her unwavering resolve? Are they concrete evidence of the pressure on her to remarry, with suitors knocking on her door? Were they actually sent to their addressee or has the suitor simply provided the context for an implied reader around whom a dialogue can be constructed to reinforce the chaste widow image? The second poem reads:

Cutting off the arm to establish one's reputation—this also is human.
Dare I use my looks to attract the dusty world?
Shutting the door, I pay no attention to the moon through the window.
Why would I care that plum blossoms have passed two springs?
(6b)

The first line alludes to the many historical examples of principled widows who disfigure themselves in order to maintain their chastity. In sum, this poetry embodies a chaste widowhood built on passionate attachments—attachment to love and sentiment, to virtue, to reputation, the constant adherence to some and denial of others point to the tenacity of the attachments. Some poems also indicate that she turns to Buddhist practices such as meditation and reading sutras for deliverance. We do not know why or how Ling Zhinü arrived at the decision to commit suicide on the fifteenth of the eighth month (the Mid-Autumn Festival), 1827. The extant couplet from her "Poem on Ending Life" reads:

Now I carefully cut out the insignificant words to be engraved on steles,[43]
A thousand years after I die my bones will surely be fragrant.
(7a)

The ultimate vindication of these passionate attachments is self-inscription and suicide.

[43] My interpretation of this enigmatic line is tentative. The puzzling term is "*pijinzi* 皮金字," literally "skin/thin metal words," which she carefully cuts out with scissors. Leaving out the *pi*, "*jinzi*" can mean either inscriptions that are carved on steles or Buddhist scriptures. My translation adopts the former meaning.

## *Conclusion: Male Mediation/Female Agency Revisited*

I have presented these texts without reference to the problem of sources because I want to foreground these women's voices and subjectivities in my reading of agency. Can my reading be challenged, itself compromised even, if their sources were brought in, which inevitably are entangled with the endemic problem of literati male intervention?[44] In order to provide an answer to the question, I will now turn to discuss the provenance, circulation, and reinscription of these texts in the hope of arriving at some conclusion regarding the possibility of women's agency in conjoining the act of writing with the act of suicide within a set of cultural determinants.

I will proceed first with Ling Zhinü's text, her case being fresh in our minds. The small collection of Ling Zhinü's extant poetry was published in 1832, just a few years after her death, by the scholar and poet Fan Kai 范鍇 in his collectanea *Fan Baifang suokan shu* 范白舫所刊書. In his colophon, Fan Kai, a native of Wucheng 烏程, Zhejiang, who liked to travel, recounts how he was shown Ling's poetry collection in Chengdu, Sichuan, by a traveler from her native county in Hunan. Much of the information he gives concerning her life history is also contained in Ling's self-postscript, but Fan does include additional details such as her childhood name Xingfeng 興鳳, "Rising Phoenix," which connects to her use of the mythical bird as self-image in her poem "Song of the Phoenix."[45] He also records that Ling was betrothed to the Tan boy in infancy and that the Tan family subsequently declined in fortune so that ten years later they were so impoverished they became laborers. Another significant detail concerns the lawsuit: the Tan lineage incited her mother-in-law to accuse Ling of having failed in her chastity (*kuijie* 虧節), but as they could not produce convincing evidence, the case

---

[44] On the most studied case of the disputed existence of a woman resulting from a unique male representation, see Paul Ropp's book-length investigation into the existence of the eighteenth-century peasant woman poet Shuangqing 雙卿 and her poetry *Banished Immortal: Searching for Shuangqing, China's Peasant Poet* (Ann Arbor: University of Michigan Press, forthcoming); see also my article "De/Constructing a Feminine Ideal in the Eighteenth Century: *Random Records of West-Green* and the Story of Shuangqing," in Ellen Widmer and Kang-i Sun Chang, eds., *Writing Women in Late Imperial China* (Stanford: Stanford University Press, 1997), 264-81.

[45] This is the name listed in Hu Wenkai 胡文楷, *Lidai funü zhuzuo kao* 歷代婦女著作考 (Shanghai: Shanghai guji chubanshe, 1985), 454. Zhinü 帙女 is her courtesy name, which she used to sign her postscript. Hu mistakenly lists her collection twice, the second time giving the author simply as Ling *shi* 氏 (nèe Ling).

was held up to over a year. So it seems that Ling was accused of sexual misconduct. Finally Ling's depression turned into illness, and she refused medical treatment and starved herself to death in the ninth month. (Here we are told about the method Ling used to commit suicide.) After her suicide, her writing was what cleared her name. The local gentry rejoiced and made a selection of her poems to be put into print; that became the edition on which Fan Kai's is based. Moved by her tragic circumstances, Fan said he decided to have her poetry reprinted to broaden the circulation.[46] Fan also includes at the beginning the original preface written in ornate parallel prose composed by the local gentry of Hengyang 衡陽 when they first published Ling's poetry collection in the fifth month of 1828, less than one year after her suicide. In it they place the date of her death precisely on the eighth day of the ninth month. Their sympathy breaks through the artificial style in a maudlin image—reading her poems causes them to "sniffle" (*bisuan* 鼻酸). Their pride in this local heroine—both talented and chaste—transforms into their sense of "responsibility to put into print this young wife's new lyrics." Finally, they expressed the hope that she would receive an imperial testimonial and archway to commemorate her virtue.[47]

To my knowledge, this original edition of Ling Zhinü's poetry has not survived. It appears that even it did not include the entire corpus of her more than three hundred poems. By reprinting a further abridged selection of her poems, Fan Kai did in fact help to circulate and preserve Ling's poetry for posterity.[48] By the same token, his selecting some and leaving out others is a representation of Ling Zhinü. We can access Ling Zhinü's subjectivity only through the choices Fan Kai made. What was left out? And what was emphasized as a result? From the poems we have read, I think we already have some answers. Fan wrote in his editorial note at the end of his small selection that, since he could not print the entire collection, he has selected some of her fine lines for preservation. Among these is the couplet taken from her poem on ending life quoted earlier.

---

[46] Fan Kai, colophon 1a-b, appended at the end of *Qingxianglou shixuan*.

[47] Preface to *Qingxianglou shixuan*, signed the Gentlemen of Heng City.

[48] Ironically, Fan Kai's own collectanea can hardly be said to be well preserved. The only copy I have discovered so far is in the Jinbun Kagaku Kenkyūjō. I have not been able to find the copy in China, which is supposed to be in the Shanghai Library. See *Zhongguo congshu zonglu* 中國叢書總錄 (Shanghai: Shanghai guji chubanshe, 1986), vol. 1, 966.

In spite of Ling Zhinü's modesty about her poetic accomplishments in comparison to *mingyuan* 名媛 (notable women of the gentry class), the *Guixiu zhengshi xuji* 閨秀正始續集 (Sequel to correct beginnings of talents in the women's quarters), published in 1836, includes her "Song of the Phoenix" and three of her *huaigu* poems written in her "apartment in spring." It also provides a brief biographical note. This work is the supplement to Yun Zhu's 惲珠 monumental anthology of women's poetry, the *Guochao guixiu zhengshi ji* 國朝閨秀正始集 (Anthology of correct beginnings) published in 1831.[49] Fan Kai's 1832 publication of Ling's poetry is quite likely the source for the four poems and the abridged biographical note. Almost a decade later, Shen Shanbao 沈善寶 (1808-62) also included Ling in a large collection of over five hundred short critical biographies of women from the late Ming to her own time entitled *Mingyuan shihua* 名媛詩話 (Remarks on poetry of notable women), published in Beijing in 1845.[50] Ling Zhinü has written herself into the ranks of those "famous women of the world" to which she did not dream of belonging.

Turning to Du Xiaoying, the earliest and also the most complete written source for her self-preface and ten suicide poems (dated 1654) is the almost contemporaneous work by Tan Qian 譚遷 (1594-1657), the *Beiyoulu* 北遊錄 (Record of travels to the North). This collection of his poetry and prose records what he had heard and seen during his travels to and from Beijing between the years 1653 and 1656, which encompass the year 1654 when Du Xiaoying committed suicide.[51] Tan Qian does not indicate how he came into contact with the text. In fact, he gives it absolutely no framing—the text stands on its own. Ji Liuqi 計六奇, another contemporary, recorded in 1671 in his *Mingji nanlüe* 明季南略 (Abridged records of the

---

[49] Miaolianbao 妙蓮保, comp., *Guixiu zhengshi xuji* 3.20a-b. Ling Zhinü's entry is given under Ling Xingfeng, her name at birth. On the *Zhengshi ji* as well as Yun Zhu's editorial authority and moral conception of women's writing, see Susan Mann, *Precious Records*, Chapter 4.

[50] Shen Shanbao, *Mingyuan shihua* 10.24b-25a (sole extant copy in Peking University Library). The biographical entry and selection of poems are based almost exactly on the *Guixiu zhengshi xuji*. On the *Mingyuan shihua*, see my study "Writing Self and Writing Lives," *Nan Nü* 2.2 (2000), 295-302.

[51] Tan Qian 譚遷, *Beiyoulu* 北遊錄 (Beijing: Zhonghua shuju, 1997), 337-38. The entry is in "Jiwen shang 紀聞上" (Recording what I heard, Part A) and is titled "Chenzhou Du lienü shi bing zixu 辰州杜烈女詩并自序" (The poems and self-preface of the female martyr Du of Chenzhou). This is the text reproduced in *Qingshi jishi* 22.15533-35.

South at the end of the Ming) that he came into possession of the ten poems in 1661, but that already he "did not know what her name was."[52] It would seem that in the rapid transmission of Du Xiaoying's poems, the self-preface that identifies her name and the circumstances of her capture and suicide had already been detached from the version obtained a few years later by Ji Liuqi. We would expect that such dramatic writings by young women of heroic stature would make a strong impact on male and female readers alike. In particular, the short quatrains that represent such intense personal feelings would circulate rapidly and widely through both word of mouth and written copies. In the process, it is almost inevitable that variants to the texts of the poems and prefaces and also misattributions or dual attributions would arise. Thus, in two later sources Du Xiaoying's poems, with slight variants, are attributed to a woman née Zhu 朱氏 from Changsha during the same period, without the self-preface but given an abbreviated life story very similar to the outline of Du's autobiography.[53]

The provenance for the self-preface and ten poems by Huang Shuhua was at first somewhat unclear to me. The *Qingshi jishi* quotes in full the biographical sketch provided by Shi Shuyi 施淑儀 in her 1922 work *Qingdai guige shiren zhenglüe* 清代閨閣詩人徵略 (Excerpts of materials on women poets of the Qing) and then Huang's ten poems and self-preface, without indicating the source. The source given by Shi Shuyi for her biographical sketch is a work whose title is missing the first two characters.[54] Huang Shuhua's biography is in fact included in the *lienü* section of the gazetteer of her native district, the 1874 edition of the *Shang Jiang liangxian zhi* 上江兩縣志 (Gazetteer of the two counties Shang[yuan] and Jiang [ning]), ten years after her suicide.[55] This entry refers to Huang's poems as its own source, and fills in many details necessarily missing in Huang's self-account, particularly concerning her actual murder revenge and suicide. According to this account, Huang wrote the poems and the self-preface after they disembarked in Xiangtan on the sixteenth of the ninth

[52] Ji Liuqi 計六奇, *Mingji nanlüe* 明季南略, quoted in *Qingshi jishi*, 22.15535.

[53] Quoted in *Qingshi jishi*, 22: 15678-79. The two works are *Lianpo shihua* 蓮坡詩話 by Zha Weiren 查為仁 (1694-1749), and *Gu sheng* 觚賸 by Niu Xiu 鈕琇 (17th century).

[54] *Qingshi jishi*, 22.15930-15932; *Qingdai guige shiren zhenglüe* (1922; photoreprint Shanghai: Shanghai shudian, 1987), 9.29b/566.

[55] I am indebted to Katherine Carlitz for discovering this biographical entry of Huang Shuhua. It initiated my search for a trail of evidence.

month (which is how Huang dates and signs her self-preface). She carried out her revenge two days later on the night of the eighteenth when they reached an inn in Guanwangqiao 關王橋, in Anhua 安化 (a village farther on). All accounts refer to hearing the commotion in their room that night. The next day it was discovered that Huang had poisoned one of the men and with one of their swords killed the other, who was drunk, before hanging herself. The owner of the inn reported the case to the authorities and was told to have Huang buried; the investigation did not go further.[56] But two travelers, one a woman from Jiangning 江甯, Huang's native district, who passed the inn (the scene of the murder) copied down her preface and poems and so they were transmitted in the world.[57] The year 1874 also saw the publication of the *Xiangxiang xianzhi* 湘鄉縣志, the gazetteer of the county in Hunan where Huang Shuhua committed suicide. In it, a brief notice on Huang Shuhua is placed at the very end of the work, in a section called *congji* 叢記 (Various records). The compilers noted how Huang's chastity, intelligence, and courage are rare in this world. Thus, they concur that even though she was not a native of the county, she had martyred herself and left her inscription on the soil of the county, so they would record her deed and words to preserve them. The entire text of her self-preface and the ten suicide poems is appended.[58]

If self-narratives by women were constructed by male literati, one can imagine that they could serve the purpose or intention of turning women's bodies and women's texts into allegorized objects that embody some of the highest ethical virtues of integrity: strength in adversity, intelligent discernment, and above all, chastity. Yet, it would be difficult to view these texts as unmitigated ventriloquist productions by male literati. In addition to the argument of the traceable records as factual proof, in my view, the specificities and force of voice and identity uttered in the autobiographical prefaces and poem series render more dependable the historicity and embodiment of these women. Huang Shuhua's practice of annotating her poems with exact details is a case in point.

It is undeniable that the literati showed strong interest in gathering, recording, and printing what appeared to be fragile, ephemeral, and virtuous, with women's writings constituting a significant but by

56 Presumably because no living person was implicated.
57 *Shang Jiang liangxian zhi* 上江兩縣志 (1874), 20.1b-2b.
58 *Xiangxiang xianzhi*, *congji*, *juanmo* 卷末: 25b-26b.

no means the only body of material attracting their attention.[59] However, their apparent interest in—even fervor for, and the common act of picking up, circulating, and reproducing these women's texts (and perhaps embellishing certain details in the process) demonstrate on some level a recognition of the power of female agency, usually hidden from view, located in the inner sphere of the home, unknown in more normal circumstances. It is a tacit admission that these out-of-place women actively demanded from them—their public—some form of acknowledgement. If we read from the women's point of view, their sentiments regarding their own writings seem to be precisely the opposite of the male recorders' concern about their perishability—like the poem that fades from the wall with age. These women see permanence and durability of their selves through the transmission of knowledge about them in texts they themselves produced. They did not worry about the ultimate material impermanence of the medium, but the exigency and efficacy of the means at the moment. I therefore argue that these instances of embodiment, when women inscribe their subject positions in texts they produce at the moment of their own disposal of their bodies, should be read and recognized as exemplary instances of female agency. This female agency also generates or precipitates a sense of male agency—it calls men into action.

To be sure, there were varied motivations in the strong male interest in these women and their suicide writings, and men did play a vital role in the preservation and circulation of these texts. There could also be commercial interest in printing some of these cases in or as dramatized and fictionalized elaborations for entertainment or instructive purposes, as in Du Xiaoying's intertextual appearance in the erotic novel *Gu wang yan*. And finally, from the perspective of the ethical values they embody, these women and their writings were cultural capital writ large—whether on a local, Han ethnic, or national level. Women themselves internalized and acted on these values and perspectives. Namely, these women saw themselves as full participants in a long tradition that placed certain values of righteousness, loyalty, and courage above the value of preserving one's own finite life. In this tradition, injustices may occur, including the

[59] Folk songs, anecdotes, vernacular fiction, epigraphs, and catalogues of various subjects all appear in the literati propensity to *ji* 集 (gather) and *ji* 記 (record). Anthologizing women's poetry is one manifestation of this interest. See Kang-i Sun Chang, "Ming and Qing Anthologies of Women's Poetry and Their Selection Strategies," in *Writing Women in Late Imperial China*, 147-70.

death (even self-inflicted) of good and innocent people, but the public recording of the injustice redeems it by giving a voice to the victim, a voice that helps transform the victim into a hero/ine. The act of writing and explaining the act of suicide, then, both ensures that the perpetrators of injustice will stand condemned in the light and the judgment of history and that the victim-turned-hero/ine will be written into cultural and historical memory.[60]

From our twentieth-century perspective, which is another level of mediation, we may critique the ideology that subordinated women, but we should recognize and make visible the agency of these women in constructing a sense of self and identity, even if their acts are inscribed within the discursive limits of the ideology. However, through all these layers of mediation, I hope to have uncovered to some degree some ordinary literate women's sense of self, subjecthood, and agency in their embodiments of violence through their textual production.

---

60 I am grateful to Paul Ropp for the broader historical perspective he brings to my paper through these points.

# BIBLIOGRAPHY

BY

PAUL S. ROPP

Note: I have compiled this bibliography as a complement to the essays in this volume, focusing on works dealing with suicide in general, and female suicide in particular, in late imperial China. I include some general publications on Chinese attitudes toward death and dying, and some on earlier and later periods, as these provide important background for our understanding of female suicide in the Ming and Qing eras. As a result of our work on this collection, the *Nan Nü* Editorial Board is now planning to organize an international conference in 2003, with a multi-disciplinary focus on the broad topic of suicide in China from earliest times to the present. If anyone is interested in more information on this conference, please feel free to contact Harriet Zurndorfer or me (propp@clarku.edu). For assistance in compiling this bibliography, I am deeply indebted to all the contributors to this volume. In addition, I especially want to thank the following: Clara Wing-chung Ho and Lo Kar Kee for supplying many of the Chinese and Japanese sources cited here; Alice Shin-Yi Kao for timely assistance in rapidly translating and typing the Chinese titles; and Harriet Zurndorfer for suggesting many additional sources and offering helpful advice throughout the process.

Ahern, Emily Martin. *The Cult of the Dead in a Chinese Village* (Stanford: Stanford University Press, 1973).

An Bilian 安碧蓮. "Mingdai dui jielie funü de jingbiao yu jielie guannian de shenhua" 明代對節烈婦女的旌表與節烈觀念的深化 (The honors list of virtuous women and the intensification of the concept of chastity in the Ming dynasty), *Mingshi yanjiu zhuankan* 明史研究專刊 12 (1998): 383-421.

——. "Mingdai funü zhenjieguan de qianghua yu shijian" 明代婦女貞節觀的強化與實踐 (The enforcement and practice of women's chastity in the Ming dynasty). Ph.D. diss., Chinese Culture University, 1994.

——. "Mingdai funü zhenjie jingbiao zhidu de jianli" 明代婦女貞節旌表制度的建立 (The establishment of the system for honoring chaste women in the Ming dynasty), in *Qingzhu Wang Hui jiaoshou jiuzhi songtao lunwenji* 慶祝王恢教授九秩嵩壽論文集 (Essays in honor of Professor Wang Hui's ninetieth birthday) (Taipei: Lexue shuju, 1997), pp. 95-122.

Bernhardt, Kathryn. *Women and Property in China, 960-1949*. Ch. 2, "The Inheritance Rights of Widows from the Song Through the Qing" (Stanford: Stanford University Press, 1999), pp. 47-72.

Birge, Bettine. "Levirate Marriage and the Revival of Widow Chastity in Yuan China," *Asia Major* 8.2 (1995): 107-46.

Blake, C. Fred. "Footbinding in Neo-Confucian China and the Appropriation of Female Labor," *Signs: Journal of Women in Culture and Society* 19.3 (1994): 676-712.

Bodde, Derk. "The Chinese View of Immortality: Its Expression by Chu Hsi and Its Relationship to Buddhist Thought," in *idem.*, *Essays in Chinese Civilization* (Princeton: Princeton University Press, 1981), pp. 316-30.

Cai Linghong 蔡凌虹. "Cong funü shoujie kan zhenjieguan zai Zhongguo de fazhan" 從婦女守節看貞節觀在中國的發展 (The development of the concept of female chastity in China), *Shixue yuekan* 史學月刊 4 (1992): 24-30.

——. "Mingdai jielie funü jingbiao chutan" 明代節烈婦女旌表初探 (Investigations into chaste women's honors in the Ming dynasty), *Fujian luntan (wenshi zhe)* 福建論壇 (文史哲) 6 (1990): 44-48.

Cao Dawei 曹大為. "Zhongguo lishi shang zhenjie guannian de bianqian" 中國歷史上貞節觀念的變遷 (Changes in the concept of chastity in Chinese history), *Zhongguoshi yanjiu* 中國史研究 2 (1991): 140-50.

Carlitz, Katherine. "Desire, Danger, and the Body: Stories of Women's Virtue in Late Ming China," in Christina Gilmartin, et. al., eds., *Engendering China: Women, Culture, and the State* (Cambridge: Harvard University Press, 1994), pp. 101-24.

——. "Shrines, Governing-Class Identity, and the Cult of Widow-Fidelity in Mid-Ming Jiangnan," *Journal of Asian Studies* 56.3 (1997): 612-40.

——. "The Social Uses of Female Virtue in Late Ming Editions of the *Lienü zhuan*," *Late Imperial China* 12.2 (1991): 117-48.

Chang, Kang-i Sun. *The Late Ming Poet Ch'en Tzu-lung: Crises of Love and Loyalism* (New Haven: Yale University Press, 1991).

Chen Dongyuan 陳東原. *Zhongguo funü shenghuo shi* 中國婦女生活史 (A history of the lives of Chinese women) (1928; reprint, Taipei: Taiwan shangwu yinshuguan, 1967).

Chen Wanyu 陳晚玉. "Song dao Ming shiqi funü zhenjie guannian de yanbian" 宋到明時期婦女貞節觀念的演變 (Changes in the concept of women's chastity from the Song to the Ming period), *Shiyuan* 史苑 37 (1983): 62-79.

Chin Seihō (Chen Qingfeng) 陳青鳳. "Shinchō no fujo zokuhyō seido ni tsuite—setsufu, retsujo o chūshin ni" 清朝の婦女旌表制度について——節婦・烈女を中心に (Concerning the system of commemorative tablets for chaste women in the Qing dynasty—especially chaste widows and heroic women), *Tōyōshi ronshu* 東洋史論集 16 (1988): 101-31.

Chow, Kai-wing (Zhou Qirong 周啟榮). *The Rise of Confucian Ritualism in Late Imperial China: Ethics, Classics, and Lineage Discourse*. Ch. 8, "Ritualism and Gentry Culture: Women and Lineage" (Stanford: Stanford University Press, 1994), pp. 204-22.

Cohen, Alvin P. "The Avenging Ghost: Moral Judgement in Chinese Historical Texts." Ph.D. diss., University of California at Berkeley, 1971.

Deng Qiancheng 鄧前成. "Mingdai funü de zhenjie wenti" 明代婦女的貞節問題 (The problem of women's chastity in the Ming dynasty), *Sichuan shifan daxue xuebao (shehui kexue ban)* 四川師範大學學報 (社會科學版) 6 (1989): 85-90.

Dennerline, Jerry. "Marriage, Adoption, and Charity in the Development of Lineages in Wu-hsi from Sung to Ch'ing," in Patricia Buckley Ebrey and James L. Watson, eds., *Kinship Organization in Late Imperial China, 1000-1940* (Berkeley: University of California Press, 1986), pp. 170-209.

Ding Yizhuang 定宜莊. "Shehui, falü, zhenjieguan" 社會·法律·貞節觀 (Society, law, and the concept of chastity), in Bo Hua 柏樺 ed., *Wang Zhonghan xiansheng bashiwu ji, Wei Qingyuan xiansheng qishi huadan jinian lunwen heji* 王鍾翰先生八十五暨韋慶遠先生七十華誕紀念論文合集 (Essays celebrating Mr. Wang Zhonghan's eighty-fifth birthday and Mr. Wei Qingyuan's seventieth birthday) (Hefei: Huangshan shushe, 1999), pp.371-78.

Dong Jiazun 董家遵. "Lidai jielie funü de tongji" 歷代節烈婦女的統計 (Statistics on chaste women in history), in Bao Jialin 鮑家麟, ed., *Zhongguo funü shilun ji* 中國婦女史論集 (Essays on the history of Chinese women) (Taipei: Daoxiang chubanshe, 1992), pp. 111-117.

——. "Ming Qing xuezhe guanyu zhennü wenti lunzhan" 明清學者關於貞女問題論戰 (Ming-Qing scholars' arguments on the issue of chaste women), in *Zhongguo gudai hunyinshi yanjiu* 中國古代婚姻史研究 (Research on the marriage system in ancient China) (Guangzhou: Guangdong renmin chubanshe, 1995), pp. 345-51.

Du Fangqin 杜芳琴. "Shangjie yu changjie: Ming Qing funü zhenjie de tedian ji qi yuanyin" 尚節與倡節：明清婦女貞節的特點及其原因 (Praise and encouragement of chastity: the characteristics of women's chastity and its origins in Ming and Qing times), *Shanxi shida xuebao (shehui kexue ban)* 山西師大學報(社會科學版) 4 (1997): 41-46.

Eberhard, Wolfram. *Guilt and Sin in Traditional China* (Berkeley and Los Angeles: University of California Press, 1967).

Ebrey, Patricia. *The Inner Quarters: Marriage and the Lives of Women in the Sung Period* (Berkeley: University of California Press, 1993).

——. "Women, Marriage, and the Family in Chinese History," in Paul S. Ropp, ed., *Heritage of China: Contemporary Perspectives on Chinese Civilization* (Berkeley: University of California Press, 1990), pp. 197-223.

Elliot, Mark. "Manchu Widows and Ethnicity in Qing China," *Comparative Studies in Society and History* 41.1 (1999): 33-71.

Elvin, Mark. "Female Virtue and the State in China," *Past and Present* 104 (1984): 111-52; also in *idem.*, *Another History: Essays on China from a European Perspective* (Sydney: Wild Peony, 1996), pp. 302-51

Fei Siyan 費絲言. "You dianfan dao guifan: cong Mingdai zhenjie lienu de bianshi yu liuchuan kan zhenjie guannian de yangehua" 由典範到規範：從明代貞節烈女的辨識與流傳看貞節觀念的嚴格化 (From model to standard: the development and rising popularity of increasingly rigid views on female chastity in the Ming dynasty). Master's thesis, National Taiwan University, 1996.

Feng Minfei 馮敏飛. "Shi lun lienüzhi de yuanyin" 試論烈女制的原因 (On causal factors in the system of heroically chaste women), *Fujian luntan (wenshizhe)* 福建論壇(文史哲) 1 (1994): 68-71.

Gōyama Kiwamu 合山究. "Min Shin jidai ni okeru jōshi to sono bungaku" 明清時代における情死とその文學 (Literature on dying for *qing* in the Ming and Qing periods), in *Itō Sōhei kyōju taikan kinen Chūgokugaku ronshū* 伊藤漱平教授退官記念中國學論集 (Festschrift for Professor Itō Sōhei on his retirement: Papers in Sinology) (Tokyo: Kyūko shoin, 1986), pp. 417-86.

——. "Setsufu retsujo ron—Min Shin jidai no josei no iki kata" 節婦烈女論——明清時代の女性の生き方 (On chaste and heroic women—women's lives in the Ming and Qing). *Chūgoku shakai to bunka* 中國--社會と文化 13 (1998): 64-87.

Gu Derong 顧德融. "Woguo gudai de renxun he xunjie" 我國古代的人殉和殉節 (Burying people alive and loyalty to death in ancient China), *Zhongguo shi yanjiu* 中國史研究 2 (1987): 57-68.

Guan Luyin 關綠茵. "Ji Mingmo zhongzhenjie de nüzi" 記明末忠貞節的女子 (Remembering loyal and chaste women of the late Ming), *Wenshi huikan* 文史薈刊 2 (1960): 91-96.

Gui Youguang 歸有光 (1506-71). "Zhennü lun" 貞女論 (On betrothed chaste widows), and "Zhenfu bian" 貞婦辨 (On chaste widows), in *Zhenchuan xiansheng ji* 震川先生集 (Collected works of Gui Youguang). Sibu congkan, vol. 85 (Taipei: Shangwu yinshuguan, 1965), 3.53a-b, and 4.69a-72a.

Hao Lianchang 赦建昌. "Shi lun Handai funü zhenjie guan" 試論漢代婦女貞節觀 (On the concept of women's chastity in the Han dynasty), *Qiqihaer shifan daxue xuebao (zhesheban)* 齊齊哈爾師範大學學報 (哲社版) 3 (1988): 79-82.

Holmgren, Jennifer. "Observations on Marriage and Inheritance Practices in Early Mongol and Yuan Society, with Particular Reference to the Levirate," *Journal of Asian History* 20 (1986): 127-92.

——. "The Economic Foundations of Virtue: Widow Remarriage in Early and Modern China," *The Australian Journal of Chinese Affairs* 13 (1985): 1-27.

Hsieh, Andrew C. K., and Jonathan D. Spence. "Suicide and the Family in Pre-modern Chinese Society," in Arthur Kleinman and Tsung-yi Lin, eds., *Normal and Abnormal Behavior in Chinese Culture* (Dordrecht: D. Reidel Publishing Company, 1981), pp. 29-47.

Hu Shi, "The Concept of Immortality in Chinese Thought," *Harvard Divinity School Bulletin* 43.3 (1946): 23-42.

Hu Wenkai 胡文楷. *Lidai funü zhuzuo kao* 歷代婦女著作考 (An examination of women's writings through the dynasties) (1957; expanded and revised edition, Shanghai: Shanghai guji chubanshe, 1985).

Hu Fagui 胡發貴. "Qingdai zhenjie guannian shuping" 清代貞節觀念述評 (On the concept of chastity in the Qing dynasty), *Qingshi yanjiu ji* 清史研究集 7 (1990): 153-70.

——. *Tongku de wenming—Zhongguo gudai zhenjie guannian tanmi* 痛苦的文明——中國古代貞節觀念探秘 (The suffering civilization—The secret of the ancient Chinese concept of chastity) (Beijing: Zhongguo shehui chubanshe, 1992).

Huang Jincai 黃金財. "Jiexiao paifang" 節孝牌坊 (The memorial archways of chastity and filial piety), *Shiyou tongxun* 石油通訊 543 (1996): 56-59.

Huang Zhanyue 黃展岳. "Ming Qing huangshi de gongfei xunzangzhi" 明清皇室的宮妃殉葬制 (The burial system of royal concubines in the Ming and Qing dynasties), *Gugong bowuyuan yuankan* 故宮博物院院刊 1 (1988): 28-34.

Ihara Hiroshi 伊原弘. "Minmatsu Shinshō no Chōshu ni okeru onna to zokuhyō—chimei ni natta josei tachi," 明末清初の潮州における女と旌表——地名になった女性たち (Commemorative tablets for women in Chaozhou in the late Ming and early Qing—women whose names became place names), in *Chūgoku no dento shakai to kazoku: Yanagida Setsuko sensei koki kinen ronshu* 中國の伝統社會と家庭: 柳田節子先生古稀記念論集 (Traditional Chinese society and family: Essays in honor of Professor Yanagida Setsuko) (Tokyo: Kyūko shoin, 1993), pp. 101-31.

Ko, Dorothy. "The Complicity of Women in the Qing Good Woman Cult," in *Family Process and Political Process in Modern Chinese History*, Part 1 (Taipei: Institute of Modern History, Academia Sinica, 1992), pp. 451-87.

Kutcher, Norman. "The Death of the Xiaoxian Empress: Bureaucratic Betrayals and the Crises of Eighteenth-Century Chinese Rule," *Journal of Asian Studies* 56.3 (1997): 708-25.

——. *Mourning in Late Imperial China: Filial Piety and the State* (Cambridge: Cambridge University Press, 1999).

Lau, Joseph. "The Courage to Be: Suicide as Self-fulfillment in Chinese History and Literature," *Tamkang Review* 19.1-4 (1989): 715-34.

——. "The Saint as Sinner: Paradoxes of Love and Virtue in 'The Predestined Couple'," *Tamkang Review* 1.1 (1970): 183-91.

Leung, Angela Ki Che (梁其姿). "To Chasten Society: The Development of Widow Homes in the Qing, 1773-1911," *Late Imperial China* 14.2 (1993): 1-32.

Li Chenggui 李承貴. "Zhenjie guannian de lishi yanbian ji qi xiandai qidi" 貞潔觀念的歷史演變及其現代啟迪 (Historical changes in the concept of chastity and its modern meaning), *Kong Meng yuekan* 孔孟月刊 75 (1998): 187-202.

Li Dazhao 李大釗 (1888-1927). "Yuansha: ansha yu zisha" 原殺：案殺與自殺 (Origins of killing: in the cases of assassination and suicide), and "Lun zisha" 論自殺 (On suicide), in *Li Dazhao wenji* 李大釗文集 (Collected works of Li Dazhao) (Beijing: Renmin chubanshe, 1984), vol. 1: 44-48, and vol. 2: 517-36.

Li Xiangqun 李向群. "Mingdai lienü de zisha fangshi ji qi xiangguan yishi" 明代烈女的自殺方式及其相關意識 (Chaste women's ways of committing suicide and related concepts in the Ming dynasty), *Weiding gao* 未定稿 6 (1989): 52-57.

Li Zhi 李贄 (1527-1602). "Wu si pian" 五死篇 (Five kinds of death), in *Fenshu* 焚書 (A book for burning) (Beijing: Zhonghua shuju, 1975), pp. 163-64.

Liang Fen 梁份 (1641-1728). "Bo zhennü lun" 駁貞女論 (Against 'on betrothed chaste widows'), in Yao Chun 姚椿, ed., *Guochao wenlu* 國朝文錄 (Literary records from the present dynasty) (1851; reprint, Taipei: Daxin shuju, 1965), 7:14a-16a.

Liang Zuoqing 梁作檠. "Jiu jiegou gongneng lilun lai kan Qingdai houqi zhengfu de jingbiao zhengce" 就結構功能理論來看清代後期政府的旌表政策 (A functionalist view of government policy on the honors list of virtuous women in the late Qing), *Zhongguo wenhua yanjiusuo xuebao* 中國文化研究所學報 10.1 (1979): 195-218.

Liebenthal, Walter. "The Immortality of the Soul in Chinese Thought," *Monumenta Nipponica* 8 (1952): 327-97.

Lin Shimin 林時民. "Dui Mingdai funü zhenjie guannian de ruogan sikao" 對明代婦女貞節觀念的若干思考 (Some thoughts on the concept of Ming women's chastity), *Zhonghua wenhua fuxing yuekan* 中華文化復興月刊 19.8 (1986): 68-72.

Lin Yu-sheng. "The Suicide of Liang Chi: An Ambiguous Case of Moral Conservatism," in Charlotte Furth, ed., *The Limits of Change: Essays on Conservative Alternatives in Republican China* (Cambridge and London: Harvard University Press, 1976), pp. 151-68.

Lin Yutang. "Feminist Thought in Ancient China." *T'ien Hsia Monthly* 1.2 (1935): 127-50; reprinted in Li Yu-ning, ed., *Chinese Women Through Chinese Eyes* (Armonk, New York: M. E. Sharpe, 1992), pp. 34-58.

Lindell, Kristina. "Stories of Suicide in Ancient China," *Acta Orientalia* 35 (1973): 167-239.

Liu Xiang 劉向. *Lienü zhuan* 列女傳 (Biographies of exemplary women) (reprint; Taipei: Guangwen shuju, 1987).

Liu Jihua 劉紀華. "Zhongguo zhenjie guannian de lishi yanbian" 中國貞節觀念的歷史演變 (The historical changes in the Chinese concept of chastity), in Bao Jialin 鮑家麟, ed. *Zhongguo funü shilun ji si ji* 中國婦女史論集四集 (Essays on the history of Chinese women) (Taipei: Daoxiang chubanshe, 1995), vol. 4, pp. 101-30.

Lu Jiexing 盧嘉興. "Ming Zheng miewang zhenlie xunsi de wufei" 明鄭滅亡貞烈殉死的五妃 (The five concubines who were buried alive after the downfall of Ming Zheng), *Gujin tan* 古今談 16 (1966): 11-18.

Maclagan, P. J. "Suicide (Chinese)," in James Hastings, ed., *Encyclopedia of Religion and Ethics* (Edinburgh: T. & T. Clark; New York: Charles Scribner's Sons, 1921), 12:26.

McMullen, David. "The Death of Chou Li-chen: Imperially Ordered or Natural Causes?," *Asia Major* 2.2 (1989): 23-82.

Mann, Susan. "Suicide and Survival: Exemplary Widows in the Late Empire," in *Chūgoku no dento shakai to kazoku: Yanagida Setsuko sensei koki kinen ronshu* 中國の伝統社會と家庭: 柳田節子先生古稀記念論集 (Family and society in traditional China: Essays in honor of Professor Yanagida Setsuko) (Tokyo: Kyūko shoin, 1993), pp. 23-39.

——. "Widows in the Kinship, Class, and Community Structures of Qing Dynasty China," *Journal of Asian Studies* 46.1 (1987): 37-56.

Mao Qiling 毛奇齡 (1623-1716). "Jin shinü shouzhi xunsi wen" 禁室女守志殉死文 (Essay on forbidding unmarried virgins from following their betrothed in death), in *Xihe heji* 西河合集 (Collected works of Mao Qiling) (N.p., 1679), 73:1a-8b.
Martin, Emily. "Gender and Ideological Differences in Representations of Life and Death," in James L. Watson and Evelyn S. Rawski, eds., *Death Ritual in Late Imperial and Modern China* (Berkeley: University of California Press, 1988), pp. 164-79.
Meijer, M. J. "An Aspect of Retribution in Traditional Chinese Law," *T'oung Pao* 66 (1980): 199-216.
——. *Murder and Adultery in Late Imperial China* (Leiden: E.J. Brill, 1991).
——. "The Price of a P'ai-lou," *T'oung Pao* 67.3-5 (1981): 288-304.
Mou Xiaodong 牟小東. "Ming huangshi de xunzangzhi" 明皇室的殉葬制 (The system of burying Ming-dynasty royalty), *Wenshi zhishi* 文史知識 1 (1985): 66-69.
——. "Qingchu de yi ren xunzang" 清初的以人殉葬 (Burying people alive to accompany the dead in the early Qing dynasty), *Wenshi zhishi* 文史知識 7 (1987): 60-64.
Muramatsu Ei 村松映. *Chūgoko retsujo ten* 中國列女傳 (Biographies of exemplary Chinese women). Tokyo: Chuo koron sha, 1968.
Ni Zhiping 牛志平. "Gudai funü de zhenjieguan" 古代婦女的貞節觀 (Ancient women's view of chastity), *Lishi yuekan* 歷史月刊 26 (1990): 19-24.
Ōtsuka Hirohisa 大塚博久. "Chūgoku ni okeru Min-Shin ki no 'Fujin dōjō ron'" 中國における明清期の《婦人同情論》('Works sympathetic with women' in China in the Ming-Qing period). *Kenkyū ronsō* (Yamaguchi Daigaku kyōiku gakubu) 研究論叢 (山口大學教育學部) 18.1 (1961): 23-35.
Paderni, Paola. "Between Constraints and Opportunities: Widows, Witches, and Shrews in Eighteenth-Century China," in Harriet Zurndorfer, ed. *Chinese Women in the Imperial Past* (Leiden: E. J. Brill, 1999), pp. 258-85.
——. "Le rachat de l'honneur perdu. Le suicide des femmes dans la Chine du XVIIIe siècle," *Études chinoises* 10.1-2 (1991): 135-60.
Pan Mingyan 潘銘燊. *Guangdong funü xunfu kao* 廣東婦女殉夫考 (On Cantonese women who sacrificed their lives for their husbands) (Hong Kong: Zhongguo xueshe, 1988).
Rankin, Mary Backus. "The Emergence of Women at the End of the Ch'ing: The Case of Ch'iu Chin," in Margery Wolf and Roxane Witke, eds., *Women in Chinese Society* (Stanford: Stanford University Press, 1975), pp. 39-66.
Ropp, Paul S. "A Confucian View of Chinese Women in the Ch'ing Period," *Chinese Studies* (Taipei) 10.2 (1992): 399-435.
——. *Dissent in Early Modern China: 'Ju-lin wai-shih' and Ch'ing Social Criticism*. Ch. 4, "Women in Men's Eyes" (Ann Arbor: University of Michigan Press, 1981), pp. 120-51.
——. "The Seeds of Change: Reflections on the Condition of Women in the Early and Mid Ch'ing," *Signs: Journal of Women in Culture and Society* 2.1 (1976): 5-23.
——. "Women in Late Imperial China: a Review of Recent English-Language Scholarship," *Women's History Review* 3.3 (1994): 347-83.
Shi Yun 石雲 and Zhang Yihe 章義和. *Rouchang cunduan chouqianlu—Zhongguo gudai funü de zhenjieguan* 柔腸寸斷愁千縷——中國古代婦女的貞節觀 (The unbearable sadness—ancient Chinese women's view of chastity) (Xi'an: Shaanxi renmin chubanshe, 1988).
Sokabe Shizuo 曾我部靜雄. "Nit-Tō no shōchoku ni mieru setsufu no zokushō" 日唐の詔勅に見える節婦の旌賞 (Honors for chaste women as seen in imperial edicts in Japan and Tang China), *Shirin* 史林 57.2 (1974): 35-69.
Sommer, Matthew H. *Sex, Law, and Society in Late Imperial China* Ch. 5, "Widows in

the Qing Chastity Cult: The Nexus of Sex and Property in Law and in Women's Lives" (Stanford: Stanford University Press, 2000), pp. 166-209.

——. "The Uses of Chastity: Sex, Law, and the Property of Widows in Qing China," *Late Imperial China* 17.2 (1996): 77-130.

Spence, Jonathan. *The Death of Woman Wang* (New York: Viking, 1978).

Teng, Jinhua Emma. "The Construction of the 'Traditional Chinese Woman' in the Western Academy: A Critical Review," *Signs: Journal of Women in Culture and Society* 22.1 (1996): 115-51.

Theiss, Janet M. "Dealing with Disgrace: The Negotiation of Female Virtue in Late Imperial China." Ph.D. diss., University of California at Berkeley, 1998.

T'ien Ju-k'ang (Tian Rukang). *Male Anxiety and Female Chastity: A Comparative Study of Chinese Ethical Values in Ming-Ch'ing Times* (Leiden, E. J. Brill, 1988).

Wakeman, Frederic, Jr. "Romantics, Stoics, and Martyrs in Seventeenth-Century China," *Journal of Asian Studies* 43.4 (1984): 631-66.

Waltner, Ann. "Recent Scholarship on Chinese Women," *Signs: Journal of Women in Culture and Society* 21.2 (1996): 410-28.

——. "Widows and Remarriage in Ming and Early Qing China," in Richard Guisso and Stanley Johannesen, eds., *Women in China: Current Directions in Historical Scholarship* (Youngstown, N.Y.: Philo Press, 1981), pp. 129-46.

Wang Wenbin 王文斌. *Fengkuang de jiaohua—Zhenjie chongbai zhi tongguan* 瘋狂的教化——貞節崇拜之通觀 (Crazed religionization—an overview of worshiping chastity) (Shenyang: Liaoning renmin chubanshe, 1993).

Watson, James L. "Of Flesh and Bones: The Management of Death Pollution in Cantonese Society," in Maurice Bloch and Jonathan Parry, eds., *Death and the Regeneration of Life* (Cambridge: Cambridge University Press, 1982), pp. 155-86.

Wolf, Margery. "Women and Suicide in China," in Margery Wolf and Roxane Witke, eds., *Women in Chinese Society* (Stanford: Stanford University Press, 1975), pp. 111-41.

Xiaozhu Wenfu 小竹文夫 (Bi Renyong 畢任庸, translator). "Qingdai jingbiao kao" 清代旌表考 (On the Qing dynasty's honors lists of chaste women), *Renwen yuekan* 人文月刊 7.1 (1936): 1-19.

Xu Bingyu 徐秉愉. "Liao Jin Yuan sandai funü jielie shijie yu zhenjie guannian zhi fazhan" 遼金元三代婦女節烈事蹟與貞節觀念之發展 (The practice of female chastity and the development of the concept of chastity in the Liao, Jin, and Yuan dynasties), *Shihuo yuekan(fukan)* 食貨月刊(復刊) 10.6 (1980): 21-33.

Yamazaki Jun'ichi 山崎純一. "Kindai ni okeru retsujoden no hensen—O Ken no Retsujoden to An Seki-shin no Reppuden o chūshin ni" 近代における列女傳の變遷--汪憲の"列女傳"と安積信の"列婦傳"を中心に (The transition of biographies of women in modern times - with special reference to Wang Xian's Lienüzhuan [Biographies of women] and An Jixin's Liefuzhuan [Biographies of women]). *Chūgoku kōten kenkyū* 中國古典研究 12 (1964):41-54

——. "Shinchō ni okeru setsuretsu zokuhyō ni tsuite - dōki retsujoden kankō no haikei" 清朝における節烈旌表について——同期列女傳刊行の背景 (On commemorative tablets for virtuous widows in the Qing dynasty - background on the publication of women's biographies in the same period). *Chūgoku kōten kenkyū* 中國古典研究 15 (1967): 46-66.

Yang Guangzhi 楊光治. *Lidai juemingshi* 歷代絕命詩 (Suicide poems through the ages) (Tianjin: Baihua wenyi chubanshe, 1996).

Yang Jianyu 楊劍宇. "Zhenjie paifang tici xiaokao" 貞節牌坊題詞小考 (Brief comments on chastity verses on memorial archways), *Huadong shifan daxue xuebao* 華東師範大學學報 4 (1982): 84.

Yang Xinxiao 楊絢霄. "Zhongguo lidai zhenjie guannian ji qi zhidu kao"

中國歷代貞節觀念及其制度考 (On the concept and the system of female chastity through Chinese history), *Zhengzhi yuekan* 政治月刊 9.1 (1945): 50-53.

Yin Dengguo 殷登國. "Gudai xingshenghuo yu zhenjieguan" 古代性生活與貞節觀 (Sexual life and the concept of chastity in ancient times), *Dangdai* 當代 2 (1980): 75-81.

——. "Zhongguo chuantong de zhencao guan" 中國傳統的貞操觀 (The traditional Chinese concept of chastity), *Dangdai* 當代 1(1980): 80-85.

Yin Zhen 殷真. "Qingdai jielie nüzi de jingshen shijie" 清代節烈女子的精神世界 (The spiritual world of heroically chaste women in the Qing dynasty), *Lishi yuekan* 歷史月刊 135 (1999): 44-51.

Yu, Anthony. "'Rest, Rest, Perturbed Spirit!' Ghosts in Traditional Chinese Prose Fiction," *Harvard Journal of Asiatic Studies* 47.2 (1987): 397-434.

Yu Zhengxie 俞正燮 (1775-1840). "Jiefu shuo" 節婦說 (On chaste widows), "Zhennü shuo" 貞女說 (On chaste virgin widows), in *Guisi leigao* 癸巳類稿 (Manuscripts compiled in the year Guisi [1833]) (Taipei: Shijie shuju, 1965), 13: 493-95.

Yu Zhimin 余志明. "Songdai funü zhenjie guannian" 宋代婦女貞節觀念 (The concept of women's chastity in the Song Dynasty). Master's thesis, Hong Kong Chinese University, 1999.

Yuasa Yukihiko 湯淺幸孫 "Shindai ni okeru fujin kaihō ron - rikyō to ningen teki shizen" 清代における婦人解放論 -- 禮教と人間的自然 (The claims for emancipation of women in the Qing dynasty - *lijiao* and human nature). *Nippon-Chūgoku gakkai hō* 日本中國學會報 4 (1952): 111-25 (English abstract, 19).

Zang Yong 臧庸 (1767-1811). "Fu si shiren ji chuqie lun" 夫死適人出妻論 (On divorce, and on remarriage after a husband's death), in *Baijingtang wenji* 拜經堂文集 (Collected works of Zang Yong) (N.p., n.d.), 1: 4 pages (unnumbered).

Zeitlin, Judith. "Embodying the Disembodied: Representations of Ghosts and the Feminine," in Ellen Widmer and Kang-i Sun Chang, eds., *Writing Women in Late Imperial China* (Stanford: Stanford University Press, 1997), pp. 242-63.

Zeng Tiechen 曾鐵忱. "Qingdai zhi jingbiao zhidu" 清代之旌表制度 (The system of honors for female chastity in the Qing dynasty), in Gao Hongxing 高洪興 et.al., ed., *Funü fengsu kao* 婦女風俗考 (On women's social customs) (Shanghai: Shanghai wenyi chubanshe, 1991), pp. 554-65.

Zhang Aidong, and Wayne Schlepp. "Xiao Guanyin: Her Tragic Life and Melancholy Poems," *Journal of Song-Yuan Studies* 28 (1998): 219-21.

Zhang Bincun 張彬村. "Ming Qing shiqi guafu shoujie de fengqi—lixing xuanze de wenti" 明清時期寡婦守節的風氣——理性選擇 (Rational Choice) 的問題 (The trend of widow chastity in the Ming-Qing period—a matter of rational choice), *Xin shixue* 新史學 10.2 (1999): 29-76.

Zhang Huaicheng 張懷承. "Zhenjie de daode yiyi jianlun" 貞節的道德意義簡論 (A brief discussion on the moral meaning of chastity), *Hunan shida shehui kexue xuebao* 湖南師大社會科學學報 1 (1994): 16-20.

Zhang Minjie 張敏杰. "Funü diwei yu zhencao guannian" 婦女地位與貞操觀念 (Women's status and the concept of chastity), in Shaanxisheng funü lilun, hunyin jiating yanjiu hui, Shaanxisheng funü lianhe hui 陝西省婦女理論、婚姻家庭研究會、陝西省婦女聯合會 (The women's theory, marriage and family research committee and women's federation of Shaanxi Province), ed., *Nüxing wenti zai dangdai de sikao* 女性問題在當代的思考 (Modern thinking on women's issues) (Xi'an: Shaanxi renmin chubanshe, 1988), pp. 138-52.

——. *Zhencao guan* 貞操觀 (The concept of chastity) (Beijing: Beifang funü ertong chubanshe, 1988).

Zhang Yihe 章義和 and Chen Chunlei 陳春雷. *Zhenjie shi* 貞節史 (The history of chastity) (Shanghai: Shanghai wenyi chubanshe, 1999).

Zheng Peikai 鄭培凱. "Tiandi zhengyi ji jian yu funü: Ming Qing de qingse yishi yu zhenyin wenti" 天地正義僅見於婦女：明清的情色意識與貞淫問題 (Justice can only be found in women: Ming-Qing consciousness and the question of chastity and lewdness), in Bao Jialin 鮑家麟, ed., *Zhongguo funü shilun ji san ji*: 中國婦女史論集三集 (Essays on the history of Chinese women) (Taipei: Daoxiang chubanshe, 1993), vol. 3, pp. 97-120.

——. "Tiandi zhengyi ji jian yu funü: Ming Qing de qingse yishi yu zhenyin wenti (xuwan)" 天地正義僅見於婦女：明清的情色意識與貞淫問題(續完) (Justice can only be found in women: Ming-Qing consciousness and the question of chastity and lewdness, continued), in Bao Jialin 鮑家麟, ed., *Zhongguo fun shilun ji si ji*, 中國婦女史論集四集 (Essays on the history of Chinese women) (Taipei: Daoxiang chubanshe, 1995), vol. 4, pp. 253-272.

Zhou Shurong 周蜀蓉. "Congyi erzhong guannian de fazhan ji qi yingxiang" "從一而終"觀念的發展及其影響 (The development and influence of the concept of "lifelong faithfulness to one man"), *Xinan shifan daxue xuebao (zhexue shehui kexue ban)* 西南師範大學學報(哲學社會科學版) 3 (1990): 18-23.

Zhou Wanyao 周婉窈. "Qingdai Tongcheng xuezhe yu funü de jiduan daode xingwei" 清代桐城學者與婦女的極端道德行為 (Qing-dynasty Tongcheng scholars and extremist views of women's moral conduct), in Bao Jialin 鮑家麟, ed., *Zhongguo funü shilun ji si ji* 中國婦女史論集四集, (Essays on the history of Chinese women) (Taipei: Daoxiang chubanshe, 1995), vol. 4, pp. 185-251.

Zhou Zhiyuan 周致元. "Huizhou zhenjie funü de xuelei" 徽州貞節婦女的血淚 (The blood and tears of chaste women in Huizhou), *Zhiyuan* 志苑 1 (1996): 11-12.

——. "Lun Ming-Qing Huizhou funü jieli fengqi de zonghe dongyin" 論明清徽州婦女節烈風氣的綜合動因 (General factors concerning chastity as a trend for women in Ming-Qing Huizhou), *Huizhou shehui kexue* 徽州社會科學 1-2 (1995): 76-79.

Zhou Zongxian 周宗賢. "Qingdai Taiwan jiexiao liefu de jingbiao yanjiu" 清代臺灣節孝烈婦的旌表研究 (Research on the honors list of chaste and filial Taiwanese women in the Qing dynasty), *Taibei wenxian* 台北文獻 35 (1976): 113-55.

Zhu Jian 朱珔 (1769-1850). "Bian zhen" 辨貞 (On chastity), in *Xiao wanjuan zhai wengao* 小萬卷齋文稿 (Prose Works of Zhu Jian) (N.p.: 1885), 5:6a-11b.

Zhu Yizun 朱彝尊 (1621-1709). "Yuan zhen" 原貞 (Origins of chastity), in *Pushuting ji* 曝書亭集 (Collected works of Zhu Yizun) (Reprint, Shanghai: n.p., 1937), 58:684-85.

Zurndorfer, Harriet T. "Bound Feet, Splendid Slippers, and the Women of Huizhou (Anhui) Who Killed Themselves: Gender and Changing Regional Identity in Late Imperial China." (forthcoming)

——, ed. *Chinese Women in the Imperial Past: New Perspectives*. Leiden: E. J. Brill, 1999.

——. "Han-hsüeh, 'Evidential Research,' and Female Chastity: A Re-examination of Intellectual Attitudes and Social Ideals in 18th Century China," in W. L. Idema and E. Zürcher, eds., *Thought and Law in Qin and Han China: Studies dedicated to Anthony Hulsewé on the occasion of his eightieth birthday* (Leiden: E.J. Brill, 1990), pp. 208-24.

# INDEX

**NEW SERIES: SUBSCRIBE NOW!**

# Brill's Inner Asian Library

MANAGING EDITOR: NICOLA DI COSMO

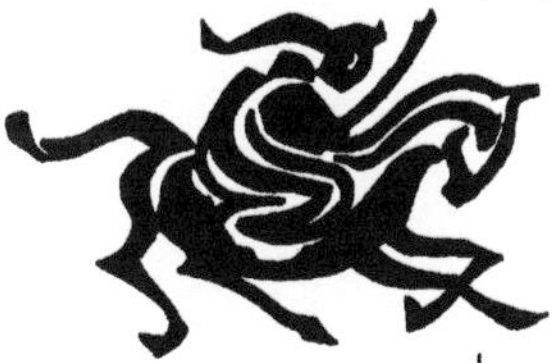

One of the most important landslides in recent World History has been the fall of the Sovjet Union. Though its consequences are felt everywhere, once again in its long history Central or Inner Asia, given its many religious, economical, and historical backgrounds and identities, will play an important role in the formation of a new balance in Asia. It is exactly the history, literature, religion, arts, economy and politics of these Inner Asian cultures and societies that *Brill's new Inner Asian Library* series will be dedicated to.

The peer-reviewed series aims at furthering our understanding of Inner Asia and enabling us to *better cope with the problems past, present and future connected with this region.*

- ISSN 1566-7162
- Two to three volumes a year.
- Subscribers to the series are entitled to a discount of 10%.

**FIRST VOLUME IN BRILL'S INNER ASIAN LIBRARY**
**PRE-PUBLICATION PRICE EUR 46.- / US$ 57.- / DGL 101.37**
**(VALID UNTIL JUNE 2001)**

## Manchu-Mongol Relations on the Eve of the Qing Conquest

### A documentary History

NICOLA DI COSMO AND DALIJABU BAO

In the 17th century the Manchu conquered the whole of China within only a few years, replacing the Ming dynasty. This unique volume for the first time shows in detail how the Manchu built the state and the military machine which enabled them to achieve their goal. With 130 original documents translated and amply annotated.

JUNE 2001.
BOUND (170 PP., 4 ILLUS.)
ISBN 90 04 11777 6
LIST PRICE EUR 50.- /
US$ 62.- / DGL 110.19
PRICE FOR SUBSCRIBERS TO THE SERIES EUR 46.- /
US$ 57.- / DGL 101.37
BRILL'S INNER ASIAN LIBRARY, 1

**www.brill.nl**

Academic Publishers

BRILL

Tel +31 (0)71 53 53 566
Fax +31 (0)71 53 17 532
E-mail cs@brill.nl
P.O. Box 9000
2300 PA Leiden
The Netherlands

Brill Academic Publishers, Inc
112 Water Street, Suite 400
Boston MA 02109
Phone 1 800 962 4406
Fax (617) 263 23 24
E-mail cs@brillusa.com

32/24/6406